WANT TO WORK WITH ROLAND + JAY TO GROW, SCALE AND/OR EXIT YOUR BUSINESS?

You might be a fit for a partnership with us if your business:

1. Generates $1M or more in profit and cash flow,

2. Has been in operation for more than a year,

3. Employs a team of 5 or more.

What's on the table? We invest our expertise, networks, and potentially our capital to help you find new leverage points, scale efficiently, and prepare your business for a lucrative exit.

This isn't for everyone. But if you meet the criteria, then let's talk business. Visit BusinessWealthWithoutRisk.com/apply and fill out the questionnaire.

We've helped numerous businesses amplify their value. Yours could be next. Plan for significant growth and potential wealth creation within the next 12 to 36 months.

WHAT THE WORLD'S GREATEST BUSINESS LEADERS ARE SAYING ABOUT ROLAND AND JAY...

TESTIMONIALS

"Roland Frasier and Jay Abraham's Business Wealth Without Risk *is jam-packed with unique insights and practical strategies that any entrepreneur can benefit from. If you're looking to achieve financial success, Roland and Jay's valuable tips will help you get there!"*

—Barbara Corcoran, Founder of The Corcoran Group & Shark and Executive Producer on ABC's Shark Tank

---

These guys are geniuses. Probably responsible for the development of more entrepreneurs than any other living people on the planet"

—Grant Cardone, Founder of the 10X Movement, Best Selling Author, Real Estate Mogul

---

"Jay Abraham is one of the world's most renowned business strategists and Roland Frasier is smart as heck when it comes to maximizing business results. Together, Jay and Roland have written an actionable blueprint that can positively transform your life. With Business Wealth Without Risk, *you will have a foundation and plan for bypassing the business hardships most entrepreneurs endure, and discover how to turn underperforming businesses into lucrative, wealth generating assets—AND—do it with very little risk. Jay and Roland are masters at this, so I recommend you read this book!"*

—Joe Polish, Founder of Genius Network

It's so rare to have the opportunity for two industry icons to collaborate. Having had the opportunity to spend considerable time with both authors, this is truly a tour de force of two of the brightest business minds of today. Whether you're looking to start, grow, acquire, or exit a business, this book will make sure it happens bigger and faster than you've ever imagined possible. Read this book NOW.

—Jonathan Cronstedt, Entrepreneur, Investor, Executive Leader and Advisor

"Jay and Roland are the world's authority on how you can make your business more profitable."

—Brian Tracy, Master Sales Trainer

"I believe Jay and Roland are the world's #1 marketing authority & business growth strategists."

—Dr. Alan Barnard, The World's #1 Authority on Constraint Theory

"Jay and Roland get businesses going and growing again."

–USA TODAY

"Jay Abraham and Roland Frasier know how to get maximum results from minimum effort."

–INVESTORS BUSINESS DAILY

TESTIMONIALS

"I strongly encourage you, if you're HUNGRY to dominate and want a sustainable competitive advantage... Jay Abraham and Roland Frasier are it!"

—Les Brown, World Leading Motivational Speaker

"When you can change your business 10, 15, 20, 30, 40% just by another human giving you advice... YOU NEED TO TAKE THAT ADVICE!"

—Chuck McDowell, Founder of Wesley Financial Group, LLC

"Imagine if you could create a leveraged way to use your unique genius to set yourself up for life. Roland and Jay have figured out a new way to create big wins for yourself, your family, your legacy and everyone you serve. I'm so excited to go further on this topic and a little sad too when I look back and see I've played too small for twenty plus years in business not knowing these ideas."

—Yanik Silver, author of *Evolved Enterprise* and founder, Maverick1000

"Jay Abraham and Roland Frasier are two of the greatest business minds that I know. I've had the pleasure to know both of them for many years, and be able to seek guidance from each of them on many projects. The ideas, strategies, and connections that they have exposed to me has helped my business and life tremendously."

—**Kevin Harrington**, Inventor of the Infomercial,
Shark on Shark Tank, Fortune 100 Investor,
Philanthropist and Autho

"Jay Abraham is one of the greatest business and marketing minds that I have ever known."

—**Stephen R. Covey**, Legendary Business Guru,
Author of *7 Habits of Highly Effective People*

"To be connected with someone who's been through so many seasons, ups and downs of life, in business, and is still here and thriving, is someone that you need to listen to and pull as much from as possible."

—**Chris Evans and Taylor Welch**, Founders of Traffic and Funnels™

What You'll Walk Away With

Imagine a world where starting a successful business doesn't have to feel so uncertain.

In this straightforward book, the authors (Roland Fraiser and Jay Abraham) present an eye-opening framework that will make you question everything you thought you knew about starting a successful business.

I met Roland over ten years ago at one of his business events. After he finished speaking on stage, I walked up to him and asked him about negotiating equity in a company I was working with. His advice led me to land my first consulting for equity deal. Every time I speak with Roland I learn something helpful.

I've learned from Jay's work and teachings for the past 20 years. He has an amazing talent for simplifying business success, better than anyone I've met. Anytime he publishes information, I devour it right away!

In this book, *Business Wealth Without Risk*, Roland and Jay challenge the conventional wisdom of starting a business from scratch with a friendly and encouraging tone. Instead, they propose a game-changing alternative: Why not acquire a company that has already proven itself to be reasonably successful?

Doing so can bypass the daunting odds of a 1-in-20 first-year success rate and a mere 1-in-10 chance of survival after five years.

The authors expertly guide you through finding these hidden gems—businesses that have already broken through the initial barriers but still have immense potential for growth and profitability.

They offer valuable insights on identifying the right opportunities and provide strategies for scaling and expanding these businesses to a successful exit.

This book is more than just a practical guide; it's a ray of hope for aspiring entrepreneurs. It empowers readers to confidently approach business ownership, knowing there's a better way to achieve success. Their friendly and approachable tone makes it a pleasure to read, and the expertise and enthusiasm of the two authors are contagious.

Whether you're a seasoned entrepreneur looking for a fresh perspective or someone dreaming of owning a business without the overwhelming risks of starting from scratch, this book is a must-read.

Prepare to be inspired, motivated, and equipped with the necessary tools to take your entrepreneurial journey to new heights.

To your success,
—Jeremiah Baker, Lifelong Entrepreneur

"Jay Abraham is one of the smartest marketing & strategy minds I know. Roland Frasier is also world-class smart in optimizing your business for growth and cash. Together their book will change your life. Without Risk gives you the shortcuts, cheat sheets, and tools to truly make any business very successful. Read it and share it today."
—Cameron Herold, Founder, COO Alliance,
Author, *The Second In Command & Vivid Vision*®

NOTE FROM THE AUTHORS

When you grab a copy of this book, you're diving head-first into the sea of proven strategies and street-smart insights on business wealth creation without taking unnecessary risks. Now, before you immerse yourself, here are a few things you need to understand.

While this book is meticulously crafted based on accurate information about the subject matter, keep in mind that the author and the publisher are not serving you personalized advice to fit your unique portfolio or specific needs. We are not providing investment counsel or other professional services like legal or accounting advice. Look, if you need expert guidance in such areas, reach out to a competent professional. After all, who would try to fix a Bentley with a Swiss Army knife?

You'll notice that this book references performance data collected over several time periods. Remember the golden rule of the investment world: past performance does not imply future returns. Things change, just like the weather and the stock market. Laws, regulations, and performance data can alter over time, affecting the relevance of the information contained in these pages.

NOTE FROM THE AUTHORS

This book is not a crystal ball. It's not predicting your financial future. It's not a personal financial advisor or a specific investment recommendation, nor is it offering to buy or sell securities. It's a treasure trove of historical data employed to clarify and illustrate essential principles. It's a mentor guiding you through the labyrinth of business wealth creation, not a genie granting your financial wishes.

While every effort has been made to ensure the accuracy and completeness of the information contained within these pages, neither the author nor the publisher are throwing out warranties. We're not taking responsibility for any liability, loss, or risk, personal or otherwise, which you might incur, directly or indirectly, from using or applying any of the contents of this book.

Enjoy the ride, keep your eyes on the road, and remember—creating business wealth without risk isn't about striking gold in an instant but about making informed decisions and learning from the wisdom of those who've walked the path before you. Happy reading!

TOOLS AND RESOURCES

Free Download

BusinessWealthWithoutRisk.com/access

ROLAND FRASIER & JAY ABRAHAM

BUSINESS WEALTH WITHOUT RISK

How To Create a Lifetime of Income & Wealth Every 3 to 5 years

FOREWORD BY TONY ROBBINS

BUSINESS WEALTH WITHOUT RISK
How To Earn a Lifetime of Income Every Three to Five Years

ISBN: 978-1-959840-79-4 (Paperback)

EP*C AUTHOR
PUBLISHING

Ordering Information: Quantity sales. Special discounts are available on quantity purchases by corporations, associations, and others. Orders by U.S. trade book- stores and wholesalers. For details, contact the publisher below:

Epic Author Publishing
EpicAuthor.com
support@epicnetwork.com

Printed in the United States of America First Printing, 2023

For those who seize the power of leverage, turn chaos into opportunity, and transform businesses into empires.

TABLE OF CONTENTS

FOREWORD
BY TONY ROBBINS

What causes someone to become an entrepreneur?

For me, it was a painful upbringing. I grew up in a tough environment. We were dirt poor. It was so bad that there was no money for food on many occasions, including Thanksgiving. While my family wouldn't have starved, we often had crackers with butter or a peanut butter sandwich.

My life was changed because someone came to the door and delivered food on one Thanksgiving Day when I was 11 years old. It became a trigger for me to want to find a way to make sure that the suffering my family went through would not happen to my future family, or anyone else I could possibly help. It became a vision for the future.

In order to accomplish that vision, I needed to have a way to be in control of my own destiny. I needed a way to be able to do more for others than anybody else, but also to be able to grow into financial security and independence.

I was clear; I was never going to let my future family go through the suffering that I experienced growing up. As a result, at an early age I fell in love with entrepreneurship. The idea that you could be your own boss, shape your own destiny, make your own decisions, take risks, find a way to help others, and grow financially free at the same time was an incredibly powerful promise.

So, at the age of 17, I started my first business and began the entrepreneurial journey that I've been on for the last 45 years. This journey has been filled with all kinds of experiences—a seemingly unlimited number of ups and downs, tremendous hard knocks, mistakes, and semi disasters.

If you're smart as an entrepreneur, you make it through, you learn from those experiences, and you reinvest that knowledge to become more effective in the future. Often, it's said an entrepreneur is a man or woman who makes enough money to pay for their mistakes. That's your true education; and that was certainly true for me.

As my skills grew, so did my business, and I began to build multiple businesses from scratch. I developed a tremendous amount of financial freedom and began to share all that I had learned with others, teaching them the psychology and skills needed to scale geometrically through my Business Mastery program, the five-day bootcamp that has become an international standard for how business owners can grow their business 30-130% or more in a short period of time.

I was feeling quite great about what I was doing until one day I sat down with one of the co-founders of MTV, a gentleman named Bob Pitman. At the time, he had just done a turnaround on the Six Flags Magic Mountain chain, as well as Century 21 real estate, and was becoming the driving force behind the massive growth of AOL in the early 1990s. When I asked him the most important distinction he made in business to that date, he said it was *not* to start businesses from scratch!

I was incredulous since this had been a very successful path for me. I remember him saying to me,

> "Tony, it took me seven years to get MTV to a point of stability... finding the right people, getting the facility set up, putting in core structures and systems from

accounting to technology all just takes time." He said, that as the years went by, "I began to realize I only have so many seven-year cycles in me."

This really struck me, and I began to see that instead of starting from scratch, I could find companies that were already successful to some extent. And instead, bring my own insight, strategy, and skills to help them grow geometrically and then sell those businesses (or my interests in them) for a multiplied profit. I could save myself all the years, especially the first five to ten most risky years that all businesses go through. He said,

> "Tony, what you've done is amazing, but what you could do with this strategy is beyond what you've imagined!"

I took what he had to say seriously and began to study how I could begin to acquire and partner strategically in companies that had momentum. As the years went by, I began to learn how to take companies from one hundred million dollars to 1.2 billion dollars in less than four years. Another company I helped to grow from 18 billion dollars AUM to 50 billion dollars AUM over the same period. Today, I have the privilege of being an owner in more than 110 companies in a variety of industries around the world that combined do over 7 billion dollars in business each year.

Why am I telling you this?

Because this book provides strategies that I wish I would have known at the beginning of my career. It certainly would have accelerated my progress. For more than 35 years, I've been training entrepreneurs and business leaders to find ways to optimize and maximize their business and profits. Along the way I've seen many charlatans offering get rich quick schemes filled with false promises and ridiculous approaches.

However, more than 30 years ago, I met a man who would become a dear friend, Jay Abraham, one of the great marketing and business minds of this generation. Jay's creativity and strategic approach to maximizing business captured my imagination. I applied his principles and brought him in to be one of the teachers at my Business Mastery bootcamp. He continues to do that to this day.

I'm writing this introduction because recently Jay joined forces with mergers and acquisition innovator and disrupter, Roland Frasier. Together in this book, they challenge the conventional wisdom on how to achieve success and prosperity.

What they show is that the road to successful entrepreneurship for many people is probably far too risky, difficult, costly, and slower than it needs to be. As I found in my own experience, starting a business of your own or growing an existing business the more traditional way takes considerable periods of time, extreme effort, and significant out of pocket investment and cash. They show that this approach to wealth building can be surpassed by acquiring businesses with little to none of your own cash, and in fact, recommend not starting a business from scratch at all.

Why? Because over any 10-year period less than 35% of businesses survive, and that doesn't even mean they're profitable. Over a five-year period, 50% are gone. Even in the first year, almost 20% go out of business.

Roland and Jay urge you not to grow your business by conventional marketing, advertising, or selling approaches. Instead, they offer an alternative path to acquire successful, profitable, but underperforming businesses—what Jay and Roland call "successfully stuck"—that you can quickly transform through a combination of eliminating overlapping functions and roles, reducing expenses, and exploding profits using their no cost, no risk, bottom line boosting methodologies.

In this book, Roland also offers many of his more than two hundred ways to acquire cash flowing businesses today—right now—anywhere in the world for no out of pocket investment.

They share how to maximize your profits by using over 90 methods to stimulate monumental increases in EBITDA.

Why do that?

Because of what hedge funds and billionaire investment titans call 'arbitrage plays,' meaning that you take maximum ethical advantage of the overlooked gaps in your value creation. You get control of one or many businesses, typically using none of your own capital, you buy it for a lower multiple, then dramatically increase its profitability so you can sell it a few years later for a significantly higher multiple. **Do this over and over (what they call "rinse and repeat") and you amass ever increasing paydays (what they call "epic exits").**

The bottom line is this: I believe this book reveals a wonderful alternative path for creating business wealth, with far lower downside risks and far higher upside gains than most other entrepreneurial strategies out there.

Whether you're just starting out as an aspiring entrepreneur, are a successful business owner or entrepreneur, or a CEO looking to dramatically grow your existing business into something more profitable and far more valuable, I believe this book is a must read. If you'll dedicate yourself to studying and applying these strategies, you can find a way to grow your business, add massive value to your client and employees, and help your own family to become financially secure and free.

Perhaps you'll also do well enough to give back to others as well. I'm proud to tell you that the simple act of kindness from a stranger to my family on Thanksgiving, triggered me to want to be successful so that I could give back.

Today, I have the privilege of providing over one hundred million meals per year through my partnership with Feeding America. And as I write this, we're closely approaching 1 billion meals after eight years—two years ahead of my 10-year goal.

I'm living proof that there is truly no limit to what you can become if you continue to learn, grow, and use strategies that can accelerate your ability to expand your business results. So, turn the page and let the journey begin...

With love & respect,
—Tony Robbins
World's #1 Peak Performance
and Business Coach

INTRODUCTION

By Daymond John, "The People's Shark"

Roland Frasier and Jay Abraham have really focused on an epic concept.

Basically, their big idea is: "Why start a business from scratch when it's got a 1 in 20 first year and a 1 in 10 five-year chance of being successful? When instead, you can acquire one that's <u>already</u> at least become reasonably successful, that's broken through the barrier, but still has room to scale and grow and expand to its full profit potential?"

Just a little bit about these two authors.

Roland is brilliant and talented in so many business-astute ways that few others can match. He's always moving through the digital age, navigating so many different industries, and finding innovative ways to maximize reach, communication, and profitability. I'm thrilled he's finally taking his proprietary expert knowledge on this business wealth-creating strategy and sharing it with the public. Prior to this, access to him was very, very private and ultra-expensive.

As to Jay, well, I probably wouldn't be at my current level of success without having the good fortune to have him as my mentor. He is a legendary marketer, but I have to say that his teachings and what he's done for me have made a profound positive impact far beyond that. He taught me how to position myself in very unique, prominent, and pre-eminent ways.

He knows how to define ways to multiply revenues in areas you can tap into from your existing customer base to resell, upsell, cross-sell, or reactivate buyers—while providing them with a better product or service. Also, his ability to get directly to the core of the challenges at hand, and then find bigger, better ways to solve, resolve, fix, mine, monetize, and maximize them is rather remarkable.

When you have the good fortune of sharing time with either of these uniquely big thinkers—as you do indirectly through this book—your mind will start thinking and rethinking at levels you never operated at before—and you'll keep doing it at all times. Life is a series of mentors, and Jay and Roland are absolutely two of the best you'll ever find.

Back to their wonderful book: Roland has nearly two hundred separate ways to structure the acquisition and control of businesses using little or none of your own out-of-pocket capital. He shares many of those in this book, along with philosophies, strategies, and actionable tactics you can use anywhere, in any country, in any economy and without the need to deploy any of your own cash or use your personal credit.

Once you gain control, Jay has crafted over 90 proprietary categories to take any business you acquire using Roland's strategies and exponentially increase its profit potential—frequently with little or no added investment or risk on your part as well.

If you want to be an entrepreneur from scratch, you must start pushing the ball up the proverbial hill, like Sisyphus in Greek mythology, and it can be daunting. If you have an existing business and you want to grow it, you would be forced to merely do good or great marketing, selling, advertising, distribution, or whatever. Either of those paths are a long, difficult haul, and most entrepreneurs never realize that it's possible to start halfway, or even almost at the top of that hill, joining the effort once the most difficult parts of gaining momentum are already done by someone else.

Now, thanks to Roland and Jay's book, you can grow through acquisition at the same time—or instead.

You can acquire competitive businesses that are in the same field as yours and consolidate them together for efficiencies of scale and expanded market reach. You can acquire products or services people buy—before, during, after, and even instead of your company's products or services—and actually very profitably compete against yourself.

And the third concept, if you're a passive investor, unhappy with today's paltry average market yields, you could instead partner, hire, or contract with someone to run the strategies outlined in this book for you and get near infinite returns because you can frequently do it with no capital outlay.

The key here is that just acquiring a business with little or no out-of-pocket capital isn't the big "play." That's just one of the three major ways that you can profit from taking action on what Roland and Jay share in this book.

Sure, you can acquire a profitable business for little or no money out-of-pocket and enjoy the continued profits that it was already generating before you acquired it. That alone can provide stratospheric returns compared to those afforded by more traditional investments, and that alone is probably enough to make most investors very, very happy.

But the bigger play comes in what you do AFTER you acquire a profitable business. Acquiring a profitable business gives you the base on which to build a truly spectacular investment vehicle. You're already starting at the top of the proverbial Sisyphus hill I mentioned above.

INTRODUCTION

The heaviest lifting of building something that has a sustainable profit is already done, now you are going to take that base and build even greater possibilities from it.

Once you acquire a profitable business, the next step is to make the business many, many times more profitable than it was when you acquired it, and as you do, generate significant additional income increases for yourself.

That's the second benefit and income boost you get from acquiring businesses.

The first is the profit that the business is ALREADY generating. The second is the ADDITIONAL profit you can make by OPTIMIZING it.

The truth is that most businesses are under-optimized, and most entrepreneurs really only understand their core product or service offering to their customers. They don't understand business itself. That's not because they are stupid or don't care, it's because they are what Roland refers to as "accidental entrepreneurs."

They got into business to serve their clients and customers. Most of the time, they had a great idea, came from some other business they worked in, or took over a business from friends, family, or someone who was retiring. They had no formal business education, and they were always so busy serving their customers and making ends meet that they never had time to really understand how business works.

And, therein lies the great opportunity that Jay and Roland point out so well in this book. Once you use their acquisition strategies laid out in the first part of this book, you will be in a position to take everything Jay and Roland share in the second part of the book to dramatically increase sales and profitability of the businesses you acquire.

BUSINESS WEALTH WITHOUT RISK

According to a study by the Corporate Finance Institute[1], the average business has a profit margin of only 10%, while a 20% profit margin is considered "good." Just imagine what would happen to any "average" business that you acquire once you apply the strategies in part two of this book to optimize it. If you could take a 10% average profit margin business and double it to become a 20% "good" profit margin business, then you literally double profitability.

That opportunity exists because so few people understand how much room the average business has to improve profitability. Of course, Roland and Jay aren't happy with just a "good" profit margin. That's why they share so many excellent strategies in part two of this book to create "exceptional" profit margins.

And, while you might already be celebrating your decision to invest in this book, thinking that just the first two ways to profit from it are more than enough to satisfy your desire to create income, you will be delighted to discover that the biggest payoff of all, the true ability to create "Business Wealth Without Risk" and "A Lifetime of Wealth Every 3 to 5 Years" lies in the final part of this book: part three.

Once you have executed the strategies revealed in parts one and two of this book, you come to the cherry on top: the ability to transfer the value that you created in parts one and two to someone else at a significant premium above what you invested in the business.

The things you did to grow the business and its profitability in part two allow you to sell it in three to five years for outsized paydays. Roland and Jay call these "the epic exits." And then they say "rinse and repeat," meaning you do it again and again and again—only each time you do it at a higher, more rewarding financial level.

---

1   Corporate Finance Institute, "Profit margin." Corporatefinanceinstitute.com, 2023.

INTRODUCTION

I went through a lot of trials and tribulations when I started my business. And my most successful business was about my tenth business. I had to learn all the things that I just talked about the hard way.

Having lived through multiple start-up businesses, I eventually got to a point in my life where I decided that I no longer wanted to start another business from scratch again because I didn't know if I was ever going to be the smartest person in the room again or discover lightning-in-a-bottle again or bite the right apple.

So, I decided at that point, well I can always invest in smarter people than me. At first, I decided to go into the market and see what businesses were available to acquire through brokers or investment bankers—but that's not always a great idea.

I quickly realized that for me to get the big payoff from the market by the time I got into it, that company that I thought was brilliant had already realized much of its value appreciation. The founders had already taken their money off the table, and my money would most likely never 10x doing it that way. It would take me a lifetime for it to 10x, if that was even possible given the growth in value the companies I found this way had already experienced.

I realized that these types of businesses were primarily either for institutional investors or for people who were happy with much lower returns than I wanted and needed to realize my personal income and wealth building goals.

So, I decided to go on Shark Tank and invest in younger and smarter people.

But the failure rate for start-ups and first-stage businesses is dangerously high.

Roland and Jay, who have seen this and done this many, many times over many years, have managed to cut through that risk factor and reduce it by orders of positive magnitude. They found the middle ground that everybody always wants to find. They've turned the tables on both the business failure rate for investors like you and me, as well as figured out how to multiply our ultimate profit payoff potential by leaps and bounds.

They say that we should look for businesses that have been built by smarter people that have taken the risk, proven it could be successful but have never been able to scale properly and never realized how to exit for maximum value.

They say to focus on businesses that can give you multiples that the market could almost never give you in a short period of time. And, more importantly, shoot for monumental, "epic exits."

Then, you can do it repeatedly and use the same fundamentals and techniques with different businesses in different industries. In fact, you don't have to do this sequentially. That is, you don't have to do this one business at a time. Because you don't need a huge bankroll to accomplish any of the acquisition and growth strategies that Roland and Jay share in this book, you can actually run their playbook on several businesses at the same time.

And, once you learn these techniques and fundamentals, they will never leave you. You will have them to use forever in your entrepreneurial and investing journeys. These tools and strategies are timeless, so while I would always keep an eye on what Jay and Roland are doing to evolve and uncover new and improved ways to achieve what they share in this book, there is no "hack" or "tactic" in this book that will expire or become unusable because other people discover it.

I think this book is long overdue. So many people who had the desire and the drive to do what Roland and Jay teach here, but not the patience, access to talent, knowledge, experience, or start-up mindset to do this, can now go in and use these methods successfully, time after time.

As they say in this book, they have done it many, many times, "rinse and repeat." That's what they do, and that's what they advise their many private clients around the world, including me, to do. And I've listened and followed that advice!

Their methods work. They really work. That's why I highly recommend this book and their methods for all the reasons stated above.

When you combine what Roland and Jay openly reveal in these pages, you have nearly three hundred irrefutable new reasons why you can now acquire, grow, and sell businesses on your terms, your way, and do it today.

Because if you aren't doing this, then you are either working on somebody else's dream or you're speculating on a 1 in 20 probability proposition by starting a new business.

But now you can acquire somebody else's partially realized dream, with somebody else's hard work through the most difficult start-up phase already done, and exit onto your prosperity pathway, then do it again and again.

Today a lot of people either are or want to be entrepreneurs. Very honestly, a ton more people are going to want to become one moving forward. That's the genius and ingenuity of being human.

But, as we have learned, start-up businesses have a very high failure rate. So, how can you be an entrepreneur, chase the entrepreneurial dream, and have a "cheat code" to mitigate that huge start-up failure risk?

Easy: you can start with an already successful business that has already crested the start-up hill and then build on it the way Roland and Jay show you to do in this book.

Remember, a typical start up may go forever and never have an exit.

This way you're building on an already proven successful business with that "epic exit" in mind, and all the while you're earning the profit the business already generates, multiplying it with proven strategies you'll learn in this book, and building wealth that you can cash in on later in the form of an "epic exit."

It's a pretty cool idea.

–Daymond John
"The People's Shark"

PREFACE

By Gino Wickman

I have spent the last 30 years helping entrepreneurs build great companies, while building two of my own in the process.

Today, over two hundred thousand entrepreneurs use the EOS tools to run great companies, and I've sold a million and a half copies of *Traction*.

My passion and love is helping entrepreneurs. The entrepreneurs I help are 'founding entrepreneurs' who created their businesses from the ground up, surviving and building through the start-up phase, or second- and third-generation entrepreneurs who have taken the family business to another level.

But that journey is not for everyone, and I want to give a shout out to Roland and Jay, because what they share in their wonderful book is a great option for someone who maybe doesn't have all six of the essential traits of a start-up entrepreneur.

Those essential traits from *Entrepreneurial Leap* are 1). Visionary, 2). Passionate, 3). Problem-solver, 4). Driven, 5). Risk-taker, and 6). Responsible.

Business Wealth Without Risk is a book for people who may not have all six of those traits, or don't have an interest in being a 'founding entrepreneur' and going through the wild ride of a start-up.

Their concept of an '**ACQUIREpreneur**' is genius for anyone who wants to jump over that start-up phase, be a business owner, and not have to build their empire from scratch.

That's not to say that being an **ACQUIREpreneur** or founding entrepreneur is better or worse. Understand as you read this that I don't want to discount the founding entrepreneur. I am one, along with millions of others. So, while Roland and Jay provide a path around (or over) that start-up building phase, for us gluttons for punishment who love creating start-ups, we're still going to do that.

That said, the **ACQUIREpreneur** idea is sheer genius for anybody that wants to jump over the start-up, founding entrepreneur steps and move directly into business ownership.

Whatever path you might choose, I can tell you for sure that Jay and Roland are two really smart, experienced, good guys, who deeply care about entrepreneurs.

This book is extremely unique, incredibly well written, and I believe that every entrepreneur can benefit from reading it.

—**Gino Wickman**
Creator of EOS,
Author of *Traction*
and *Entrepreneurial Leap*

OUR INVITATION TO YOU

HOW TO ACHIEVE EXPONENTIAL GROWTH
AS AN INVESTOR AND BUSINESS OWNER

I **magine you just received a text from your private bank-er informing you that $2 million was received into your bank account today from the sale of** part **of one of your businesses.**

You swipe up to dismiss the text notification from your phone, and then continue to sign the digital signature request you just received via email to sell yet another interest in a different business you acquired just about a year ago.

You are interrupted again when your phone rings, and the seller of a different business to whom you submitted an offer yesterday calls to tell you that she has accepted your terms (which, by the way, required no money out of your pocket). You congratulate and thank her. Then you disconnect the call and whisper to yourself, "YES!" as you take a drink of the freshly squeezed tropical fruit drink served by your private butler at the exclusive beachfront villa you purchased last month for you and your family to enjoy for one of your three-month long vacations that you take each year.

Your phone vibrates again with news from your accountant that profits across your portfolio of businesses are up 80% for the year. Again, you dismiss the message as you look out to see your children playing in your villa's pool and then to the sea beyond. "Ahhh, this is nice. Why did it take me so long to do this?" you ask yourself.

This is the life of a new type of entrepreneur, the "**ACQUIRE-preneur**," and it can be yours as well if you would like to claim your spot.

ACQUIREpreneurs do not get bogged down with operating the businesses they own. They only acquire businesses that already have qualified managers to run them.

They don't spend sleepless nights wondering if their latest start-up is going to finally figure out how to make money. They only purchase existing, profitable businesses.

And they don't kowtow to a group of investors or a board or a boss or live in fear of losing everything if they fail to please their bankers, because they have mastered the art of Zero Out-Of-Pocket acquisitions and the use of little-known business structures called "special purpose vehicles" or SPVs (more on those later) to provide limitless capital for acquiring businesses with zero personal risk to their personal credit and assets.

They also hold the keys to build any business they work with by implementing exponential growth strategies. They know that linear growth provides only limited returns (and takes way too long), but exponential growth creates opportunities for continuously compounding growth upon growth upon growth. They take advantage of a corollary to what Albert Einstein said was "the 8th wonder of the world," compound interest by invoking the benefits of compound profits.

Lastly, these **ACQUIREpreneurs** understand that generational wealth (wealth that lasts for multiple generations) requires the mastery of building "exit ready" businesses that can sell for 3x, 5x, 10x, or even 15x or more their annual profits.

It's not a pipe dream. It's real. And it's within your grasp.

Over the past 50 years or so, we have not only discovered that this is possible, but we have also mastered the specific models by which to accomplish it. We know how to do it, and we live it every single day.

And, now, we, Roland Frasier and Jay Abraham, want you to know what we know.

And the first thing that we want to share with you is this simple fact: *we are all investors.*

Maybe you don't call yourself an investor just yet. But you are.

We are intellectual investors. We are emotional investors. We are investors in our own lives and the lives of those we care about. We invest our time in our children, we invest our time in our relationships, we invest our time in our hobbies and in our careers. These are investments because we do these things in the hope that we and those we serve will reap rewards. This is a kind of investment that largely happens on a subconscious level; it's inborn.

When you ferry the kids to baseball practice, you're not consciously saying "I'm investing in their personal development, so I get more than what I put in." But deep down, you do so because you hope that the sweat equity (not to mention the financial expense) of child-rearing means that your kids are going to turn out to be great people who live happy lives, find joy, and give back to the world, and you're going to be satisfied as a result because you did well investing in them.

OUR INVITATION TO YOU

You are all trying to invest in yourself, in all areas of your life, so you reap the greatest rewards out of the things that you put your time and your energy into. This is particularly important in terms of your time because you have so little of it.

Consider this, take out a piece of paper and pen and write this number down: 27,740 if you are a man and 29,565 if you are a woman. Now, multiple your current age times 365 and write that down underneath the first number. Subtract and see what you have left. What number did you come up with?

That number is the average number of days that you can expect to continue to be alive. So, if you are 45 years old and a woman, you would write down 29,565 and subtract 16,424, which leaves 13,141. That's how many days you have left to live.

Every single day, you make an investment of your time and wake up the next day with one fewer day to remain among the living. When you think of your time this way, what you do each day takes on a new meaning, and you realize that every day, every single thing you do is in some form an investment in time or in money.

When it comes to money, investing as described above is something more than taking money and contributing it to a company or a person hoping for a financial return. Investing is the exchange of capital for some expected return.

That capital can be money, like an investment in a stock, and the expected return can also be money, which for stock investors is usually realized in the form of a dividend and/or capital gain.

But capital can be so much more than money. Capital can be relationships, knowledge, skills, talents, time, or any number of things. And the expected return can be money, but it can also be joy, impact, legacy, or one of a hundred other things. In this book, we are focusing on investments of capital in all its forms, and the expected return in all its forms as well.

We will talk about investing other people's money ("OPM") to acquire interests in businesses, and we will also explore investing using the assets already owned by the businesses you want to acquire. You will discover that in many cases, you will be able to acquire ownership in businesses without the need to invest a single dollar of your own cash—that you can use a combination of tools and strategies to literally acquire businesses for zero dollars out of your own pocket.

This book is written for people with an entrepreneurial drive—people who want to acquire and grow businesses to staggering heights. But it's also written for those who just want to earn an extra $5,000, $10,000 or $20,000 per month to supplement their income or escape the 9 to 5 grind. It's also for those who are looking to create a retirement, or emergency nest-egg, or just some additional wealth to feel more at ease, to help their friends or family or to start a personal philanthropy program.

Of course, these are investments of a different sort, different from the meaning people normally associate with the word, "investment." But to be successful as a financial investor and business owner, you must never lose sight of the fact that what really counts is that emotional, intellectual, social, and "life" investment whose returns are unquantifiable but whose value is indispensable.

And now is the time to get your investments right because there is a wave approaching. A wave of opportunity that is only just beginning to crest and will continue to provide unprecedented opportunities for the foreseeable future, as it is unlikely that all of these current opportunities will expire any time soon.

This book is targeted at three groups of readers:

Group #1: First-time entrepreneurs who are quitting their day jobs to join the ranks of the ***ACQUIREpreneurs*** (Note: ***ACQUIREpreneurs*** are far better off than those who are simply "self-employed." ***ACQUIRE-preneurs*** create wealth and passive income, while self-employed people are still bound by a job they cannot escape to unlock passive wealth, even though they technically work for themselves).

Group #2: Established entrepreneurs who have achieved a modicum of success in a business or two but whose growth has been limited, or who have plateaued because they've been doing the same things and don't know how to progress to the next level (usually because they are still "owner/operators" or have bumped up against the wall of opportunity in their existing businesses).

Group #3: Experienced and/or wealthy investors who have succeeded in amassing considerable savings from working in a traditional job, or investing in real estate, the stock market, or some other asset class, but who want to add a few more zeroes to their incomes and net worth by venturing into new and profitable terrain: acquiring, building, and selling small and medium-sized companies, namely those with under $50 million in sales and/or $2 million in profits.

In the chapters to come, we'll lay out a distinct, three-part journey for you. This journey comprises three potential paths. Any of these three paths will produce massive profit, but integrating all three creates the possibility to generate unimaginable wealth.

The First Path

The first is a detailed program for acquiring established, profitable businesses, often with little or none of your own capital.

Start-ups fail at an astonishingly high rate (20% fail in the first year alone, 45% fail within the first five years, and about 65% total fail over time), but already established, thriving businesses involve much less risk to the **ACQUIREpreneur**-owner.

There are literally millions of such businesses whose owners are motivated to sell at any given time, and the market is highly inefficient, which means opportunities abound for the savvy investor.

Using the strategies and skills that you will learn in this book, you will find that you can actually acquire many of these businesses without using your own money or personal credit, while also providing significant cash to the sellers at closing.

The Second Path

The second path is about how to rapidly grow a business that is under your control (whether you are starting from that position already, or whether you acquire one via the first path we just described).

Here, we're not talking about incremental growth; 3%, 5%, 20% a year. Most entrepreneurs would be euphoric at the prospect of 20% growth. But why settle for less? What we're teaching is beyond linear—it is *exponential* growth. And even beyond that, *hyper-exponential* growth (a term we'll explain later).

How is this achieved? There are myriad strategies, but a common thrust is finding underutilized channels and unseen opportunities in adjacent or parallel industries, products, and services—such as selling complementary products and services that people buy before, during, or after they buy your product.

For example, if you're selling a supplement for weight loss, you might want to buy other supplement companies or other supplements people buy, along with related products in related businesses: exercise equipment, diet-friendly food products, personal trainers, books, health clubs, and gyms. You're monetizing what is being overlooked, undervalued, or unsold to achieve blockbuster growth.

But beyond growth for growth's sake, we also venture into examining how to make the businesses you acquire and/or own more profitable. Growth for growth's sake is a fool's errand, and many erstwhile successfully growing businesses have foundered on the rocks of profitability when they made the mistake of seeking growth without paying attention to its demanding cousin, profitability.

And while many entrepreneurs aspire to have their businesses appear on the well-known *Inc. Magazine* list of 5,000 fastest growing businesses, a study by that very magazine presents a cautionary warning for those pursuing growth and growth alone. The Kauffman Foundation and *Inc. Magazine* conducted a follow-up study of companies five to eight years after they had appeared on the magazine's list of the 5,000 fastest-growing companies.[2]

What they found was startling: about two-thirds of the companies that made the list had shrunk in size, gone out of business, or been disadvantageously sold. Why? Because they failed to make it through the fourth and final stage of enterprise maturity, where a company finally becomes self-sustaining.

---

2 Wanda Thibodeaux, "Here's why growing your business too fast is disastrous..." Inc.com, December 16, 2016.

Now, if you follow the advice in part one of this book, you will only deal with already self-sustaining businesses that you acquire using all of the strategies that we share. But, as you begin to take control and operate the businesses you acquire, and as you begin to implement the growth and optimization strategies contained in part two of this book, remember that it is important to always be wary of prioritizing growth over profits.

The Third Path

The third path is that of selling (or in the vernacular of the mergers and acquisitions community, "exiting") the businesses you acquire and/or build. This is the tremendously exciting phase where you are paid for many years of the business's profits, in most cases all at one time, and all from one single transaction.

To reiterate, that is the magic formula: 1) acquire existing businesses from motivated sellers—without committing your own capital—that have already been validated, that are already profitable, or are strategically beneficial; 2) blow them up in two to five years for tremendous profit increase through optimization of the existing business and implementation of the strategies presented in part two of this book; and 3) then sell them for a multiple of many years of profit, usually paid all in one day, at closing.

The ability to create a flywheel of interlocking businesses using this three-step formula allows you to create truly generational wealth. With it, you can achieve a lifetime of business profits in a single year, year after year. You can then use those profits to acquire a new business, then grow that business exponentially, and then sell that business for many years of profits.

OUR INVITATION TO YOU

This creates the wealth building hat-trick that is one of the most closely guarded secrets of private equity funds, the family offices of the ultra-wealthy, and self-made millionaires and billionaires worldwide. It isn't merely life changing. Its impact can be multigenerational. There is no limit to what you can dream or do when you acquire that kind of wealth.

In this book, we are pulling back the curtain to reveal, democratize, and disseminate these strategies because we believe that everyone deserves the opportunity to live the life of their dreams, and because we share a prosperity mentality, knowing that the opportunity to create wealth using this formula is not diminished by the number of people executing it.

You will be amazed to discover that you do not require advanced degrees, coding skills, a coterie of Ivy League fraternity brothers, mountains of capital, or even good credit to implement them. Truly anyone with the formula can do this. We have seen it with our own eyes: single mothers, life-long employees, and failed entrepreneurs are all among those who have used this formula to their great delight and success. They sit alongside investment bankers, attorneys, private equity managers, and other sophisticated players, all equal when wielding the power of the three-step formula.

All you need to make this yours, dear reader, is an open mind, an eagerness to learn, and the ability to take consistent, enthusiastic action on what we are about to share with you.

Welcome to the big leagues. Welcome to the game of advanced wealth creation.

That's the game we are playing. It's all about exponentiality (exponentially easier, exponentially less expensive, exponentially less risky, and exponentially more profitable). It's not just about performance, but the wealth you're creating, the velocity of wealth creation, and moving you out of the day-to-day, operational minutiae of ownership (a low-yield use of your time) into the more high-yield, strategic, scalable, limitless growth potential type of entrepreneurship, what we call "**ACQUIREpreneurship**."

It is time to embark on the path of your choosing.

As you read through this book you will find many tools and resources that we refer to, including worksheets, checklists, and more. All of these have been gathered in one place for your convenience at BusinessWealthWithoutRisk.com/access. Visit that site at any time to access these resources, additional materials, and media that would not fit in this book. You will be pleasantly surprised.

We also suggest that you take the time to follow us on social media and our podcasts where we share a continual stream of content on the subjects explored in this book.

You can find Roland at the following:

- Facebook.com/RolandFrasier
- TikTok.com/@RolandFrasier
- Instagram.com/RolandFrasier
- YouTube.com/RolandFrasierEpic
- Twitter.com/RolandFrasier
- LinkedIn.com/in/RolandFrasier
- BusinessLunchPodcast.com
- RolandFrasier.com

25

And you can find Jay at the following:

- Facebook.com/JayAbrahamMarketing
- Instagram.com/RealJayAbraham
- YouTube.com/@JayAbrahamOfficial
- Twitter.com/RealJayAbraham
- LinkedIn.com/in/JayAbrahamOfficial
- Ultimate Entrepreneur Podcast
- Abraham.com

Download the resources and links related to this book here:

BusinessWealthWithoutRisk.com/access

PART ONE

$0 Out-of-Pocket
Business Acquisitions

CHAPTER 1

EPIC OPPORTUNITIES

Now is the Time.

The coming years will create unprecedented opportunities for you to acquire businesses for no money out of pocket and reap enormous financial rewards. We are so excited to share how our insights and strategies can benefit others that, quite frankly, we just can't stop talking about it. We are both passionately obsessed with business and entrepreneurship and how to help entrepreneurs create, build, and sell successful businesses, and if you asked either of us what our favorite hobby is, we would both answer without hesitation: "Business!"

But because our families get mad and ask us, "Is there anything else we can please talk about besides business?" we're writing this book to convey what we've learned and share it with you, to open your eyes to the life-transforming possibilities that we have made into realities in our lives, and provide you with a road-tested system for taking advantage of them.

CHAPTER 1 - EPIC OPPORTUNITIES

If you follow the methodology we describe, you're on your way to becoming what we call an "EPIC investor": people who *ethically earn enormous profits in a time of crisis* because they have the vision and skills to turn what looks like a predicament into long-term prosperity. The "crisis" in EPIC can be global, such as the COVID pandemic, a military conflict, economic crisis, disruptive innovation, or changing market dynamics, or it can be local to the business or the entrepreneur who owns it, such as personal challenges (health, divorce, retirement, etc.), or financial issues specific to the business (cash mismanagement, supplier issues, competitor encroachment, supply chain issues, etc.).

These EPIC investors are primarily focused on acquiring businesses, growing them, and then selling them at a nice profit. We call people who specialize in acquiring business in this way "**ACQUIRE-preneurs**," an apt portmanteau of "acquisition" and "entrepreneur."

Ethical Profits in Crisis create the E.P.I.C. acronym. Oh, and spoiler alert, there is ALWAYS a crisis, whether a fully recognized in your face crisis or the early warning signs of a crisis brewing. Crisis brings opportunity for those savvy enough to realize it and take action. Ethicality in crisis means that you can be an agent for change, an agent for good, AND make a healthy profit. That's what it means to us to be an EPIC investor, an EPIC **ACQUIREpreneur**.

To begin, we want you to understand that our system works across any industry, in any country, in any economy, and it doesn't require any capital, any monetary investment, or any of your own personal credit.

There's no snake oil, hocus pocus, or voodoo here.

What we're presenting is a clear and logical system for increasing wealth; one we've applied ourselves across myriad industries with many companies with sales ranging from a few million to several billion. There's no reason you can't do the same because, as you'll see, our system isn't about investors competing for a limited number of transactions in which your success demands some other person's failure.

This is simply smart, savvy business at its best.

There's room for everyone under the **ACQUIREpreneur** tent. Why? Because the number of deals waiting to be made is virtually unlimited—provided you learn and apply the proper principles. By the time you finish reading this book, we promise you'll have the tools you need to generate exponentially increasing wealth and income as we do in one of the greatest wealth-creation pursuits of our lifetimes—as an EPIC **ACQUIREpreneur** investor.

Why is now the best time to acquire businesses? Because of the opportunity created by three crises (the "C" in Roland's EPIC investor acronym). And remember, there is ALWAYS a crisis.

1. Baby Boomers are Aging out of Their Businesses.

Many no longer want to run their companies; others are no longer able to because of health or other reasons. The first step is to keep in mind that roughly 60% of the seven hundred million Boomer population—420 million people—have yet to retire and that fifty million of them will do so in the next ten years, according to the Insurance Research Institute and the Pew Research Center.[3]

Next, consider that 12 million (i.e., 24%) of those Boomers own businesses, 4.5 million of which are going to transition over the next

---

3   Richard Fry, "The Pace of Boomer Retirements Has Accelerated in the Past Year," pewresearch.org, November 9, 2020.

decade. Their cumulative value is worth over $10 trillion. So, the years ahead will be full of opportunity. We've been doing this for decades, so we can assure you that investing is both long and short. It can generate short-term profits and it can continue to do so over the very long-term. It is not dependent on any state of the economy or limited opportunity. But the market is drenched in rocket fuel right now and ready to explode. Change is afoot, and that means opportunity for those willing to seize it.

And for those of you who are concerned that the baby boomer opportunity will only last for 10 years, just remember that we have been using the strategies we are sharing with you in this book for over 40 years. The current baby boomer "crisis" is but one of a continual string of interlocking crises/opportunities that create an ever-renewable source of opportunities for EPIC *ACQUIREpreneurs*.

2. The Market for Selling These Businesses is Inefficient.

You don't need a PhD in economics to know that when supply exceeds demand by 400%, prices are going to go down, and buyers will get more value for less money. The data thus supports our contention that now may be the best time in history to buy a business, and that opportunity is likely to continue for at least the next 10 to 25 years.

Combine this with the ever-repeating economic cycles of growth and recession and you will see a historically undeniable trend for opportunities to "buy the dips" and "exit the peaks" as you apply our strategies.

As you can see from the upcoming chart, over a recent 70-year period, the United States saw 12 recessions, or one every 5.8 years on average. Paying attention to these cycles alone can produce tremendous returns for the wise investor.

Buy when the market is down and everyone is panic selling; sell when the market is up and everyone forgets that recessions even happen.

When markets are down, sellers understand that they will have to accept less for their companies than in good times, and despite that fact, for whatever reason, many sellers decide that they need to sell when things get tough and happily accept those lower prices. The media is only too happy to stoke the fires of uncertainty during times of economic turmoil with all sorts of speculation about how long and how bad the trying times will last, and this unearths a veritable treasure trove of highly motivated sellers ready to cash in their chips and move on to the next greener pasture.

When markets are up, a frothiness develops where everyone sees only upside. Even when bellwether key economic indicators show the economy is slowing, the media continues to trumpet the siren's song of never-ending appreciation, providing ample notice and opportunity for the savvy **ACQUIREpreneur** to time the perfect exit to maximize sales price and cash out before the inevitable next downturn.

Check out the chart below to glimpse the continual cycle of economic peaks and troughs over a 70-year period.

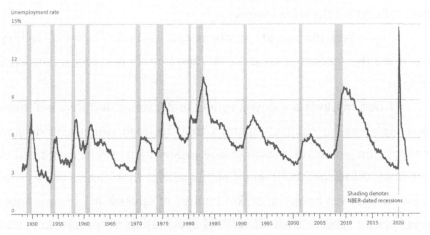

Unemployment rate. NBER-dated recessions in gray.
Source: Bureau of Labor Statistics via the Federal Reserve Bank of St. Louis.

Despite the best efforts of business brokers, investment bankers, and Silicon Valley coders, no one has yet cracked the combination to defragment and unify the huge universe of would-be sellers and place them in an efficient market where they can be matched with willing buyers. The current and continuing state of this inefficient market creates outsized returns for those who know where to find motivated sellers for years to come.

3. Due to Various Reasons, Millions of Businesses Each Year Simply Fail or Close.

According to the U.S. Bureau of Labor Statistics, every year 6.5 million businesses start up, and every year, 1.6 million fail. 20% will fail within the first year, 45% will fail within the first five years, and 65% or more will fold within ten.[4] And while that high failure rate means that there is a tremendous opportunity for "turnarounds" where someone acquires the business and then sets it on the right path to a healthy recovery, that is NOT what we are talking about here.

We have extensive experience in business turnarounds, where you acquire or take control of a business that is experiencing existential challenges and take action to right the ship, save the day, and hopefully, make a nice profit in the process. However, having experienced the joys and challenges of turnarounds as compared to the ease with which you can acquire an existing profitable business for little or no money out of pocket, we now choose the much easier, much more certain to be profitable, path of only executing these strategies on non-turnaround businesses that are comfortably profitable and free of all of the challenges you must face in turnaround situations.

We give you these data points on start-ups and failures simply to help you understand the tremendous risk in those other paths. Why start a business from scratch or put it all on the line to turn around a failing business when there are so many currently profitable businesses available for you to acquire?

In other words, why *start* a business when you can *acquire* one? And before you answer, consider that, depending on the age of the business you acquire, only about 10% of *acquisitions* fail as compared to 90% of *first-time founders*. So, you have a choice: a 90% chance of success through acquisition or a 10% chance of success with a start-up as a first-time founder—and a 65% chance of start-up failure no matter

---

4   U.S. Bureau of Labor Statistics. "Entrepreneurship and the U.S. economy." April 28, 2016. bls.gov/bdm/entrepreneurship/entrepreneurship.htm

what your experience level. In the face of these odds, our question becomes rhetorical.

Aside from reduced risk, you'll also have far more financing options if you buy a company rather than start one. Over many decades and a thousand deals, we've identified over 220 different funding options for acquiring businesses vs. the roughly 17 funding options for those just starting up.

Other advantages include the following:

- **Brand recognition.** Rather than starting from scratch, you can build on the branding efforts of the previous owners or put the acquisition through a more popular brand you already own. Brand recognition creates customer confidence, increases buying frequency, and creates goodwill that translates into increased sales, profits, and customer satisfaction. Why invest in creating a brand when you can simply acquire one that already exists and comes along with the business that you acquire?

- **Instant customers.** Tapping into a pre-existing customer base is a huge advantage. Those of you who've studied physics (or pushed a car) know that—because of momentum—it's far easier to keep an object moving than to initiate movement from a standstill. The same law applies in business.

- **Instant sales.** In part two of this book, you'll learn how to exponentially expand the previous owner's sales, but for now just understand that the benefit of the difference between starting with *some income* vs. *zero income* is impossible to overstate.

- **Instant employees.** Although you'll want to sift the wheat from the chaff here, having a team of experienced employees who know the business—and feel invested in it—will vastly reduce your learning curve and increase your chances of success.

Motivated Sellers

Every year, just in the United States 595,000 businesses simply shut down without being bought. That's in the USA alone. Worldwide the number is well over a million. The figure below shows the top ten reasons for these closings.

Top 10 Reasons for Business Closings:

Money	Many people make the mistake of thinking that businesses that close due to money reasons close because the business is losing money or going bankrupt. While some businesses close for these reasons, many more close because either the business does not provide enough money to satisfy the needs and desires of the owners despite already being profitable, or the owner finds another opportunity that can provide a more secure or guaranteed path to receiving the money they desire. We do not seek out troubled businesses, only those that are already profitable and many of those exist for financial reasons beyond losing money.
Retirement	Many entrepreneurs have lived most of their entire business life inside one business that they started and built. It is not uncommon to find businesses where the entrepreneurs have owned and operated it for 10, 15, 20 years or more. Often, these entrepreneurs have no legacy plan for what happens when they leave the business and no idea how to make a transition into retired life. Acquiring their business in these types of situations provides them the security of income continuity from a seller-financed sale or the ability to receive the cash they need to transition to the next stage of their lives.

CHAPTER 1 - EPIC OPPORTUNITIES

Relocation	Life holds many unexpected twists and turns and, frequently, the need or desire to change location is one of them. Often, we find entrepreneurs who need to change locations to live near children, grandchildren, friends, relatives, or others who have moved away or live too far away to visit regularly. In other cases, entrepreneurs want to retire to a different climate, lifestyle, or lower cost of living to enjoy their later years. For others, a new business opportunity may present itself that requires a relocation to fully take advantage of it.
Burnout	For entrepreneurs who pour their lives into their businesses, a common refrain is a desire to get some rest, take some time off, or just escape the day-to-day demands of a daily grind they have endured for the past years. These entrepreneurs have great businesses but are either just tired of them or have not been able to scale themselves out of the business to the point where they can enjoy life as they want to live it. These are excellent acquisition opportunities.
Can't Sell	The statistics are undeniable: 80% of businesses that are listed for sale do not sell. That means that even if you are dealing with an entrepreneur who wants to sell their business, many times you will discover that they have tried in the past and failed. These are excellent opportunities to serve the entrepreneur by providing them with an exit at a very favorable price and/or terms to yourself. The entrepreneurs will be motivated and grateful to you for helping them to finally realize their vision of exiting the business.

Shiny Object	Walk into any roomful of entrepreneurs and you will find a roomful of people itching to find the next big thing for themselves. One of the challenges of being an entrepreneur is a continuing drive to discover, innovate, and try new things. That makes it hard to stick with running a business that you've been in for a few years, and very often that entrepreneurial restlessness leads to a motivated seller longing to escape their existing business to try something new. We love buying from these entrepreneurs and helping them get out of the old and into the new.
Death	Sadly, to the best of our knowledge to date, no one gets out of here alive. We all come with expiration dates, which as of this writing run about 76 years for the average man and 81 years for the average woman. Often, entrepreneurs pass on without any viable plan of succession for their businesses, leaving their heirs with a business that they do not understand, have no skills or experience to run, and most likely just want to sell to move on with their lives. This presents an excellent opportunity to step in and help the decedent's family by removing the onus of continuing to operate the business and providing them with cash or terms for cash in exchange for transferring ownership of the business.

Partners	Ah, partners. There are so many wonderful benefits to having a good partner. You can partner to fill in the knowledge, experience, skill, and connection gaps in your own entrepreneurial skill set, or to have someone who actually enjoys doing the things in a business that you do not.
	Either way, partners can be wonderful things. But not infrequently, people make poor choices with respect to who they partner with. They don't think through how it will be to work so intimately with someone in such a challenging environment as operating a business. Or they jump in with a friend, family member, or even a total stranger, without properly vetting and exploring values, or defining duties, expectations, and responsibilities. When they are poorly executed or hastily created, partnerships can be an absolute nightmare.
	So, when you find a business that has quarreling partners, or in a case Roland has experienced with partners that want to buy out another partner, you find an excellent opportunity to acquire a business that will exit one owner and continue to benefit from another who is usually the primary operator. These make excellent acquisition opportunities.
Health	Many entrepreneurs begin their entrepreneurial journey in the best of health and have no expectations that it will ever change. Then, after operating their business for many years, they experience some unanticipated health challenge or simply decide that as they age and their health changes, they no longer can or want to own and operate their business.
	These situations provide an excellent opportunity for you to come into the picture and acquire the business to help the ailing or aging entrepreneur shed the responsibilities of owning and/or operating their current business to move on to their next adventure.

Divorce	With divorce rates as high as 50% or more in different areas, it's not surprising that often one of the casualties of a failed marriage is an entrepreneurial business. This may result from a distracted owner/operator no longer being able to focus on the business, a couple who started a business together no longer being able to work together, or the need for an owner to sell the business to meet property settlement or ongoing child support obligations. No matter what, it's not an ideal situation, but it happens regularly, and you can serve the people who are going through divorce by providing them with an option to sell their business so that it can continue to serve its clientele and provide jobs for its employees. Because divorce sales are usually subject to timing pressures, very often both the terms and the price of the businesses in this situation are quite favorable.

Why are we presenting this list?

Because people who close up shop for these reasons are what we call "motivated sellers." Just as in real estate, you're looking for people eager to sell their business. You're not interested in anyone listing with a business broker and trying to get an auction going to get the highest price for his or her company. You want people who are driven by one— or ideally several—of these ten reasons.

Now, having done this for quite some time and having helped thousands of students learn how to acquire businesses for little to no money out of pocket, we can tell you that not just some, but most, of you will ignore our advice about avoiding business brokers and will go off and start making offers to business owners who have listed their businesses for sale through brokers on one of the many online businesses selling sites. This, we find, is inevitable because most people do not want to take the time to find off-market businesses for sale.

Just understand that while most of what we teach applies to businesses listed with business brokers, the job of the business broker is to create an auction environment for the business where multiple would-be buyers compete to purchase the business that is for sale. They want to drive multiple offers to get the highest price for the business, and you will have a much more difficult time getting a great price and great terms for your acquisition if you choose this path. As in almost every case in life, when you are willing to put forth the effort (in this case to find off-market businesses with motivated sellers), you reap the greatest rewards.

Keep that in mind as you work through the subsequent chapters and we get more specific about the kind of businesses you want to buy. Your ideal seller should be someone highly incentivized to make *a deal*, not someone on the fence with the leisure or temperament to make the *best possible deal*.

People who want to relocate to be near their grandchildren are generally interested in moving quickly, not spending months trying to ratchet up their selling price. People going through a divorce or facing health issues prioritize their time and emotional well-being over finding the perfect buyer at the perfect price.

The same is true for those who have grown tired of the business and want to pursue a shiny new object. In all these cases, your interests coincide with the sellers': they want a quick exit, and you want a fair, and likely low, price for your willingness to act quickly. You've heard the expression "going-out-of-business sale." One of the first things to understand is that this phrase doesn't apply just to the products a company sells. It also refers to the business itself.

There is ALWAYS a crisis

The fact that there's always a crisis means there are always opportunities for those of us who seek to acquire businesses at favorable, but fair, prices.

Here are just a few that have presented themselves over the past several years:

Tax Changes

Sellers are also motivated by changes in the tax code. The avalanche of excellent deals happening at any given time may be driven, in part, by owners who fear that if they delay, they're going to lose money should certain countries, including the United States, follow through on proposals to repeal the tax advantages that traditionally have applied to business sales.

The good news here is that there is ALWAYS some crazy proposal in the US Congress or state legislatures to increase taxes, so there are ALWAYS concerns for sellers to move now and take advantage of the known tax situation vs. waiting and possibly being subjected to a far worse tax burden as a result of a delayed sale and closing.

As Jeffrey Levine points out with respect to the United States, "Those considering the potential sale and exit of a business (that may potentially have a lifetime of growth all taxed in a single year of sale) will seriously want to consider liquidating the business ... in an effort to 'harvest' capital gains at current rates, and avoid potentially substantial capital gains income from being subject to the proposed top tax rate in the future."[5]

The key takeaway here is that such sellers will be motivated to act quickly since haggling over the sale price will bring them less money than they'll save in taxes. Again, this spells opportunity for an investor like you, and it does so in an ethical manner since the buyers are also benefiting. It's a non-zero-sum transaction.

Health Scares

We also need to consider the impact of any global health scares, like the COVID pandemic of 2020, which caused over one hundred thousand businesses to close forever[6]. In his insightful *Post-Corona: From Crisis to Opportunity*, NYU professor Scott Galloway presents two central theses, "First, the pandemic's most endurable impact will be as an *accelerant*...to dynamics already present in society. Second, in any crisis there is *opportunity*; the greater and more disruptive the crisis, the greater the opportunity."[7]

Given the number of businesses that have closed their doors in troubled times and health panics, investors often have enormous opportunities as society moves back (as it inevitably always has) toward a new normalcy or what the biologists call 'homeostasis.' These include (but are not limited to) businesses involving travel, hospitality, entertainment, dining, and so on.

---

5   Jeffrey Levine, "Accelerating 2021 Business Sales To Navigate Biden's Proposed Capital Gains Tax Increase," *Nerd's Eye View*, June 2, 2021.

6   Heather Long, "More than 100,000 small businesses have closed forever as the nation's pandemic toll escalates," The Washington Post, May 12. 2020.

7   Scott Galloway, *Post Corona: From Crisis to Opportunity* (New York: Penguin, 2020).

Many pundits suggest that we have not seen the last of health scares and pandemics, so it is unlikely that potential sellers will become unaware or unafraid of the possibility of these events in the near future.

Wars and Military Operations

It seems that there is always someone somewhere who would like to annex the land or resources of someone else. Frequently, this leads to saber-rattling, and, from time-to-time, it can also lead to military action.

For example, when Russia invaded Ukraine in 2022, millions of people and thousands of businesses were impacted. Interruptions to the supply chain for oil, grain, and IT professionals created higher costs for those services and for businesses that previously depended on them as they searched throughout the world to find alternative supplies.

Economic Turbulence

In recent years, multiple factors (government stimulus programs, excessive demand, inflation, and supply shortages) caused severe economic shocks that had a tangible impact on people's well-being. Many businesses experienced an inability to secure personnel, raw materials, or inventory to sell cash-flush buyers who were increasingly willing to pay ever higher prices to obtain the goods and services that they desired.

Similarly, the daisy-chain effect of the pandemic created a need for many businesses to "go remote." Freed from geographical chains, many of these workers fanned out to less expensive places to live, and many realized that they simply no longer wished to work for the companies that they never really liked working for in the first place.

This was one factor behind the "Great Resignation" that has seen millions leaving their jobs permanently to find work elsewhere, which then led to the phenomenon of "Quiet Quitting" where workers simply stopped working or worked the least amount possible without getting fired, yet they continued to draw pay and benefits from their employers.

The one thing you can always count on is that there will always be some turmoil creating challenges and crises for business—and with those challenges comes great opportunity as well.

A Word about the "Ethical" of our "Ethical Profits In Crisis"

Despite the tremendous opportunities that exist to acquire businesses from motivated sellers, we do not ever advocate "taking advantage" of the position these sellers find themselves in. While you could use these motivated sellers' situations to acquire their businesses at rock-bottom prices, we prefer that you instead think of this as an opportunity to do good for BOTH you and the seller whose business you would like to acquire.

We like to think of operating within a "Zone of Fairness" where the amount that you will pay is within a price range that provides the seller with a price that reflects the value of the business and the speed at which they may want to sell it.

To accomplish this, you determine the maximum fair market price that you are willing to pay for any given business as lying between a low-fair price equal to, close to, or just under one times the last 12 months' profits (often referred to in the mergers and acquisitions world as TTM for "trailing twelve months'" profits) and the high-fair price as the last 12 months' profits from the business multiplied by an average multiple of what similar businesses sell for.

Don't worry too much about the valuation aspect of the Fairness Zone right now, as we will explain in much more detail when we talk about business valuations later in this book. For now, just understand that you want to help the seller realize a fair return for the sale of their business, at a price that is also advantageous for you, the buyer/ *ACQUIREpreneur*.

Huge Potential

The market for what we are talking about is absolutely huge. As the table at the end of this section shows, there are 57.1 million small- and medium-sized businesses (SMBs[8]) in the US, Canada, Australia, and Europe. SMBs are the ones you want to target—as we'll explain more fully in subsequent chapters. Of those, at any given time, about 4.32 million are for sale, and of those, only about 719,170 will sell—leaving you with approximately 3.6 million businesses you can target to acquire.

That's a lot of opportunity!

We are completely comfortable sharing this information because we have a *prosperity* mentality, not a *scarcity* mentality. We believe there's room for everyone—us and all of you—to do anything we want in this world. So, we are not trying to protect some narrow fiefdom.

It's not as though there are only a hundred gold mines in the world, so we need to hide our maps from you. The world is full of far more possibilities than we could ever hope to harvest on our own—and the numbers of acquisition targets replenish themselves each year!

---

8   SMBs are synonymous with SMEs (small- and medium-sized *enterprises*).

CHAPTER 1 - EPIC OPPORTUNITIES

There's no way that we could ever share this with so many people that we would run out of companies and start bumping into each other. We live in a cynical age, but we promise you that our motive is simply to share our fact-based insights into a nearly infinite opportunity to increase your income and your net worth.

Plus, we often find opportunities for partnering with those who adopt our approach. As a matter of fact, we are most hopeful that you will read this, and find yourself in a situation where you have an amazing deal and would like some help to fully optimize its value. In that case, we encourage you to reach out to us, and perhaps we can help you with that deal and create a big win-win for all of us!

You can do that at our BusinessWealthWithoutRisk.com/access website where you will find, not only numerous valuable resources and more information we could not include in this book, but also a form to submit deals that you have that you think might fit our acquisition criteria so that we might do some deals together!

HOW BIG IS THE MARKET?

	# of SMBs	FOR SALE	# THAT WILL SELL	# WE CAN TARGET TO ACQUIRE
USA	28.8 MILLION	2.59 MILLION	431,670	2.16 MILLION
CANADA	1.1 MILLION	99,000	16,500	82,000
EUROPE	25.1 MILLION	1.5 MILLION	250,000	1.25 MILLION
AUSTRALIA	2.1 MILLION	126,000	21,000	105,000
TOTAL	57.1 MILLION	4.32 MILLION	719,170	3.6 MILLION

Position Yourself as an Investor

In later chapters, we'll clarify how to pre-position yourself to find promising businesses, what kind of owners to contact, when to do so, and how to interact with them to ensure that you make an effective deal. For now, however, we want to introduce the crucial first step of our five-step plan for acquiring a business: *Positioning Yourself as an Investor.*

That means seeing and presenting yourself in a new way. In essence, we want you to become the thing that sellers want most: someone who can add value—not just cash—to their businesses.

The fact that you will do these deals with *no money out of pocket* differs from doing them with *no money down.* That's a key distinction.

What you'll learn throughout this book is that you can find a combination of inside money (cash to acquire the business created from within the four walls of the business itself) and outside money (i.e., not yours) to fund these deals in such a way that the seller may very well receive a large cash payment at closing, only it will come from sources entirely separate from your pockets, and you will not have to use any personal credit to fund your acquisitions.

Declare Yourself as an Investor

Before you begin reading Chapter 2, we want you to follow our lead and update all your social profiles (e.g., Twitter, YouTube, LinkedIn, TikTok, Instagram, Facebook, etc.) to let the world know you see yourself as an investor.

From this moment forward, start repositioning yourself in this new role so that when prospective sellers begin checking you out—and they will—you're represented as a serious player in this marketplace.

Your life is about to change, and you need to convey that changed mindset to the world—and to feel it in your bones. Begin with social media because that's the first place business owners will check. The next image shows how we've done this:

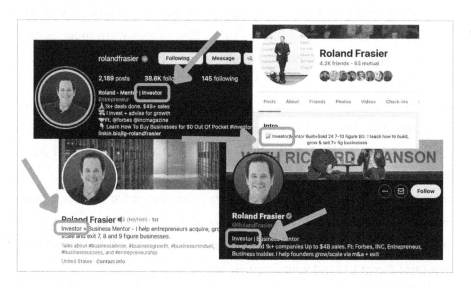

Make the same change to your email signature, your business cards, and any other biographical information you present to the public.

Start referring to yourself as an investor in your conversations. Don't worry if this feels artificial at first. It won't for long—certainly not after you make your first deals. What's crucial is to make all your self-references congruent with how you'll present yourself to prospective business owners. Unless you see yourself as a serious investor, neither will they. So, start reshaping your self-image—today!

And just in case you are having trouble identifying yourself as an investor, because perhaps you do not have a huge pile of cash sitting in your bank account with which to make cash investments in companies, consider this: an investor is defined as "a person that allocates capital with the expectation of a future financial return or to gain an advantage."

Capital is broadly defined as "relating to or being assets that add to the long-term net worth of a corporation." Do you possess assets that add to the long-term net worth of a company with the expectation of a future financial return or to gain an advantage?

Capital is broader than just money or cash. There is intellectual capital, social capital, human capital, etc. Capital is any asset or resource that you can bring that will help the business you are interested in working with. When you bring your skills, talents, resources, connections, strategy, know-how, labor, plans, and such to a business, you are bringing capital. Therefore, you are an investor.

Another way to think about yourself as an investor is to think about what the business you intend to work with would do with an infusion of cash. Most businesses are not looking to have investors contribute cash just to sit around and look at it. Rather, they want cash to buy the things that they believe their businesses need to grow and thrive, typically in the form of labor, management teams, inventory, attorneys, accountants, business equipment, advertising, or more.

So, when you bring these things to the business directly, you are bypassing the middleperson, the cash investor, and bringing the value and assets the company needs directly. You are an investor.

The other thing we want you to do before starting the next chapter is to read a bit about the kind of deals you're preparing to make.

Doing so will get you thinking creatively and help to cultivate the mindset you'll need to succeed.

Thrasio is a really interesting company that used a strategy called a "roll-up" to acquire a lot of different companies that were selling their products via FBA (Fulfillment by Amazon) on Amazon.[9] Many copycat companies have done this now—and you may soon join them. Thrasio was one of the fastest companies in history to reach a valuation of $1 billion. That makes it a unicorn.

Also, it went public, and the owners at the time forecast that it would be worth as much as $10 billion. Regardless of the long-term success of the Thrasio strategy, the concept is one that has prevailed for years. Companies find a "platform" business to acquire and then aggregate similar businesses around that platform company through a series of acquisitions (called "roll-ups" or "tuck-ins") to build a much larger company that then sells to strategic investors, family offices, private equity firms, or goes public.

As you read, think about whether you might be able to imitate the roll-up model if you had all the money you needed—because when you employ our EPIC strategies, you're going to have a blank checkbook to acquire as many companies as you want, along with the resources, skills, technology, and know-how needed to blow each acquisition up many times over.

Then you simply aggregate them, employ the "beyond exponential" growth tactics that we will describe in part two, and package them in a deal worth a whole lot more money than the companies were worth individually.

---

9   AJ Horch's "Thrasio," *CNBC Disruptor 50*, May 25, 2021. cnbc.com/2021/05/25/thrasio-disruptor-50.html.

That's the whole strategy of a "roll-up," which we will explore more fully in Chapter 3. But we want you to start getting an idea of what's possible through "arbitrage," a fancy word investment bankers and attorneys use for buying low and selling high. Thrasio's goal, and possibly yours as well, was to acquire these companies at low multiples, rolling them all into one giant company, and selling them for significantly higher multiples of their earnings. You can do the same and you may just find that you can earn more money than you've ever dreamed of making.

Think Big

To ward off any lingering doubts you may have, consider what we've accomplished using the same strategies you're about to learn. The next figure shows the diversity of business industries in which we've acquired with no money out of pocket and/or grown using exponential strategies.

You will find 24 different industries listed out of thousands that we have worked with, several in the $10 million, $100 million, and $1 billion sales ranges. We are not in an ivory tower passing on abstract ideas that should work in theory. We've been in the trenches living these strategies for decades, and we're still in the trenches! All the methods we're going to pass on have proven themselves in practice.

A PROVEN SYSTEM FOR GROWTH

Medical Billing**	Machine Manufacturing**	CPG**
eLearning*	Sporting Goods*	Corporate Training
Commercial Real Estate*	Legal Services	Document Preparation
Residential Real Estate***	Mastermind Groups*	Medical Equipment*
Trade Show/Events	Supplements*	Telecom Infrastructure*
Motorcycle Equipment*	Real Estate Training*	Beauty + Cosmetics*
Direct Response*	Online Casinos*	Tax Services
Digital Marketing Agency	eCommerce*	Software As A Service*

Why should you listen to us?

When you're evaluating surgeons, the first thing you should ask is how many times they've performed the procedure you need. We're the equivalent of a surgeon who does the operation you need every day. We've done over a thousand purchases and exits in our careers. Over the years, we've done so many deals and helped so many people do the same that it turns out we're not as young as we thought!

Here's Roland's backstory:

- Back in the 1980s, he was doing manufacturing company acquisitions using leveraged buyouts starting with a well-known Wall Street firm and a friendly investment banker mentor who took Roland under his wing and showed him how leveraged buyouts work.

- In the 1990s, Roland did retail workouts and turnarounds.

- In the 2000s, when the dot-com crash happened, he did reorganizations to help put companies together and build value.

- In the Great Recession from 2007 to 2009, he was doing real estate roll-ups, which (as noted previously) is where you acquire a lot of properties or companies and combine them into one so that you can sell them for a lot more than you could sell them for individually.

- And now he's doing software-as-a-service (SaaS) deals and acquiring media companies, real estate, service, and publishing operations—as well as pursuing opportunities that provide monthly recurring revenue (MRR). He recently acquired a webinar software company, and he's working on a recap deal with a $75 million financing and a $6 billion roll-up. While there is no guarantee the deals in process will ultimately pan out, the track record and experience are undeniable.

So, if you're wondering, "Does this work?" **The answer is an emphatic, _Yes!_**

A few years back, Roland acquired a company called DigitalMarketer, which is the leading training company in the world for teaching people how to market online. He acquired that company using none of his own cash through a combination of the strategies shared in this book. That company alone has spun out four different exits to date, including a sale to a Blackstone-owned company, another sale to a different billion dollar acquirer, a SaaS exit, and a media company exit, and Roland believes there are still five more exits to go from this one acquisition.

CHAPTER 1 - EPIC OPPORTUNITIES

Also, for no money out of pocket, Roland acquired part of a company that is one of the fastest-growing real estate brokerages in the US—with about 1,100 agents that work with it and whose most recent year's sales volume was approximately over $6.2 billion—again all acquired with no money out of pocket. And as we've shown above, there's an almost unlimited number of these deals.

Roland owns an interest in a publishing company that writes books for other people, a company that provides real estate software for investors, a company that provides major corporations with the ability to create standard operating procedures, and another SaaS software service that allows people to see how their employees are performing. He also owns a marketing software company, has an interest in a chain of over three hundred restaurants, a company formation business that forms thousands of new businesses per month for its clients, an accounting firm, a tax practice, a franchise company, a chain of auto repair shops, and a guitar player training company that teaches people online how to play. These are all business interests that Roland acquired for little or no money out of his own pocket.

For decades, Jay has been one of the most successful marketing authorities in the world, having created billions of dollars of wealth for clients across the planet. He has worked in more verticals than any other marketing expert, which means that he has always been able to provide fresh ideas to clients—ideas that may have been standard in other fields but were never before used in the field of that particular client.

We could go on, but you get the idea: we're not sharing theory with you here. This isn't something that we did 10 or 20 years ago and now make our money teaching it. We are practicing what we preach, living it, doing it, in the trenches making deals constantly.

We did not write this book to make money selling books. In fact, there's a good chance you received the copy that you are reading because we bought it for you and sent it to you ourselves.

We created this book to share our knowledge and help others enjoy the success that these strategies have brought to us, but there's another more selfish reason that we created it as well. We know that there will be those who read what we have written and decide that they would like to partner with us, to have us become part of their businesses, or to participate with them as they do larger deals, and those people will invite us into their companies and into the deals that they are doing so that we can all create income and wealth without risk together.

Even now, while we write, our profits are increasing—with a wide range of companies. And the reason we're sharing this with you is so you can see that it really works for anything. Whether you're in manufacturing, retail, services, product development, or event planning, online or offline, Business-to-Business or Business-To-Consumer, in whatever country, in whatever economy—it works across the board.

In the next chapter, we'll get specific about our five-step plan for acquiring businesses with no money out of pocket. If you doubt that this is possible, we're about to change your mind in a way that can change your life, creating business wealth without corresponding risk while earning you the income of a lifetime in a matter of years, not decades.

Remember as you read through the book and see examples, worksheets, checklists, forms, scripts, and other resources, that all the resources provided in this book and many more, including quite a few that we simply could not fit in the book itself, are all available and waiting for you at BusinessWealthWithoutRisk.com/access. Visit the site now and enjoy a huge collection of resources at absolutely no money out of pocket for you!

Chapter Highlights

Let's circle back to a thought we introduced at the onset of this chapter, "Now is the Time." That statement warrants repeating because it perfectly captures the essence of the moment we find ourselves in.

Right now is a moment—when the doors to unprecedented opportunities are swinging wide open for you. You can acquire businesses and unlock colossal financial rewards, while at the same time helping those who are in crisis. All without taking a penny out of your pocket!

If these words are dancing before your eyes right now, then there's a good chance that you share in our excitement. That's crucial because that flame of anticipation will light the path ahead.

The best part? You're not walking this path alone. We're right there with you, sharing in your journey every exhilarating step of the way.

And, if your excitement is tinged with a dash of doubt, you're not alone. Some people might be thinking, "Will this work? For me? In any industry? In my country? In this economy?" Or the notion of doing this without any personal investment strikes you as too good to be true. That's only natural.

But rest assured, we're not peddling illusions. Our aim is to hand-deliver a method that's stood the test of time across diverse industries and business sizes. We're not just going to tell you it works. We're going to show you how it's done.

The time is ripe for us to shift gears from theory to practice, from anticipation to action. We're eager to demonstrate just how attainable and pragmatic this journey is.

In the next chapter, we'll break down our five-step plan for acquiring businesses without dipping into your pockets. We won't simply hand over a roadmap; we'll give you exactly what you need to navigate this thrilling terrain.

Get ready to turn the page and take the next transformative step toward becoming an Epic *ACQUIREpreneur*.

Let's get this show on the road.

BusinessWealthWithoutRisk.com/access

CHAPTER 2

THE FIVE-STEP PLAN

As a musician, Roland has always loved Miles Davis's classic tune "Seven Steps to Heaven." We can't make any promises about the afterlife, but we can offer you a roadmap to a kind of financial paradise—and do it in two fewer steps than Miles needed. What we're going to reveal is precisely the way we work—a recipe we've proven again and again in our own financial kitchen.

Once you understand the framework, you can really dig into the specifics of acquiring businesses that make you money. So, think of this chapter as the bedrock upon which you're going to begin your new life as an *ACQUIREpreneur*.

We're going to pay special attention to your acquisition criteria before buying a business. One thread that will connect these five steps is the goal we articulated in Chapter 1: you always want to come as close as possible to the goal of completing your acquisitions with zero money out of pocket, because when you do, you have a virtually unlimited "checkbook" to acquire as many businesses as you like without the capital and credit constraints that hamper and limit even the largest private equity funds or family offices as they pursue their acquisition plans.

STEP 1. Work as an Investor "Above" Your Business

In the last chapter we encouraged you to begin thinking of yourself as an EPIC investor, as an **ACQUIREpreneur**. As part of your new mindset, we now want to add that you should devote your energy to working above the business rather than "on" or "in" it.

What may seem like a minor shift in prepositions will have a major shift in your earning trajectory.

Let's look at the few ways we can place ourselves in a business.

Working *in* the business is nice if you're content to be an employee, but we don't want you to do that. We don't want you doing the actual work of the business, like opening the store, making the coffee, that kind of stuff.

Michael Gerber in his excellent book, *The E-Myth Revisited*, takes us part way to our point by clarifying that when a barber or a software developer starts a business, the core task shifts from cutting hair and writing code to *running a business* in which others do those things.[10] Thus, the job becomes working *on* the business (e.g., installing systems, creating processes) rather than *in* it. Gerber's is a great book, but his audience isn't you. It's the person you hire to run your business.

As an EPIC investor and **ACQUIREpreneur**, we want to shift the paradigm a step beyond what Gerber describes. The key here is to

---

10   Michael E. Gerber, *The E-Myth Revisited: Why Most Small Businesses Don't Work and What to Do About It* (New York: Harper Business, 2004).

recognize that, for you, the product isn't what the business sells. Instead, the business *itself* is the product. You want somebody else doing all of the day-to-day work and supervising the employees. Your goal is to have a portfolio of businesses that you are able to rise above. They're the things you ultimately want to sell. That's an essential mindset shift, and it's what gets you to the next level as an investor.

In short, we want you to consider the possibility of working ABOVE the business, not on it, not in it. Working above the business is where the high-level financiers that run the trillion-dollar hedge funds and corporations play.

With the tools you're learning in this book, you'll be able to acquire as many businesses as you want with no money out of pocket. We've had clients acquire 16 businesses in their first few weeks. We'd like you to go a little bit more slowly, but you can set the pace. Once you're armed with these principles, you'll be like a kid in a candy store. You'll effectively have an unlimited checkbook to acquire businesses. But if your focus is working *in* or *on* a business—rather than *above* it—you'll be limited in your ability to make multiple acquisitions because you won't be positioned to scale yourself.

STEP 2. Never Risk Your Credit or Personal Assets

Why? Because you don't have to.

Unfortunately, however, many talented people fall into this trap. Roland's father risked and lost all his wealth. Yes, ALL of it. He came from absolutely nothing. His father's father was a minister and had no money at all. Roland's father came along, worked very hard, and built up a great investment portfolio. But he kept doing bigger and bigger deals, and he never stopped being personally liable for the debt associated with those deals. In fact, he frequently pledged his personal financial guaranty as a way to get brought into deals to have an equity stake, but he was also personally liable for the businesses where he did this.

In effect, he began to create wealth by betting the farm in every deal, and he never stopped. He never learned how to use SPVs and protect his personal and other business assets from liability and it cost him everything. Ultimately, he lost it all. He went from a multi-millionaire set for life to virtually bankrupt. This is and was for Roland a poignant, cautionary tale, and one that he has remembered in all of his dealings in business ever since.

Remember, if you are daisy-chaining your businesses and your finances to fund your portfolio's growth, if one business goes bad, you're going to suffer a lot of harm and possibly lose everything that you've worked for over your entire career. We've seen this countless times with investors who use their existing investment portfolio to secure their entry into the next deal. They do this deal after deal until, eventually, just one misstep in one deal brings the whole house of cards tumbling down. Don't let this happen to you!

There's a way to eliminate that risk. Recently, Roland asked an enormously successful friend, Gary Vaynerchuk, "What is the one thing that you know now that you wish you'd known when you got started?" His response was immediate and emphatic, "I wish I'd known about the SPV because it would've saved me *tens of millions of dollars.*"

An SPV is a "special purpose vehicle." Essentially, it's a way of isolating financial risk by ensuring that you aren't personally liable for the debts of your companies—and that debts from one company don't jeopardize the profits of your other companies. That way a single bad apple doesn't spoil the bushel.

You can form the SPV as a limited partnership, a trust, a corporation, or a limited liability company (LLC), among other options in the United States, or one of any number of limited liability entities in other countries. We'll talk more about how to set up an SPV later in the book. For now, however, be aware that *you want to have one in place before you do your first deal.*

STEP 3. Source and Analyze Deals You Want to Acquire

This is about finding and assessing buying opportunities to create what we call "deal flow." We'll get into the specifics in Chapter 3, but before that, we need to clarify your acquisition criteria, so you know what specific type of business you're trying to find. In the figure below, business profits increase as you go from left to right, and the amount of effort you need to expend increases as you go from the bottom to the top.

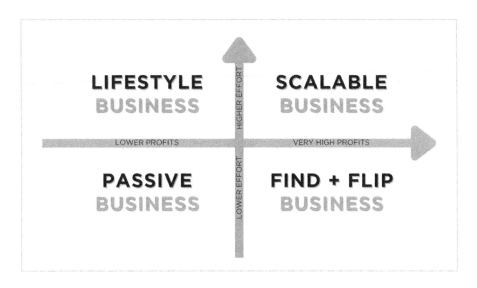

You may say that lower profits are acceptable provided you don't have to invest a lot of time and effort.

In that case, what you're shopping for is a passive business—one that's already profitable with someone who runs it for you. It's effectively like having a stock that pays a dividend, a property that pays you rent, or an invention that pays you a monthly royalty.

Next, if you're a little bit more ambitious and willing to exert more effort, you might want to consider a lifestyle business. It, too, brings in lower profits—though we should qualify that "lower" is a relative term. We have friends who make tens of millions of dollars per year from these businesses. And although they require effort, they're doing what they love and getting paid for it.

In the lower-right quadrant, you have high profits and low effort. That's a beautiful combination! In this case, you're finding and flipping businesses. So, it's not completely passive: you need to put some work into them. Later in the book, we'll talk about how to acquire these high-profit businesses at low prices and then sell them for a lot of profit to a really hungry crowd of private equity investors, Amazon aggregators, family offices, and other corporations and investors. These people don't want to do the work of finding companies, so they reward you for doing so. And the rewards are substantial—as they often are when you flip a house.

In the upper-right quadrant, you have our favorite: **Scalable Businesses**. We do all four kinds of deals, but we focus on these "buy-and-build" opportunities more than anything else. We love getting in and adding value by deploying our exponential growth strategies, and then adding even more value to increase the price at which the businesses can be sold to private equity funds, family offices, SPACs (special purpose acquisition companies), and larger companies.

The goal is to acquire a business at a very favorable and ethically fair price using our $0 out of pocket strategies, enhance it using our exponential growth strategies, and then sell it to a private-equity firm or other investors for a whole lot more than we paid for it using our "exit ready" strategies (more on those in part three of this book).

A key concept here is called EBITDA (i.e., earnings before interest, taxes, depreciation, and amortization). That's a fancy word we use in the investment banking M&A (Mergers and Acquisitions) community to talk about profit.

Businesses typically sell for a multiple of EBITDA. Buyers typically purchase a business by paying the owner/seller a certain number of years' worth of profit in the company as part of the sale. The number of years of profit the buyer pays for a business is generally referred to as a "multiple" and the higher the multiple, the better the price realized by the seller.

So, let's say that a business is making $120,000 a year—$10,000 a month—in EBITDA, and you buy it for a multiple of 1X EBITDA (i.e., $120,000). Then you deploy our exponential growth strategies and add value for three to five years increasing the EBITDA by 5X, from $120,000 per year to $600,000, and then sell it for a multiple of 10X the then-current EBITDA of $600,000. That would mean your original $120,000 acquisition investment would return you $6 million!

That's what we love about these deals!

Imagine this: Every five years, you sell a business and make ten years of profits! Over 20 years, you'll have sold four businesses (20-year time period divided by five years every sales cycle = four business sales). That means that you will have sold four businesses at a multiple of ten years of profits, which means that you will have received 40 years MORE profits than if you had held onto the business and taken the profits every year. This is a huge breakthrough that we had several years ago, and one of the major aims of this book is to share it with you.

Let's break that down to be sure you fully appreciate the impact of it, because this is truly life changing and something that almost no one outside of the top tiers of Wall Street hedge fund masters truly understand AND implement.

If you simply held onto a business for 20 years, you would receive 20 years of profits from that business. However, if you held and sold four different businesses over that same 20-year timespan, then you would have the 20 years of profits from those four businesses PLUS the proceeds from four exits, each of which paid a 10x multiple on profits, an equivalent of 40 years of profits. In effect, you would have 20 years of holding profits PLUS 40 years of "exit profits" giving you a grand total of 60 years of profits as opposed to the 20 years of profits you would have had simply by holding the business without ever selling.

This is why investment bankers and people on Wall Street are able to accumulate so much wealth so fast: they aren't playing the game of only getting paid one year, every year.

Every few years, they're getting paid 7 to 20 years or more of income. **Imagine being 60 years of profits ahead of where you are right now!**

And then, of course, you still get the profits in all the other years that you continue to hold and own the business. So, a person who held a business that made $100,000 a year for 20 years would only have made $2 million. You would have made $6 million plus $2 million (i.e., $8 million). That's four times as much net worth.

Most people fail to cash in on these opportunities for three simple reasons:

1. *They don't know the strategy exists, or*
2. *They don't know what or how to acquire it, or*
3. *They're overwhelmed by the range of possibilities, and they either get paralyzed or choose unwisely.*

We created the worksheet below to help you avoid these problems and develop the specific acquisition criteria that will lead you to success. The worksheet starts out completely blank so you can then fill in the blanks. We have also included an example worksheet that has already been completed for you so you can see how we might fill this worksheet out.

You can download a free copy of the worksheet at BusinessWealthWithoutRisk.com/access along with all the other resources referred to in this book.

WHAT TO ACQUIRE WORKSHEET

HOBBIES/INTERESTS/PASSIONS	EXPERIENCE, SUPERPOWERS, + SKILLS
_____	_____
_____	_____
_____	_____
_____	_____

BIGGEST CURRENT NEEDS/DESIRES		FINANCIAL (PRICE TARGET 1-5X EBITDA)
MARKET SHARE	LEADS	INCOME FOR YOU _____
CAPABILITY	HIGHER AOV	GROWTH BUDGET _____
HIGHER LCV	MORE MARGIN	EBITDA TARGET _____
INNOVATION	1st PLATFORM	PRICE TARGET _____ TO _____

And a completed version:

WHAT TO ACQUIRE WORKSHEET

HOBBIES/INTERESTS/PASSIONS

Photography, Travel, Cooking, Fashion, Wine,

Pets, Real Estate, Home Decor, Remodels,

Crypto, Coding, Entrepreneurship, Design, Music,

Alternative Investing

EXPERIENCE, SUPERPOWERS, + SKILLS

Negotiating, Networking, Simplifying,

Accounting, Finding Partners, Excel, Finance,

Raising Capital, Marketing, Copywriting,

Buy/Sell Businesses, Events, Creating Courses

BIGGEST CURRENT NEEDS/DESIRES

MARKET SHARE | LEADS
CAPABILITY | HIGHER AOV
HIGHER LCV | MORE MARGIN
INNOVATION | 1st PLATFORM

FINANCIAL (PRICE TARGET 1-5X EBITDA)

INCOME FOR YOU — $120,000

GROWTH BUDGET — $120,000

EBITDA TARGET — $240,000

PRICE TARGET $240,000 TO $1.2M

The first thing we want you to do is fill in the section called *Hobbies, Interests + Passions*. To give you a model for completing this essential exercise, Roland filled in the form for himself.

Before you start reading Chapter 3, we want you to open a spreadsheet or a word processor file or get a blank piece of paper and fill in the four sections for yourself. Remember, you can also download a blank copy of this form at BusinessWealthWithoutRisk.com/access. The new ideas we introduce in the coming pages will be vastly more helpful if you complete this step. Trust the process! Don't skip ahead!

So, begin by identifying, "What do I love?" Given the wide range of business possibilities, why would you choose one you're indifferent to? We sure wouldn't.

In the example form, Roland filled in a wide and varied range of interests—from cryptocurrency (although he skews more into infrastructure than coins) and investing to music and dogs. Don't censor yourself here. Just be honest. You can make money with any kind of business that's driven by passion. Roland has a friend turning big profits by manufacturing organic horse biscuits. Talk about a niche company!

Next, move to the upper-right quadrant: *Experience, Superpowers + Skills*. Here we're basically answering the question, "What have I done?" Write down those areas in which you have special insights that will add value to any company you acquire. As you can see, Roland has experience in accounting, events, raising money and so on. But because he doesn't have the desire to turn photography into a business, he concludes—even though he loves it—this might not be the place to invest.

What you're looking for as you fill in the sheet is how to combine your answers under all four headings into an investment thesis. An investment thesis is a written analysis laying out the case for why an investment opportunity should generate a compelling return. Roland's investment thesis using the worksheet above could be "Using my passion for pets and my experience in buying and selling businesses, negotiating, networking, and finding partners, as well as my extensive network of connections, I will acquire pet manufacturing, sales, and distribution businesses to create a vertically integrated pet company."

When you are brainstorming your "Superpowers + Skills," you're answering the question, "What am I great at?"

You want to acquire a business that will let you unleash that greatness. Michael Jordan loved baseball and basketball, and he had experience playing both, but he was a mediocre baseball player and a superstar on the basketball court. So instead of continuing to bat a pathetic .202 with the lowly Birmingham Barons, he ultimately followed his greatness and won six NBA titles with the Chicago Bulls, signed insane endorsement deals, created a legacy shoe brand with Nike, and built a net worth approaching $2 billion. Had he ignored his superpower and spent the rest of his career trying to make baseball's major leagues, he would have a whole lot lower net worth than he does now. Lean into your natural talents and skills, enhanced by your practice and experience.

Roland's best skills include negotiating, networking, building one-on-one relationships, simplifying complex ideas, composing music, and so on. Now not all of these skills will overlap, but when thinking about acquiring a business, he always asks, "Is this enterprise going to amplify or negate my superpowers?" And he chooses those that play to his strengths and rejects those that don't.

If you're a chess champion, why would you want to play poker? Jay, too, is considered preeminent, virtually unequaled as a strategist and value creator. So, he, too, plays to his strengths.

When you've finished the worksheet and filled in all of the boxes (although we may not have covered them all here), step back and ask, "Where do these criteria overlap?" To give you a concrete example, Roland might ask, "Can I take my interest in dogs and apply it to any experience I have?" Well, sure. He can apply it to buying businesses, selling businesses, negotiating deals, creating and running events, or raising money. So, he has a lot of experiences he can summon, thanks to his passion for dogs.

What about Roland's superpowers and skills?

Marketing, finding partners in these deals, negotiating, networking—he can do that all to amplify his canine passion. He can reach out to his social media connections and say, "Hey, I'm interested in doing deals related to pets, particularly dogs. Does anybody have anything they can share with me?"

Okay, enough about Roland and man's best friend! Let's talk about you!

As you look at your own completed sheet, begin to cross off the categories or items that do not appeal to you as a potential business acquisition category. You are likely to find several things that you wrote down that are fun and interesting, but you would not enjoy doing as your job or even as an investment or for money, just like Roland did when he eliminated photography from the list.

That's okay, and it's one of the big benefits of going through this exercise—to identify areas of interest, experience, superpowers, or connections that you just do not want to explore as a business option.

That's your assignment after you finish reading this chapter. Because if you don't know what you want to do, you won't move forward. This is a step that will hold you back. We want to get you over this hump so you'll be able to say, "Wow, I actually can go after this thing I have a passion for, and I can have my experience, my network connections, superpowers, and skills to support me in this thing I love to do."

Step 4. Fund Your Deals with $0 Out of Pocket

As you'll see, you can buy businesses that are worth millions of dollars using little or no money out of your own pocket. One recent graduate of Roland's 5-day EPIC Challenge seminar acquired an $88 million dollar business with no money out of pocket, and another created a $100 million dollar funded private equity fund deal.

While the size of these two deals is unusual, creating million-dollar deals with no money out of pocket is most definitely not an anomaly. Legions of graduates have learned how to acquire businesses from the very small to multimillion-dollar legacy businesses, almost always without anteing up any of their own funds.

We'll share proven ways to do this in later chapters.

For now, we just want to make it clear that your purchases aren't limited by your personal assets—nor are you going to put those assets at risk. (Notice that Roland didn't include gambling in his list of Hobbies, Interests + Passions). He wouldn't do something risky with his money, and he'd never present financial strategies that require you to do it with yours.

To give you a sense of where you're heading, a good target size for your first acquisition would either be 1) a media asset like a Facebook or LinkedIn group, podcast, YouTube channel, or newsletter which has somewhere between zero trailing 12 months' profits up to about $200,000, or 2) a business with between $100,000 and $1 million in annual profits. But you can certainly go much bigger or smaller. The beauty of our system is that it allows you to move at your own pace.

Step 5. Earn Profits, Get Paid, and Build Wealth

Before we get you started making deals in the next chapter, we need to clarify another part of your acquisition criteria: How much money do you want to earn from your initial deals? A common answer is $10,000 per month ($120,000 per year). So—for the sake of this example—let's say that's your goal.

One option is to own the business and have it pay you $10,000 a month—and that would be great. In that case, you'll need an EBITDA (or target profit) of $120,000 a year. But our hope is that you'll also want to grow these businesses.

So, let's say you want another $10,000 a month to be able to invest for growth. In the worksheet below, we simply add your income target and what you intend to spend for growth. That gives us a target EBITDA for the business you want to buy. Now that you have your acquisition criteria, you know that if the EBITDA of the acquisition target you are presented with isn't $240,000 or more, then you aren't interested.

Note that the worksheet below, and all the other materials contained in this book, are available digitally for you at BusinessWealthWithoutRisk.com/access, along with a host of other valuable and free resources. Visit that site now to download your copy of the worksheet below.

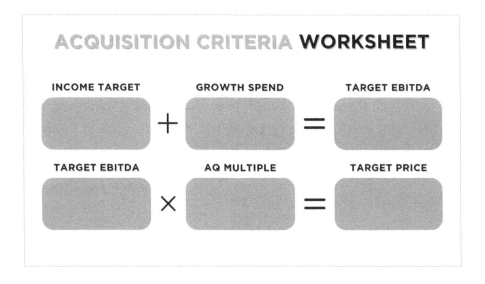

Now multiply the target EBITDA by the acquisition multiple[11]. Set that figure between one and five—and as close to one as possible. Our goal for you is to sell these businesses for a significant profit.

So, with the possible exception of SaaS, we don't want to exceed 5x. That sets your target price between $240,000 (1x) and $1.2 million (5x). As with the *What to Acquire* worksheet we looked at earlier, we'd like you to run your own numbers for the *Acquisition Criteria* worksheet before you start reading Chapter 3.

11   These multiples help buyers estimate a business's value based on the multiples used in a similar group of transactions. An acquisition multiple of 1x would be identical to the EBITDA.

Overview: Three Major $0 Out of Pocket Strategies

TYPE 1. Advisory Deals.

These involve getting paid for using your superpower skills to advise companies. Roland does this all the time. This week, as we write this, Roland completed three half-day advisory consults for $25,000 each. So that's $75,000 from people who just wanted to get together for four hours to talk about what he knows to accomplish their business goals. Last month, he had 11 of these $25,000 half-day consults. He currently completes 3 to 12 of these consults per month.

Roland uses these consultations much more for deal flow and a chance to get an inside look at potential acquisitions than as a source of income. He targets between 40 and 80 of these consults every year, so, if you're doing the math, that means that as a side-benefit to his deal finding activities, Roland gets to earn somewhere between $1 million and $2 million.

Doing this, you can basically get paid quite well just to vet deals! But that would be a terrible waste of an opportunity, because just one deal could mean $2 million every year to you, plus a huge exit.

And that is a very cool thing because as we've always said, "Every extra two million dollars helps!"

You have special expertise, too. If you don't feel you have any skills or knowledge that would allow you to do this, you're wrong!

Combine your superpowers with what you're learning in this book and you can add a lot of value. As a matter of fact, as of today, we want you to start referring to yourself as an "investor" and a "consultant" and all the while always remember you are an **ACQUIREpreneur!**

CHAPTER 2 - THE FIVE-STEP PLAN

Think how often you've given away your time for free helping someone else solve business problems. That's not fair to you, and people may value your help less because they aren't paying for it. It is often said that in the mind of someone receiving advice, "Free has no value!"

With the information in this book, you are, at a minimum, becoming a mergers and acquisitions consultant, or at least by the time you're done reading it, you will be qualified to consult in that area. We recommend that you charge at least $2,500 a day for your time. As you get more confident, you'll find that you can do this for more money than you think you are worth right now, because we are all worth more money than we think we are. As with most things, it is our mindset that limits our success and altitude.

We promise that's true. It is for you, and it is for us as well. We have all graduated through countless levels of thinking too small to where we are now, and then we find that we are still thinking too small. At least we see that we are constantly growing in our mindset!

You can also trade your expertise for partial ownership of a company. Some of our friends, like the investors on *Shark Tank*, make their whole living doing this.

They just say, "I'll be a consultant for your company for an hour a month." And the companies give them equity—typically between 1-5%.

Think about this. If you had 20 consultancy deals at 5% each, that is like owning 100% (20 companies multiplied by 5% ownership in each) of a company. It's like getting an entire company for free, plus it is diversified because instead of owning one company and bearing 100% of your risk there, you own 20.

TYPE 2. Equity Deals.

This differs a bit from being a consultant: you're going to invest a bit more time and effort, but the payoffs are correspondingly bigger.

Typically, you might be a growth consultant, using the skills you're acquiring from this book. You can approach people who already have businesses and say, "I'd like to help you grow this business and acquire companies with no money out of pocket." And in exchange, you're going to receive 10-50% ownership.

Roland recently did two deals: one was a 10% ownership in a business services company, the other a 10% ownership in a chain of auto repair shops. You can do the same.

People will value what you learn in this book, and they'll offer you equity in exchange for your knowledge. One caveat: we don't recommend that you try to get more than 50% ownership. Why? Because when someone offers you that much, they expect you to do 100% of the work, and if you are going to do 100% of the work then you might as well own 100% of the company through a full acquisition.

TYPE 3. Self-Funding Acquisition Deals.

In these transactions, the company pays for itself using the kind of creative financing we'll describe in subsequent chapters. Several of the strategies let the company pay for itself out of the value that's already there—and that gets really, really exciting.

If we wanted to create a course to give out all the information in this book, we could charge college-like tuition fees of $20,000 or more and deliver it over two years like an MBA program. But we're more interested in a movement that helps the economy, makes a lot of millionaires—you among them, and that creates tremendous deal flow for us in the process. All part of our win-win philosophy!

In the next chapter, we're going to start getting down to the heart of the matter: finding deals you can acquire. Be sure to complete the *What to Acquire* worksheet and the *Acquisition Criteria* worksheet we shared previously so that you'll have a clear picture of what you want and—equally important—so you can filter out all the deals that don't meet your criteria.

Remember that you can download free copies of all the worksheets and all the other materials in this book at BusinessWealthWithoutRisk.com/access, along with additional supplemental content that can help you as you begin your journey as an **ACQUIREpreneur**.

Key Takeaways

While we're unsure if you likened this five-step plan to the "Seven Steps to Heaven" we mentioned at the start of this chapter, we hope you see it as your straightforward roadmap to financial success.

Now that you've grasped the core of it, your transformation into an accomplished *ACQUIREpreneur* is in motion.

Take a moment to appreciate your journey. This framework has guided many to financial prosperity. Now, we're going to step from theory into practice as we enter the captivating world of deal-making.

In the next chapter, we will guide you through spotting lucrative opportunities, crafting your approach, and making your case persuasively. You won't just be following a roadmap; you'll be equipped to navigate confidently and precisely.

As you turn the page, we're stepping into the nitty-gritty of finding the right targets to acquire and turn what you've learned into money.

BusinessWealthWithoutRisk.com/access

CHAPTER 3

FINDING TARGETS
TO ACQUIRE

In this chapter, we're going to talk about turning what **you've learned into money.** More specifically, we'll clarify five crucial aspects in the life cycle of a deal: how to find deals the right way, drill down and identify specific targets, single out the key players, contact those players, and make your most effective case to them through what you say and do.

To begin, let's look at three strong monetization strategies.

The first is *CASH-ON-CASH*. Here, you're acquiring an already profitable business—perhaps one that's closing or fits some of your other criteria from Chapter 2. What's crucial is that you acquire it at the right multiple or price.

Let's look at three examples in the figure below: *Good, Better, and Great*. In each option, we are buying 100% of the company with no money out of pocket. Remember we don't say "no money down" because you'll often give money to the seller at closing. It's just not going to be out of *your* pocket! It's going to come from the business or some other place, which we'll talk more about in Chapter 5.

Suppose the business is valued at a multiple of 3.6x its profit (or EBITDA) by the market, as determined by recent sales of similar businesses. That would mean that the business with $360,000 of EBITDA has a market value of $1.3 million ($360,000 EBITDA x 3.6 multiple). For our first example, you are going to buy the business with 100% seller financing and a 10-year interest only note, meaning you pay nothing down to acquire the business and pay simple interest at 10% of the purchase price for 10 years, with a single payment for the full amount of the purchase price due at the end of the financing term in 10 years.

ROI: CASH-ON-CASH RETURN

	GOOD	BETTER	GREAT
100% NO $0 OUT-OF-POCKET	$1.3M	$540k	$360k
EBITDA OF TARGET	$360k	$360k	$360k
100% FINANCED @ 10% INTEREST	($130k)	($54k)	($36k)
NET CASH FLOW YEAR 1	$230k	$306k	$324k
YEAR 1 CASH-ON-CASH ROI	177%	567%	900%

As you can see, you have an annual payment for the first 10 years that you own this business equal to 10% of the $1.3 million purchase price, which makes your annual payment $130,000. Fortunately, you have acquired a business that makes a profit (EBITDA) of $360,000, so to see how much cashflow you have after the acquisition debt interest is paid you subtract the $130,000 interest payment from the $360,000 EBITDA and discover that you have a $230,000 profit.

Keep in mind that at the end of 10 years you will also have to pay back the $1.3 million acquisition price, so you should probably set aside a sinking fund to pay that off. If you wanted to set aside 10% per year of the total amount that is due in 10 years, that would mean you would need to set aside an extra $130,000 per year ($1.3 million due in 10 years divided by 10 years). Deducting that additional set aside from your initial $230,000 net profit calculated above still leaves you with $100,000 per year in clear cashflow. $360,000 EBITDA - $130,000 annual interest - $130,000 annual principal reduction set aside = $100,000 net positive cashflow.

But let's say that the seller was not willing to finance for the full 10-year period to receive their $1.3 million in a lump sum at the end of 10 years. Let's assume that you're still able to buy the business with 100% seller financing, but this time the seller wants you to amortize your payments using a 10-year, 6% loan with straight amortization.

Under those terms, you can use a calculator to determine the amount per month that you will be making in payments on the purchase price of $1.3 million over the 10-year purchase term. You will be financing $1.3 million dollars at 6% interest for 10 years, which creates a monthly payment of about $14,500. Multiplying $14,500 x 12 months gives you your annual interest payment of $174,000. (Note: we rounded these numbers for ease of reading)

By the way, if you're thinking, "well, no seller would ever finance millions of dollars on a business that they were selling," we can tell you that it is done quite regularly, both in business sales and real estate. For example, Roland's house is seller financed over 10 years with 3.5% interest. He doesn't pay the whole balance of the $2 million loan the seller made until the end of that 10-year period. We do the same with businesses, and so can you!

In this example, you can take the $1.3 million purchase price and say, "Over 10 years with the payments made monthly at 6%, this will cost me about $174,000 a year." So, the COST of the debt used to acquire this business totals $174,000 per year for the next 10 years. At the end of those 10 years, you will have paid off 100% of the debt and owe nothing on the business.

But the business is earning $360,000 of profit every year, which is $186,000 more than the loan payment. Your year-one cash-on-cash return on this investment (ROI) is 207%. That is calculated by dividing the business's profits/EBITDA of $360,000 by the cost of the acquisition loan debt service of $174,000.

So, $360,000/$174,000 = 2.07. That means that the business earned 2.07 times what it cost to service the debt, thereby creating a cash-on-cash return on investment of 207%.

Now, for you math types, you will realize that the true return is actually infinite because this was a 100% seller financed deal, meaning that you actually did not have to invest any money at all to acquire this company. That's pretty good!

Let's shift to the *Better* column. Here you are able to buy the business at a lower price: $540,000, which represents a purchase multiple of 1.5x EBITDA. The EBITDA is still earning the same profit/EBITDA or $360,000, but because of the lower purchase price, your payment drops to $54,000 a year if you can get the seller to agree to a 10-year financing with interest only at 10% interest, which means your cash-on-cash return is $306,000 ($360,000 EBITDA minus $54,000 debt service)—which equates to a 567% ROI.

ROI: CASH-ON-CASH RETURN

	GOOD	BETTER	GREAT
100% NO $0 OUT-OF-POCKET	$1.3M	$540k	$360k
EBITDA OF TARGET	$360k	$360k	$360k
100% FINANCED @ 10% INTEREST	($130k)	($54k)	($36k)
NET CASH FLOW YEAR 1	$230k	$306k	$324k
YEAR 1 CASH-ON-CASH ROI	177%	567%	900%

Even if you have to straight-line amortize the payments like a traditional house mortgage, your payment drops to $72,000 a year, which means your cash-on-cash return is $288,000 ($360,000 EBITDA minus $72,000 debt service)—which equates to a 500% ROI.

To calculate that 500% ROI, simply divide the business's profit/ EBITDA of $360,000 by the $72,000 cost of the annual debt service and you can see that the answer is five. That means that the business is generating 5x the cost of the debt service that was used to purchase it. Now, you have gone from good to better.

Finally, in the *Great* column, you buy the company for your ideal price—one times $360,000 profit/EBITDA (i.e., 1x).

ROI: CASH-ON-CASH RETURN

	GOOD	BETTER	GREAT
100% NO $0 OUT-OF-POCKET	$1.3M	$540k	$360k
EBITDA OF TARGET	$360k	$360k	$360k
100% FINANCED @ 10% INTEREST	($130k)	($54k)	($36k)
NET CASH FLOW YEAR 1	$230k	$306k	$324k
YEAR 1 CASH-ON-CASH ROI	177%	567%	900%

At that purchase price, you're paying only $36,000 a year to service the debt you incurred to purchase the business, assuming the 10-year interest only financing scenario, which leaves you with $324,000 in profit and a 900% ROI.

Even if you have to use straight-line amortization like you would if you were buying a house, you're paying only $48,000 a year to service the debt you incurred to purchase the business, which leaves you with $312,000 in profit and a 750% ROI.

Determine that ROI by dividing the $360,000 that the company earns in profit/EBITDA by the $48,000 annual debt service incurred to acquire the company and you can see that the answer is 7.5. That means the business earned profits that were 7.5x the cost to service the debt, thereby creating a 750% ROI.

But, as we mentioned earlier, these returns are actually infinite because you're paying no money out of your own pocket to acquire the business.

Consider how this compares to the ROI on other investments you might make. For a savings account, while returns fluctuate greatly, they are generally quite low with the figure as of this writing averaging somewhere around 1.09%. Stock investments have historically returned about 8% per year over time, and real estate has historically generated approximately 10.6% per year. And even in a white-hot real estate market, where properties routinely sell above market rate, nothing we've ever found earns anything close to the kind of returns that you can make from acquiring a business. The whole purpose of this book is to show you how to (literally) capitalize on this fact.

Strategy 2 is *MAKE MONEY ON THE BUY*. Now your focus is instant intrinsic built-in profit: that is, how much your net worth goes up when the deal closes. In the first case of your hypothetical acquisition described in the previous section, you had three different potential purchase prices: a "Good" scenario where you purchased the business at its full market value, a second, "Better," scenario where you purchased the business at a lower value of 1.5x EBITDA and a third, "Great," scenario where you purchased the business at a significant discount to market value at a multiple of 1x EBITDA.

In the "Good" example, you were paying full market value, so the business cost you $1.3 million to acquire and as soon as you closed the deal it was still worth its full market value of $1.3 million. Accordingly, the immediate profit was $0. You paid $1.3 million for a business that was worth $1.3 million. This was a good deal, but not a better or great one. The fact is that this is how most people buy companies.

Here we're talking about built-in wealth. In strategy one, you're able to make a lot of money because the business earns substantially more than it costs to service the debt payments on the acquisition price, but you don't have any built-in equity (equity in this case is the same as profit or value). That's why the table below shows $0 under the *Good* column.

In the *Better* column, you paid 1.5x the profit rather than full market value. That means you receive the same value at closing—a business whose fair market value is $1.3 million—but you've paid only $540,000 for it. Thus, the day you close the deal, your immediate wealth gain is $760,000, the difference between the business's fair market value of $1.3 million and what you paid $540,000.

In the *Great* column that gain is $940,000 since the purchase price multiple was still lower, at 1x, resulting in us paying only $360,000 for a business that was worth $1.3 million.

ROI: MAKING MONEY "ON-THE-BUY"

	GOOD	BETTER	GREAT
EBITDA OF TARGET	$360k	$360k	$360k
PURCHASE PRICE MULTIPLE	3.6x	1.5x	1x
PURCHASE PRICE	$1.3M	$540k	$360k
VALUATION POST CLOSING	$1.3M	$1.3M	$1.3M
IMMEDIATE WEALTH GAIN	$ -0	+ $760k	+ $940k

Why would anyone sell for less than market value? For the reasons we clarified in the last chapter: because they're a motivated seller.

In fact, if you recall, we listed the ten most popular reasons that people become motivated sellers. The business is simply worth less to them than it is to the market if you were to take the time to prepare it for sale, solicit buyers, receive offers, and negotiate a sale over the course of four to six months.

When you sell, you will not be similarly motivated. Your aim is to buy low and sell high (or at least to buy below market and sell at market)—to get the most money you can for the business. If you're able to acquire companies for significantly less than they're worth because you're willing to act quickly, you instantly pick up profit in the form of cash and equity that's built into the business.

Some of you may be thinking, "Well, Roland and Jay, you're experienced, so you can make 1x deals, but I'm never going to be able to do that." To which we say, nonsense!

This issue is 100% mindset, which you're developing as you read this book. And if owners have gone through the process of trying to sell and failed, or if they need to sell quickly and don't just want to close the business and get $0 for it, your 1x offer is going to be a godsend. It's all about making offers to create an EPIC win-win transaction: ethical profits in a time of crisis.

In Strategy 3, you're going to MAKE MONEY ON THE EXIT (where you buy businesses with the intention to flip them or to build them to even higher profits and then flip them). Either way, you're planning to cash out with an exit. And for mergers and acquisition (M&A) deals, there's more cash than ever out there searching for great businesses to acquire, a total as we write this of about $5 trillion.

Apple, Tesla, and other big companies have a ton of money on the sidelines, waiting to figure out what to do with it, and private equity funds, SPACs (special purpose acquisition companies), family offices, high net worth individuals, and high net worth investors are all sitting on the sidelines with literally trillions of dollars in "dry powder" or cash on hand, ready to buy. One thing they love to do? *Buy companies!* Private equity, family offices, and retiring entrepreneurs who cash out of bigger companies are all looking to buy businesses you turn around, roll up, or explode in EBITDA.

Let's step back a bit and look at the four columns in the next figure—each of which represents a class of business buyer with a purchase-price multiple that increases as you move from left to right. You're looking to play in the business acquisition world by searching for and closing your deals in the two columns on the left, the #1 and #2 boxes.

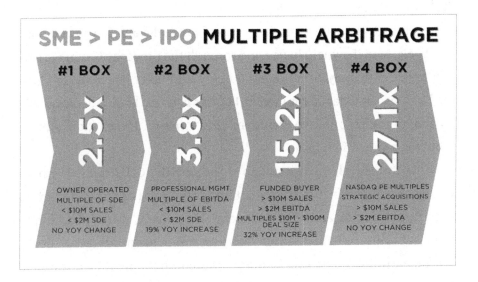

SME > PE > IPO MULTIPLE ARBITRAGE

#1 BOX	#2 BOX	#3 BOX	#4 BOX
2.5x	3.8x	15.2x	27.1x
OWNER OPERATED MULTIPLE OF SDE < $10M SALES < $2M SDE NO YOY CHANGE	PROFESSIONAL MGMT. MULTIPLE OF EBITDA < $10M SALES < $2M SDE 19% YOY INCREASE	FUNDED BUYER > $10M SALES > $2M EBITDA MULTIPLES $10M - $100M DEAL SIZE 32% YOY INCREASE	NASDAQ PE MULTIPLES STRATEGIC ACQUISITIONS > $10M SALES > $2M EBITDA NO YOY CHANGE

The #1 box represents owner-operated businesses, those which require the presence of the owner to continue operating at their current level, and in which the owner typically plays a critical role as the operator of the business. The #2 box represents professionally managed businesses, that is those that do not require the owner's presence to earn the revenue and profits that they generate.

Owner-operated businesses (what we call the "#1 box businesses") trade on multiples similar, but slightly different from, the EBITDA multiples we have been discussing so far. Instead of EBITDA, these businesses trade on multiples of SDE, or Seller Discretionary Earnings. SDE is the same thing as EBITDA, only you add back any special benefits the seller/owner-operator is paying themselves that are not required to operate the business.

Typically, this would include things like salary in excess of what a third-party manager would expect to earn doing work that is similar to the work the seller does in the business. For example, maybe the seller pays herself $400,000 per year in salary, but a manager brought in to do the same or similar work would only cost $200,000 per year. The excess $200,000 per year over and above the market cost of a similar manager must be added back to SDE to reflect the real and actual operating costs associated with the business.

Similarly, expenses typically written off by entrepreneurs like the cost of a family retreat, automobiles primarily used for the owner or their family, subscriptions, meals, and other expenses that are not necessary to the earning of the profits for the business, all must be added back to SDE to determine EBITDA.

Many owner-operator entrepreneurs pay what should perhaps otherwise be characterized as personal expenses from the business account in order to reduce their taxable income and save money on taxes, or they may simply treat the business checking account similar to a personal account using the money to pay bills when needed, but none of these personal expenses are necessary to operate the business. These personal expenses all get added back to SDE to arrive at a true EBITDA number for owner-operated businesses.

The #2 box businesses are those that are professionally managed, meaning that the owner's presence is not required within the business for it to generate its earnings and profits. The owner is not performing any critical role in #2 box businesses and therefore there are generally no add-backs to the business's profits like there are with owner-operated #1 box businesses. In #2 box businesses, profits are already stated in the form of EBITDA.

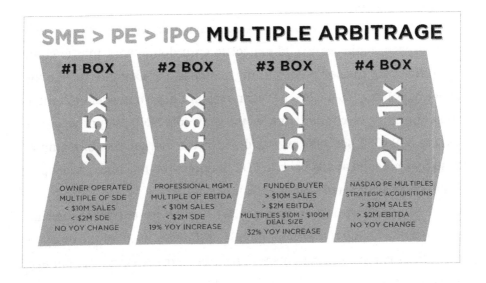

Note in the graphic that #2 box businesses typically sell for much greater price multiples than #1 box businesses, even after the add-backs to convert from SDE to EBITDA. #2 box businesses sell on average across all industries for a multiple of EBITDA equal to 3.8x as of this writing and have ranged from about 2.9x to 4.5x EBITDA over the past few years.

That means that a #1 box business with SDE of $1,000,000 would sell for $2.5 million ($1,000,000 x 2.5) but a similar business with a professional management team and no need to have the owner operating that business would sell for $3.8 million ($1,000,000 x 3.8). That additional $1.3 million in sales price represents a premium of 52% in additional value that the seller could realize from the sale of their business simply by installing a professional management team.

Now that you know this, consider a very easy and common arbitrage play (remember, arbitrage just means buy low and sell high) that many business flippers use to generate quick profits.

Here's how it works: a buyer acquires an owner-operated business generating $1 million in SDE, then installs a professional management team. The professional management team typically costs about the same as what the previous owner/seller was paying themselves, so expenses remain relatively constant before and after the sale and installation of the new professional management team.

That means that the business continues to enjoy a profit, or EBITDA, of $1 million. However, now the business that was previously worth only 2.5x SDE is worth 3.8x EBITDA. The new owner now sells the business for $3.8 million and pockets the 52% return on their investment, even with no additional growth in the business above and beyond what it was previously earning.

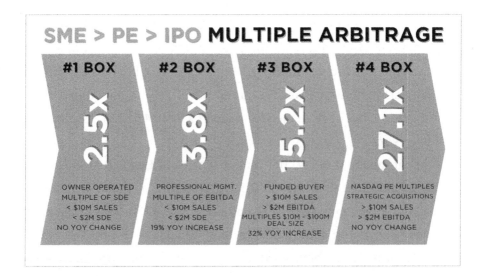

Moving on in our graphic, the columns further to the right, the #3 and #4 boxes, represent private equity and public market multiples, respectively. Ideally, you want to be acquiring businesses that are owner-operated and fit in the #1 box category on the far left of the graphic or in the #2 box next to it.

These SME (small to medium-sized enterprises), also known as an SMB (small to medium-sized business) typically sell for about 2.5x SDE (Seller Discretionary Earnings) and 3.8x EBITDA, respectively. Note that this is an average selling price for these types of businesses across all industries and this number fluctuates from quarter to quarter.

Some businesses like software as a service (SaaS) or ecommerce businesses may sell for significantly more as a category than this average, while others like education and publishing may sell for substantially less. Nevertheless, the 2.5x #1 box number and 3.8x #2 box number provide a good general rule of thumb for our purposes to illustrate the difference in valuations among the various #1, #2, #3 and #4 box business categories.

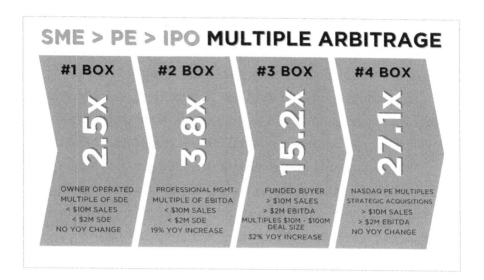

Now, with a motivated seller, these average multiple numbers go way down. Because you are looking for off-market businesses (that means not listed for sale with a business broker, investment banker, or business selling website), you are able to identify motivated sellers and you are able to acquire these #1 and #2 box businesses for multiples far lower than the average market of 2.5x or 3.8x. In fact, very often we find that you can acquire these types of businesses from motivated sellers for multiples of 2x, 1.5x, or even 1x or less.

Finding these types of deals requires a little bit of effort, but the return is worth it. One additional thing to note is that you want smaller deals that are generally not appealing to the very well-funded private equity firms, family offices, SPACs, and high net worth individual buyers who occupy the #3 box. #1 and #2 box acquisitions typically generate less than $10 million in sales and $2 million in profit (SDE or EBITDA).

Now, as you consider all that we have been discussing so far with respect to these companies and the graphic with the various numbered boxes, you may be asking yourself, why is there an opportunity to sell the #1 and #2 box businesses for significantly more, typically within a three- to five-year period, to the buyers in the #3 and #4 boxes?

The answer is that the third box from the left, where buyers are paying an average multiple of 15.2x, houses a different type of buyer than the typical #1 or #2 box buyer, and the same is true of the #4 box buyer.

The good news is that you can potentially generate huge profits acquiring #1 and #2 box multiples and selling at #3 or #4 box multiples. For example, if you buy a #1 box business at 2.5x SDE and sell it to a private equity fund at 15.2x EBITDA, that's an increase of 508%!

Why would that opportunity exist? Because buyers in the two columns on the right are typically private equity companies, ultra-rich people, corporations, special purpose acquisition companies (SPACs) (collectively the #3 box buyers), or publicly held buyers (the #4 box buyers).

They don't want small deals. They know that the effort to identify and acquire a smaller business is about the same to identify and acquire a substantially larger business, and they simply do not want to expend the time and resources needed to sift through all the smaller deals to find the few that meet their ideal acquisition criteria. Therefore, they're typically going to be looking for more than $10 million in sales and $2 million in profits.

But if you acquire a couple of smaller but related companies and merge them together into one company, the big players will now pay you a lot more money to acquire that combined enterprise than you paid for each of its component parts.

It's as though they only want to buy expensive flowers, and you buy low-cost seeds, nurture them until they bloom, and then earn enormous profits by selling your self-made bouquets. You don't want to *compete* with these powerful companies. You want to *sell* to them—at their prices, after buying at yours.

Buying in the #1 and #2 boxes on the left and selling in the #3 and #4 boxes on the right—that is a huge opportunity for you. Why do the private equity people pay so much? Because their goal is to go public, sell to a public company, or grow the business and flip it to another private equity firm later. At the time of this writing, the average multiple of a company on the Nasdaq exchange in the US is 27.1x its EBITDA.

Private equity and similar funds generally find that they're able to exit through initial public offerings (IPOs) or sales to public companies or other private-equity, family offices, SPACs, high net worth individuals, or similar companies that are planning on taking the target business public. Public companies, the #4 box category acquirers, typically buy businesses at multiples lower than what those #4 box companies are currently trading at, knowing that they can add those acquisitions' earnings to their own and instantly benefit their overall valuations. And so it goes, so that everybody along the way gets to make money. Win-win, just the way we like to do business.

The next figure clarifies why buying and selling is better than buying and holding. This gets pretty exciting.

WHY BUY + SELL IS BETTER THAN BUY + HOLD?

YEAR	EBITDA @7%	EV: HOLD	SELL @ 7X	YEAR	EBITDA @7%	EV: HOLD	SELL @ 7X
1	$500,000	$3,500,000		9	$859,093	$6,013,652	
2	$535,000	$3,745,000		10	$919,230	$6,434,607	
3	$572,450	$4,007,150	$4,007,150	11	$983,576	$6,885,030	
4	$612,522	$4,287,651		12	$1,052,426	$7,366,982	$7,366,982
5	$655,398	$4,587,786		13	$1,126,096	$7,882,671	
6	$701,276	$4,908,931		14	$1,204,923	$8,434,458	
7	$750,365	$5,252,556		15	$1,289,267	$9,024,870	
8	$802,891	$5,620,235	$5,620,235	16	$1,379,516	$9,656,610	$9,656,610
CASH REALIZED	$0		$9,627,385	CASH REALIZED		$9,656,610	$26,650,977

HOLD STRATEGY CREATES EXIT AT	$9,627,385	100%
SELL/BUY OR REFOUND STRATEGY CREATES	$26,650,977	276%

Let's consider how this works across a 16-year period. Let's say that you hold the business for one year. It would earn $500,000 during that year, plus an additional $35,000 if you assume that it can grow at a 7% annual earnings growth rate. That would mean at the end of that first year of owning the business, it would have returned $535,000 in EBITDA.

However, what if instead of holding, you decide to sell it, and you can sell it to a private equity fund at a 7x multiple. Remember from our discussion of #1 box, #2 box, #3 box, and #4 box buyers previously, these private equity funds typically are willing to acquire at more than double this 7x rate.

If you can sell the business for 7x EBITDA, how much will you receive for the business? All you have to do to determine the answer is multiply the business earnings after that first-year times 7.

In this case, that is 7 x $535,000 which equals a total sales price of $3,745,000, as shown in the "Year 2" row of the graphic above. Notice how that compares to the $1,379,516 annual income that you might make each year after holding and growing the business for 16 years and growing it 7% in each of those years!

But suppose you sold this business after owning and growing at 7% per year for three years. You would receive $4,007,150 at the end of year three. That means that you would receive seven years of profits all at once in the year of that sale.

Now, let's say that you took the proceeds of that sale and bought another business and held that one for say five years, then sold that business and bought another and so on. In other words, what if you held the first business for five years and then sold it for $4.7 million (i.e., 7x).

Now you go out and buy a business that's making $600,000 with no money out of pocket (using several of the strategies we will teach you later in this book), or you financed it using traditional sources of capital. Again, let's say that you hold that business for five years and then sell it at a 7x for $5 million. Well, during that eight-year period, you've received $9.65 million more than if you'd just held onto it.

If we continue this process for 16 years, we end up acquiring and selling four different businesses and receiving a total of $40,595,006 ($26.6 million from sales of those four businesses, plus $13,944,029 from the earnings of those businesses over that 16-year period).

Had you simply owned and held that first business during that same 16-year period, even with annual growth of 7% per year in earnings, you would have only received a total of $23,600,639 ($9,656,612 from the sale of that one business, plus $13,944,029 from the earnings of that business) over that 16-year period.

The earnings remain constant over those sixteen years in both cases. However, the sale of four businesses where you were able to receive seven years of profits in a single transaction via the 7x sales multiple, compared to the sale of just one business at the end of that period where you were able to receive seven years of profits in a single transaction, provided us with 21 *years* of additional profits. That is 4 sales at 7x = 28 years of profits from selling four businesses.

In terms of dollars, that meant that your total cash received as earnings from operations from holding the business was equal in both scenarios; however, your cash received from the four sales vs. the one sale netted you an additional $16,994,365. That's a significant amount of extra money to realize compared to hanging on to the one business during that time.

In fact, selling those businesses four times and reinvesting to acquire replacement businesses using the strategies we teach nets you a whopping 276% more total cash. If that doesn't motivate you to read on and learn how you can do this yourself, we don't know what will!

The Acquisition Wheel

The next image illustrates the various ways that acquisitions can increase the value of a business. For everyone who owns a business, think about the biggest area that would increase your value and profits.

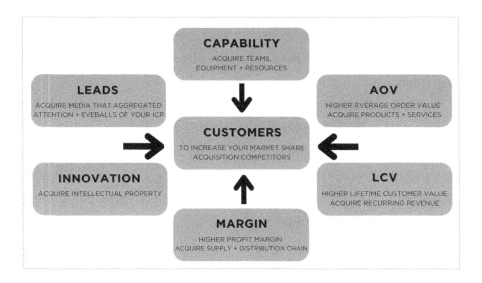

If you don't already own a business, think about any of these places as an entry point for brainstorming what type of business to acquire as your first acquisition. Either way, the Acquisition Wheel can help you decide, "What is my most important next step?"

The real magic of the Acquisition Wheel is that you can return to it again and again to solve pretty much any business problem or challenge you might face. Want more market share? The Acquisition Wheel helps you see that you can achieve this by acquiring a competitor.

Need more leads for your business so that you have more people to sell your products and services to? Easy, just acquire media and you've got as many as you can handle.

CHAPTER 3 - FINDING TARGETS TO ACQUIRE

Having a hard time handling all the business you are generating and need to scale your team or infrastructure rapidly? No problem, just acquire teams and resources through an "acqui-hire."

Want to get more out of all the customers that you already have without having to generate a whole bunch of new customers? The Acquisition Wheel can help you do that too. Just acquire new products and services that already exist and that your existing customers are already buying from someone else and offer them up to your existing customers.

That will definitely increase your Lifetime Customer Value or LCV (the amount that each customer you acquire is worth over the lifetime of their doing business with you), and it may just increase your Average Order Value or AOV (the total dollar value of the order your customer places with you each time they transact with your business), and Initial Order Value or IOV (the total amount the customer pays to you on their very first transaction with you).

All of these increases—LCV, AOV, and IOV—will go to increase your total sales revenue and profits, and that will ultimately allow you to be able to afford to spend more to acquire a customer than your competition, which can provide an enormous competitive advantage.

But you're not done yet extracting value from the Acquisition Wheel. Let's say that you want to increase your profit margins or even turn around a negative profit situation. Just look to the Acquisition Wheel and you discover that you can use Vertical Integration (the acquisition of your supply and distribution chain) to capture a greater portion of the value chain where profits are being lost to other businesses that assist in the creation of the total value that your product or service ultimately provides to the customer. Acquire their businesses, or their assets that produce the value they add, and you also capture the profit margin that you have been ceding to them.

Having challenges with product life cycles that are running their course? Need to breathe new life into aging products or services? Losing market share to innovative upstarts who are luring your customers away with exciting new offerings? Not to worry, the Acquisition Wheel can help you here as well. Just look to acquire intellectual property assets, or the businesses that own them, and you can acquire innovation, adaptability, and new products and services that will wow your customers, win them back from those upstarts, and breathe new life into your business.

Last but not least, what if you are tired of always having to find new customers and wish that you could just start every month or year with all of your expenses already paid for and a healthy amount of profits already guaranteed and baked in?

While technically a part of the acquisition of new products or services, we break this solution out into a separate category because of the special value that it can add to your business. The answer to this challenge or desire is to add recurring revenue to your business, whether through the modification of how you offer your existing products or services to your customer or through the acquisition of products and/or services that provide monthly recurring revenue (MRR) or annual recurring revenue (ARR).

As you can see, whatever your challenge, need, or desire, the Acquisition Wheel stands ready to provide value at scale on a continuing basis. Let's dive into each of these categories a bit deeper, and we'll also give you a worksheet you can use. You can download the worksheet shown below at the BusinessWealthWithoutRisk.com/access site so you can complete it and use it for your acquisitions brainstorming.

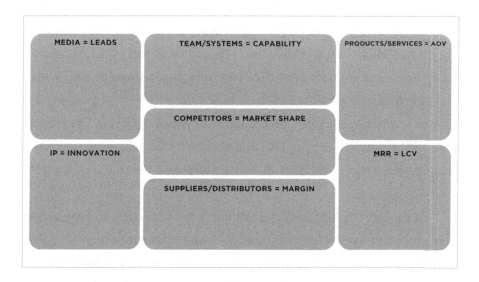

Competitors for Market Share

We like to think of the Acquisition Wheel as a problem-solving tool; it provides answers for your most vexing questions.

Even if you don't yet have a business and are trying to decide what kind of business to buy, you can use the Acquisition Wheel to help generate ideas.

Let's start with the idea of how to capture a larger market share for your existing business. Can you think of how you might literally double your current market share overnight? We can. Just acquire competitors that are approximately equal to the size of your existing business.

Having a difficult time deciding what business to approach about an acquisition after determining your acquisition criteria using our acquisition criteria tools? Just imagine that you already own a business that meets your acquisition criteria and then use the Acquisition Wheel to brainstorm as many businesses as you can think of that might be competitors of that business.

When you're trying to brainstorm a list of companies to acquire, think about direct competitors (those who provide the same products or services to the same markets as your business), substitute providers (those that provide products or services that your existing customers might purchase from someone else to achieve the same utility or benefits that your products or services provide them), replacement providers (those that provide products or services that completely replace or eliminate the need for your products or services because they subsume the value and utility of your products or services or completely eliminate the need for your products altogether), geographically divergent providers (businesses that provide the products or services that you provide only in geographically diverse markets that you do not currently serve), price point divergent providers (businesses that provide products or services that are relatively similar to yours but that target consumers of those products at higher or lower price and quality points), and market divergent providers (businesses selling the same products or services that your business does, only selling into different markets or audiences than you currently sell into).

You might want to focus first on your competition. As mentioned previously, if you acquire a direct competitor that's the same size as your company, you instantly double your business.

Can you think of a better way to increase your market share more quickly than that? We sure can't. Remember, if you don't own a business yet and you're trying to filter out the universe of options into a few key possibilities, one of the best ways to do that is to consider your acquisition criteria, identify a company that you might want to acquire, and then say, "Who are the competitors?" All of the competitors you identify are then potential acquisitions for you.

It's extremely important that you approach this creatively. For example, don't limit yourself to thinking only about direct competitors. Consider companies who sell products that substitute for yours (e.g., fans vs. air conditioners, motor scooters vs. bicycles). Also consider companies who sell similar products or services in different geographical markets or to different types of customers.

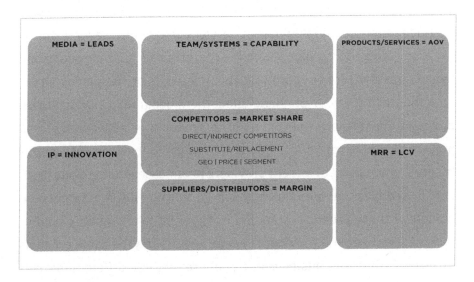

A great example here is The Gap. The company wanted to go upstream and sell to higher-income customers, so they bought Banana Republic. Then they went downstream to find lower-income customers and bought Old Navy. So rather than looking at competitors for *exactly* similar customers, they broadened their target to *approximately*

similar customers at different price points. The key takeaway? Don't define your competition too narrowly.

Media for Leads

Leads help generate customers and create more sales for your business. So, if you would like to have more opportunities to place your product or service in front of your ideal customer, then you will want to consider acquiring media.

For our purposes, the term "media" means anything that has aggregated the attention and eyeballs of your Ideal Customer Profile (ICP).

Your ICP is often referred to in marketing circles as your customer avatar. If you'd like help figuring out just who your ICP is, then you're in luck, because we have another tool for you that can help you do just that.

One of the companies that Roland acquired using several of the strategies outlined in this book provides marketing instruction to people who want to learn how to be better digital marketers. The aptly named company that Roland acquired is called DigitalMarketer.com and one of its premier tools is called the Customer Avatar Worksheet, which is provided here for you to use to help determine yours.

If you would like more in-depth instruction on how to complete the Customer Avatar Worksheet, you can simply Google "DigitalMarketer Customer Avatar Worksheet" or visit our resources site for this book at BusinessWealthWithoutRisk.com/access, where you will find a whole host of resources and materials, including all the worksheets and forms provided in this book as well as many additional tools and information you can use to help you move forward as an *ACQUIREpreneur*.

CUSTOMER AVATAR WORKSHEET

Company/Product Name:

GOALS AND VALUES

Goals:

Values:

Name:

Age:

Gender:

Marital Status:

#/Age of Children:

Location:

CHALLENGES & PAIN POINTS

Challenges:

Pain points:

SOURCES OF INFORMATION

Books:

Magazines:

Blogs/Websites:

Conferences:

Gurus:

Other:

Quote:

Occupation:

Job Title:

Annual Income:

Level of Education:

Other:

OBJECTIONS & ROLES

Possible Objections:

Role in the Purchase Process:

DIGITALMARKETER

What you're looking for when you are trying to identify media to acquire is a company or service that has already captured the attention and interest (the "eyeballs") of potential customers. If you can find that, then you can have as many leads as you want. You simply go and acquire the businesses or the assets that have already aggregated that attention.

As you are brainstorming the various types of media and other categories on the Acquisition Wheel worksheet, remember that not only can you acquire businesses, but you can also acquire assets that people have created that are NOT YET businesses, that do not yet generate profit, or that are assets that are owned by businesses but that can be purchased in and of themselves, separate from the businesses that own them.

This is especially the case with digital assets that were created as passion projects and have garnered a following but are not necessarily profit-generating ventures. Their creators may not, in fact, even have intended to profit from them. But that doesn't mean you can't.

Media covers a broad range of potential acquisitions that include email lists built by others containing customers, buyers of specific products, opt-in emails who requested certain information, newsletter subscribers and more. One thing to be aware of when purchasing an email list is whether it was built in compliance with all applicable privacy and spam laws.

While you may want to check with an attorney specializing in this area, you will for sure want to take a look at how the email list was built and examine the terms of service (TOS) and privacy policies (which vary depending on jurisdiction) applicable to the creation of the list.

You may find it much more productive and much easier to consider acquiring complete email accounts rather than just lists of names. If you acquire the email service provider account that is owned by a business that has an email list that you would like to acquire, then you will save yourself the time and effort of migrating the names into a new account, which is prone to loss of email addresses.

Acquiring print or email newsletters can provide an excellent source of leads, particularly if the newsletter is affinity based around your ICP and, even more so, if the subscribers are paying for their subscriptions.

One of the most powerful forms of media to acquire is blogs that rank high in Google and other search engines for your targeted keyword terms. If you have identified buyer keywords (keywords that purchasers of your product or service use to find and purchase your type of product or service), then Google each of your best keywords and find out which websites or blogs or search results appear in the top five organic search engine results for each of those keywords.

Have an assistant, intern, or VA (virtual assistant) research each result to determine who owns the sites that rank in each of those top five positions for each of your target keywords. Then, approach the owners and see if you can acquire the domain, blog, site, or page that ranks. When you acquire these sites, you now control the traffic that goes to them, and you can make offers or direct that traffic to offers in any way that you like.

This is an excellent strategy for rapidly dominating the search engine results for your ideal keywords, and it is one that a good friend of ours, Neil Patel, used to become the pre-eminent search engine optimization (SEO) expert online.

Neil brilliantly concluded that the easiest way to own the search words and phrases around search engine optimization was not to try to outrank all the other SEOs who were already vying viciously for those choice spots. Instead, he found out who already owned the sites that ranked for those coveted terms and started buying them all up.

He would acquire a site and then point that towards his main site, capturing all the rank authority from the already ranking site and also boosting the authority of his main site. Eventually, he acquired so many that he ranked for all of the key terms that he wanted to rank for, and he never had to spend a ton of time trying to outrank everyone else. He was GUARANTEED to win because he was playing a different game.

He was playing chess and his competitors were playing checkers, and he won massively. You can do the same thing with your companies to your competition. All it takes is some research time on Google and a willingness to do some outreach.

Popular social media groups also merit your attention as potential media acquisitions. Unlike most of the other types of media we discuss, you cannot actually acquire ownership of Facebook or LinkedIn groups because they are always owned by the platforms that host them. However, you can still acquire control of those groups by acquiring the administrative rights to run them. When one of the companies that Roland owned wanted more leads for a do-it-yourself (DIY) project, it acquired a Facebook group with 250,000 DIYers in it.

That group had a better name "DIY Projects" than the group Roland's company initially owned, "DIY Ready," and after the acquisition, which was completed for only $1,500, Roland's company reached out to Facebook and asked to have the two groups merged into one under the DIY Projects name. Facebook agreed and did this at no charge and when it was done, Roland's company controlled a Facebook group with over half a million members and the better name, DIY Projects.

Take a minute and go do some research on your favorite social media and find out who has already aggregated the attention and eyeballs of YOUR ideal customer. Follow this strategy and reach out to see if you can acquire these types of media for your own company.

Once you are the administrator, you control the group and can operate it as if you owned it, subject of course to the terms of service of the platform on which it exists.

Keep in mind that the terms of service of social media platforms are ever evolving, so you'll want to be sure that whatever acquisitions you make on those platforms comply with the then-applicable terms of service.

One often overlooked form of media that can be extremely lucrative to acquire is podcasts. Podcast devotees are generally high income, listen frequently, are brand loyal, and in general are good customers for products and services aligned to their interests as determined by their listening or viewing choices.

Social media pages, trade shows, live and virtual events, associations, masterminds, meetup groups, networking groups, radio, television, print media, and other forms of media also merit your attention as you brainstorm to identify all of the places that your ICP spends their time, so that you can acquire as many of those media as possible.

We've completed some ideas in the Media section of the Acquisition Wheel worksheet to give you more ideas below:

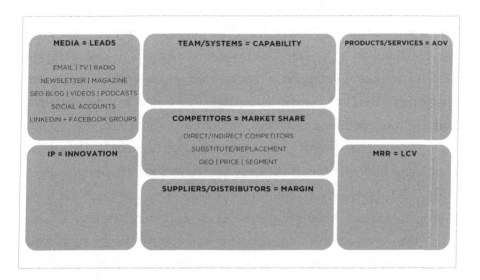

Teams/Systems for Infrastructure

Trying to build everything from the ground up is a fool's game. If nothing else, we certainly hope we have convinced you of that by now.

If you need a pair of shoes, do you make them yourself? If you don't have a sales team, or an effective operations system, or a software development team, you don't need to build them from scratch. That's a long and expensive process with plenty of opportunities to fail.

We spent and lost millions of dollars trying to build a sales team, something that none of us had done from scratch before. Ultimately, we failed and simply went out and acquired a company that had already done that.

Similarly, we squandered three million dollars trying our inexperienced hand at building a software development team from scratch. Save yourself the headache and just go out and acquire already proven teams to help expand your business resources and team.

Instead of trying to build from scratch, acquire a company that's already solved this problem. We recently acquired a software development team to fill a gap in one of our companies and we did it, as usual, with no money out of pocket.

You don't need to reinvent the wheel. Just acquire someone else's wheel! This applies to software teams, sales teams, manufacturing operations, leadership teams, in-house legal or admin teams, rep networks, business development teams, call centers, customer service teams, overseas teams, finance teams, acquisitions teams, integration teams, product development teams, launch teams, training teams, research and development teams, and pretty much anything else along these lines that you can think of.

Here is a sample Acquisition Wheel with the Infrastructure section completed to give you ideas for this section:

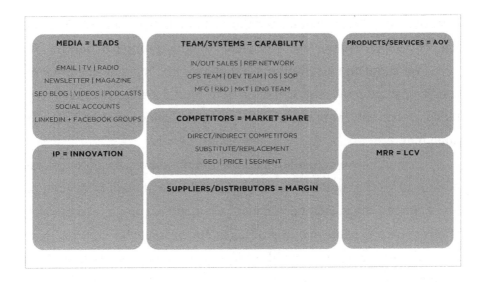

Products/Services that Increase Lifetime Customer Value (LCV)

Here you're answering this question: "What products or services are my customers buying before, during, and after the time they interact with me?" We call these "BDA" products and services.

The easy way to increase LCV is to add additional products and services. You can acquire a product or service that already exists as a standalone asset, or a company that's selling products or services that your ideal customer wants to buy and is already buying. Then, you can sell those products and services to your existing customers in addition to the other things they are already buying from you.

One of the most often missed opportunities businesses incur is failing to maximize sales to existing customers, but an existing customer is much likelier to make a purchase than new prospects.

Similarly, consider acquiring related products to the products your customers are already buying.

Amazon is absolutely one of the very best examples of this. They have perfected a "recommendation engine" that can tell you that people who liked some product or book that you just purchased (and even that you are considering purchasing while lingering on the product page) bought these other books or products.

So, you read about them, and in 30 seconds they have three sales from you instead of one because we are buyers "in the market" for books or products like the one you just bought. And every time you buy a book, you go through this same process. Your LCV to Amazon increases 300%.

Another type of product or service to consider acquiring is an enabling product or service. Enabling products help people get more from the product that they just purchased.

Think of a milk frothing tool for someone who just purchased a coffee maker, or a pasta attachment for a high-end mixer, software that helps a digital marketing agency client manage their media purchase budgets, fuel additives that make engines run cleaner or even snow chains to help tires increase traction in the snow and ice.

Upsells and downsells provide a powerful opportunity to increase LCV as well. Think of McDonald's question, "Would you like fries with that?" That is a classic upsell that dramatically increased average order values at the Golden Arches by increasing sales of a low-cost add-on. More recently, McDonald's has installed AI to read the license plates of customers' cars as they wait in line at the drive-through. The AI then populates a recommendation screen on the drive-through menu board suggesting recommended items for you to buy, tailored specifically to what you have bought before!

How much additional revenue does the "would you like fries with that?" upsell strategy net McDonald's every year? Reports show increases of up to 40% in total sales revenue, all attributable to those six little magic words!

Similarly, bundles like those Combo Meal options at pretty much every fast-food restaurant increase average order value and profit margins. While the food cost of a hamburger can be significant, the food cost of fried potatoes and especially of soft drinks is negligible.

The profit per order on a combo is hugely greater than the profit per order on a hamburger. You need to identify the opportunities for upsells in your business to find the opportunities to not only increase average order value, but also average profit per order. In other words, you need to discover and acquire your businesses' equivalent of those fries, Cokes, and combos!

Downsells provide you with the ability to capture sales from potential customers who might not be able to afford your flagship or more expensive products or services. What products or services might provide your potential customers with the results or utility they desire at a lower cost? Look at what customers who cannot afford your current offerings are buying and go out and acquire those products or services to offer in your marketing funnels.

Can you acquire brands that are up-market or down-market from your current brand? Once you start exploring the possibilities for adding products and services to increase your LCV, you will find a virtually limitless number of options for acquisition.

Another wonderful thing about would-you-like-fries-with-that ("WYLFWT") offers is that they have proven to be substantially more effective than cross-selling strategies. Cross-selling involves making offers of complementary products or services to your customers or clients. Upselling the WYLFWT way simply offers additional value to what the customer or client is already buying. If you haven't yet crafted your WYLFWT offer, do it now, then go and acquire whoever makes your industry's "fries."

We completed the Acquisition Wheel with some ideas for you below:

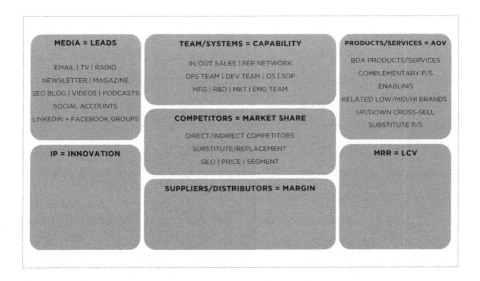

Supply + Distribution to Increase Margin

Many businesses find themselves wondering "How can I become more profitable?" To be more profitable, you really have two major options: you can increase your prices or you can reduce your costs. When exploring cost reduction, you also have several options. One is to look to your current operations to discover ways to increase efficiencies that can reduce waste and reduce labor costs.

The other is to determine whether there are ways to increase your business's share of the overall profit in the value chain that exists from the very beginning of the creation of the component parts of whatever product or service you are selling, all the way through the final sale and delivery of that product or service to your end customer.

This is called *vertical integration*, which is a fancy way of saying that you're going to buy up and down the supply and distribution chain of whatever products or services that you sell.

Vertical integration is effectively cutting out the middleperson so that you can keep more of the profit that is currently being siphoned off by your manufacturers, wholesalers, ingredient or component suppliers, distributors, affiliates, outsourced service providers, etc. In other words, you are seeking out and capturing (by acquisition) for your business each instance in the creation of the ultimate value for your customer where someone else is currently making profit.

For example, a few years back we acquired a company (for no money out of pocket, mind you!) that was selling water filters, and we thought, "Wouldn't it be better if we could manufacture our own filters?"

So, we sought out and bought (also a no money out of pocket acquisition) a company that we renamed "Rapid Filter" which manufactured water filters from scratch. This allowed us to recapture the profit that was previously taken by our supplier/manufacturer in China.

Now, you may be thinking that this whole supply and distribution, vertical integration thing does not apply to your business because you don't sell physical products or you are not a manufacturer or distributor, but that is simply not the case. Almost every business has a supply and distribution chain. They just don't realize it.

For example, let's say that you are a digital marketing agency or other service provider. While it is true that you don't have a manufacturer taking profit from your business, if you outsource any part of the services that you provide, then you have the equivalent of a manufacturer.

Using the digital marketing agency example, perhaps you provide Facebook advertising to your customers, but when they ask you to also create content for them, you outsource to a content marketing agency.

Or maybe you do create content, but you outsource editing the content to independent contractors. Maybe your clients that ask for you to run their Google ads or TV ads are outsourced to another agency whose services you white label, etc.

Any third party providing any part of the services that you are selling to your clients is taking profit in the value chain. If you acquire those businesses, then you capture the profit they are making and thereby increase your total profits without having to sell a single additional thing to your clients.

One often overlooked profit increasing opportunity using vertical integration is to acquire your affiliates. Many businesses allow affiliates to sell their products or services and pay significant commissions to those affiliates. For example, one of our private consulting clients sells courses on public speaking and pays affiliates who sell their program a 50% commission.

When we were looking for acquisition opportunities for that client to help them increase their profit margins, we looked at the historical sales for all of their affiliates and discovered that their number one affiliate earned over $1 million per year selling the client's products. We approached that affiliate and were ultimately able to work out a deal to acquire them for about $2.5 million.

Now, they were already a profitable company earning a little over $1 million in net profit per year. Combining the profit they were already making plus the $1 million in affiliate commissions saved, and adding additional products and services to their product line through cross-selling, we were able to effectively pay for the acquisition in a little over two years with no money out of pocket.

Here is a sample of the Suppliers/Distributors section of the Acquisition Wheel filled out to give you some good brainstorming ideas for your business:

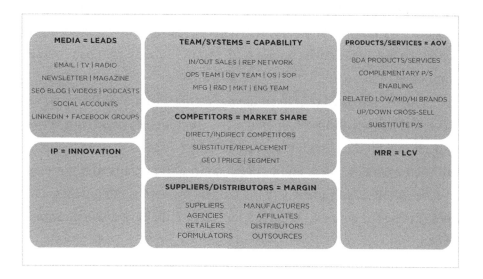

IP for Innovation/Adaptability

Suppose you find that your products are getting stale, and you need to become more creative. You can acquire innovative companies. Problem solved. You can also license things from other people, or you can acquire a company that has something other people might want to license and then sell that. You can acquire other people's patents, copyrights, trademarks, and trade secrets. We've done all these things more times than we can count.

Maybe there is a best-selling book that is directly related to your product or service. What if you acquired that book and used it as a frontend to attract people by giving it away for free or adding it to a free plus-shipping offer, then upselling your book buyers into your higher level, more costly, and more profitable products?

When we wanted to start a line of courses to teach trades for a project that we called "Start-Up Jungle" (e.g., cosmetology, truck driving, etc.), we knew that we needed content and courses for each of the topics we wanted to cover, but we didn't want to create all those courses from scratch.

At an estimated cost to create per course of about $5,000, it would have cost us over $500,000 to create the one hundred or so courses we had on our product roadmap. We could have licensed those courses, but then we would have had to pay a continuing royalty and not even own the intellectual property that would be the core of our business. We could create the courses ourselves, but that would have taken hundreds of hours.

So, we searched online to find several publishers of the types of courses that we wanted to sell, and ultimately, we identified and acquired a business that had already created 128 of them, including software templates—and it won't surprise you to know that we also acquired that in a no money out of pocket deal!

We completed the IP and Innovation section of the Acquisition Wheel for you below to give you ideas for IP acquisitions to help stoke innovation at your business:

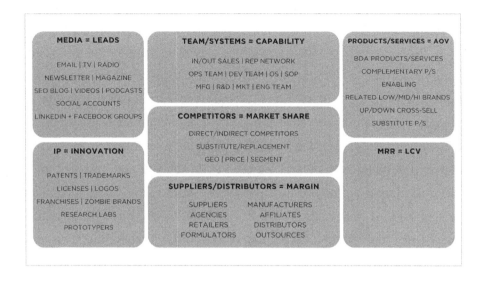

Monthly Recurring Revenue (MRR) for Capital

If you want to acquire a company and you need to raise money for the purchase, you are ultimately going to want to start to think about recurring revenue.

Recurring revenue can recur on an annual basis, in which case we refer to it as ARR (annual recurring revenue), or it can recur on a monthly basis as MRR (monthly recurring revenue).

Investors are always looking for lower risk, and when it comes time for you to think of selling your business, you're going to want to think about how you can reduce investor risk so that your business can command a higher selling price. If there's money that's coming in every month, the risk level to investors plummets.

Why?

Because your survival doesn't depend entirely on new sales. Customers are already committed to you. People with a subscription to Audible.com make an automatic monthly payment that they've stopped thinking about.

How many times have you joined a gym, an online streaming service, subscribed to a magazine or other publication, or otherwise signed up for some product or service that you no longer use but continue to pay for every month or year because it's either not worth the effort of canceling (low cost service and the joyful inertia of taking no action to cancel it outweighs the effort required to do so); you plan to eventually use it (that gym membership) so you don't want to cancel it, surrender to your lack of fitness, and have to resubscribe; or you keep thinking every time you see the charge that you need to cancel it, but then you forget until you are reminded the next time the charge processes.

These are just a few of the reasons that recurring revenue can continue even when it provides no ostensible value to your customers. While that is not an ideal situation, it does provide for recurring revenue.

A much more positive situation is one in which you have tailored your products or service in such a way as to provide continuing value to your customer, ideally while becoming virtually indispensable to them.

In this case, you have a win-win situation where your customer receives continuing value, and you receive continuing payments without the customer acquisition cost you would incur if you had to resell those products or services every single time.

Any additional sales you make above and beyond your recurring revenue income are icing on the cake (i.e., money you can use to grow the company or take in distributions to do all the things you want to do). ARR and MRR are the investor's equivalent of a paycheck from an employer—except that you get more frequent raises as business increases.

We completed the MRR Recurring Revenue section of the Acquisition Wheel for you below to give you ideas on what types of Recurring Revenue businesses you might want to acquire for your business.

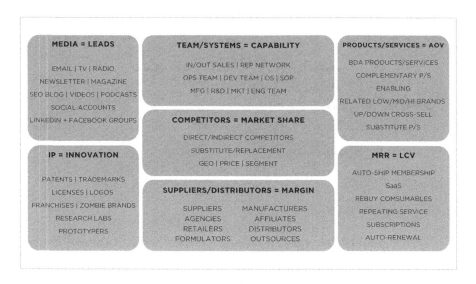

MEDIA = LEADS	TEAM/SYSTEMS = CAPABILITY	PRODUCTS/SERVICES = AOV
EMAIL | TV | RADIO	IN/OUT SALES | REP NETWORK	BDA PRODUCTS/SERVICES
NEWSLETTER | MAGAZINE	OPS TEAM | DEV TEAM | OS | SOP	COMPLEMENTARY P/S
SEO BLOG | VIDEOS | PODCASTS	MFG | R&D | MKT | ENG TEAM	ENABLING
SOCIAL ACCOUNTS		RELATED LOW/MID/HI BRANDS
LINKEDIN + FACEBOOK GROUPS	**COMPETITORS = MARKET SHARE**	UP/DOWN CROSS-SELL
	DIRECT/INDIRECT COMPETITORS	SUBSTITUTE P/S
IP = INNOVATION	SUBSTITUTE/REPLACEMENT	
	GEO | PRICE | SEGMENT	**MRR = LCV**
PATENTS | TRADEMARKS		AUTO-SHIP MEMBERSHIP
LICENSES | LOGOS	**SUPPLIERS/DISTRIBUTORS = MARGIN**	SaaS
FRANCHISES | ZOMBIE BRANDS	SUPPLIERS MANUFACTURERS	REBUY COMSUMABLES
RESEARCH LABS	AGENCIES AFFILIATES	REPEATING SERVICE
PROTOTYPERS	RETAILERS DISTRIBUTORS	SUBSCRIPTIONS
	FORMULATORS OUTSOURCES	AUTO-RENEWAL

Zero Dollar Traffic: Never Pay For Traffic Again

As we discussed above, you don't have to acquire whole companies. You can also acquire *traffic sources*, a media category that describes connective internet paths by which you find customers and they find you.

The next chart shows the seven most important of these intersections: 1) groups, 2) social sites, 3) SEO pages that have already been ranked, 4) people who have lists, 5) products, 6) shows, and 7) intellectual property. The chart also includes subcategories under each heading so you can start thinking of specific opportunities to explore. So, for example, you can find Meetup groups of like-minded people all over the country (meetup.com).

Remember that you can obtain a digital copy of the worksheet shown above so that you can complete it yourself at our resources site at BusinessWealthWithoutRisk.com/access where we have all of the resources and worksheets in this book along with many additional resources that we either created after the book's publication date or that we just couldn't fit in the book in the first place. Go there now and download the worksheet shown above so you can complete it yourself.

Here's what the fillable version of the worksheet looks like:

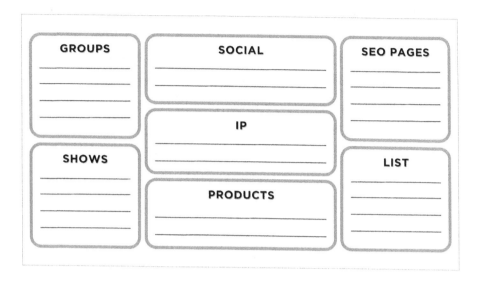

And for good measure, here's a completed sheet example so you can get some ideas for the types of traffic assets you may want to purchase:

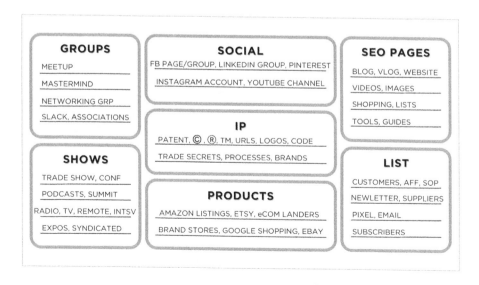

Looking at the sheet above you see that you can also acquire Amazon listings or accounts, Etsy stores, e-commerce landing pages on Shopify or BigCommerce, Google accounts, and eBay stores—all places that have built product-specific followings you can acquire.

We sold a trade show to a Blackstone company a couple of years ago, and now we're building another one to sell. Trade shows are great places to get together with everyone interested in a particular topic. Conferences, podcasts, summits, radio or TV shows, online or satellite shows, events, syndicated shows, intensives, expos—these are all things you can acquire.

Finding Unlisted Businesses and 29 Other Deal Sources

The figure below provides nine of the best ways to find unlisted M&As as well as 29 additional ways to find deals. To date we have identified over two hundred different sources of deals. We've covered much about these nine already—and the rest need little clarification, but we want to say a few words about some of the key deal sources.

HOW TO FIND UNLISTED M&As

1. Use the "Acquisition Wheel" + 29 Deal Sources
2. Search Facebook Groups, Pages, Places, + Events
3. Search YouTube Channels + Videos
4. Search LinkedIn Groups
5. Search Instagram Accounts
6. Search TikTok Accounts
7. Search Clubhouse Clubs, Spotify Green Room + Facebook Audio
8. Search Apple Podcasts, Spotify, etc. (for Podcasts)
9. Search Google for Un-Updated Sites

29 MORE DEAL SOURCES

FRIENDS	COMPETITORS	CUSTOMERS
FAMILY	DISTRIBUTORS	SUPPLIERS
PHONE CONTACTS	PEOPLE YOU MEET	MASTERMINDS
INSTAGRAM FRIENDS	NETWORKING GROUPS	CONTRACTORS
LINKEDIN CONTACTS	MESSENGER CONTACTS	EMPLOYEES
FACEBOOK FRIENDS	BUSINESS APPRAISERS	ANGEL NETWORKS
EMAIL SIGNATURE	FINANCIAL PLANNERS	EO + YPO + VISTAGE
DUE DILIGENCE FIRMS	DIRECT MAIL	HOOVERS
LINKEDIN SEARCH/SN	TRADE ASSOCIATIONS	TRADE EVENTS

First, friends and family might sound obvious or stupid to you, but they are really important and an often-neglected source of deals. Be sure they know you're an investor and that you're interested in acquisitions. These people have your best interests at heart, and they can form an immediate, cost-free network of eyes and ears working on your behalf. This can lead to deals. What's the downside?

CHAPTER 3 - FINDING TARGETS TO ACQUIRE

One of our favorite stories is how one of our students found the deal of a lifetime by listening to his nine-year-old son. His son was playing board games at a local board game store and was told by one of the employees that the store was going out of business so soon he would not be able to play there anymore.

The boy went home to his father and told him what was happening about the store going out of business and asked his dad if there was anything that could be done about it. His father talked with the employee and learned who the store owner was and approached the owner about acquiring the store before the owner shut it down for good.

After some negotiations, the owner agreed to sell the store inventory at cost and the rights to the store and everything in it for a few thousand dollars, and the seller agreed to finance the purchase and be paid as existing inventory was sold.

Well, as it turns out the lease was not just for the space occupied by the store, but for the whole building and when our student took over the space, he relocated his office to the top floor and leased out the second space next door. Not only that, but upon meeting and negotiating with the landlord, our student was able to acquire the entire building.

So, from his nine-year-old son asking to help save the game store, our student acquired the game store, saved thousands of dollars in rent by moving into the space upstairs, created a passive income from leasing the space next door to a sub-tenant and acquired a valuable piece of real estate, all for no money down!

It just goes to show that you never know where your next once in a lifetime deal might come from. Maybe it will come from your nine-year-old child.

We go through our phones regularly and look at the hundred most recent messages and calls to see if there's anybody with whom we should reconnect. If you're working your contacts and your social media connections, you'll have an army of people exponentially expanding your reach and letting people know that you are interested in a deal.

Due diligence firms will look at financial statements for people buying companies, and a lot of those deals don't ultimately work out and close. Those failures can be opportunities for you.

Also, consider using Sales Navigator to research potential acquisitions and contacts at acquisition targets. Sales Navigator is a separate service owned by LinkedIn that allows you to deep search LinkedIn data—a fantastic resource although it is a paid service. We will say that we subscribe to Sales Navigator and find it extremely helpful in finding deals as well as operators to run the companies we acquire.

As we mentioned, reach out to competitors, distributors, everyone that you meet. Join networking groups like Business Networking International (BNI), which has over 280,000 members.

Scour your contacts on Facebook Messenger or WhatsApp. Talk to financial planners and business appraisers. Why? Because people who want to sell businesses often consult them when they need money to fund their lifestyles. That makes them extremely motivated sellers.

Recently, one of Roland's companies looking to acquire a business sent out 760 letters to digital marketing firms in the Minneapolis-St. Paul area. They received about 60 replies, 10 of which turned into phone calls. They ended up buying two of those companies. That was a straight result of buying a list of digital marketing companies in the geographic area they wanted to target for acquisitions.

Trade associations are great because you can be specific about your target. If you want to buy a pottery company, for example, just contact their trade association and ask, "Do you know of anyone who may be interested in selling right now?"

D&B Hoovers is an excellent resource, maintaining a database of 330 million companies with thirty thousand global data sources updated five million times per day. Or, you can ask a company's customers, "What else are you buying?" The more of these options you exploit, the more deal flow you'll have.

Another paid service subscription we subscribe to and use for finding deals is ZoomInfo. While the subscription we have is expensive at about $3,000 per month, we use it regularly to source deals because it has all of the income, employee, location and contact information and details that we need to build marketing outreach lists.

We highly recommend that you consider using ZoomInfo, Crunchbase, and Sales Navigator as a powerful one, two, three punch in finding your prospects for acquisitions. Combine those services with the Acquisition Wheel and you should never be at a loss for detailed company contact information and acquisition targets.

Finding and Contacting Owners

Don't make this step needlessly complicated; we typically just call the company and ask who the owners are. Most people will tell you. If they don't, go to their website and look at the *About Us, Team, Founders, Our Story, Contact Us*, or similar pages or links. Very often, it will list the owners and provide photos. Or, you can open LinkedIn, search the name of a company, and generally, voila, you'll find what you need.

Here's a graphic with six proven easy ways to reach most owners you will be looking to contact:

6 WAYS TO IDENTIFY **THE OWNERS**

CALL THE COMPANY + ASK WHO THE OWNERS ARE	CHECK ZOOMINFO.COM
CHECK "ABOUT US", "TEAM" + "CONTACT" ON THEIR WEBSITE	CHECK SECSTATES.COM FOR STATE BUSINESS INFORMATION
WHOIS	LINKEDIN SEARCH

Next, start your three-step outreach plan. The first is what we call *personalized bulk outreach.*

3-STEP **COMMUNICATIONS**

STEP #1: "PERSONALIZED" BULK OUTREACH

STEP #2: INITIAL RAPPORT-BUILDING CONVERSATIONS

STEP #3: DATA GATHERING CONVERSATIONS

Just remember this is a numbers game. You absolutely have to do this at scale: for every hundred outreaches, you might receive about 40 to 60 initial responses; 10% of those will likely turn into a conversation of some sort. You'll probably identify three to five businesses to whom you decide to make offers, and you can expect that in the end you will end up completing one to three deals.

If you experience no or poor initial results, please don't despair. Accept this as the nature of the business. Also, these numbers will get better as you have more deal flow and more people know who you are.

If you have existing connections to the owners, it's best to use those first. Below is a scale from the easiest to the most removed way to reach out to owners:

HOW TO MAKE CONTACT

GET A WARM INTRO - Ask your network. Have someone who knows the person you want to contact connect you via phone, email, + text.

MAKE A PHONE CALL - Call the person you want to contact and follow the rapport-building strategy that follows.

WRITE A LETTER - Write a letter to the person you want to contact, then follow up with a meet, call, or Zoom.

LINKEDIN - Find them on LinkedIn, make a connection request or InMail, then try to move the conversation to meet, call, or Zoom.

REACH OUT ON SOCIAL - Find and message them on social media, then move to live chat, call, Zoom, etc.

All of these methods work and have worked for us. Try for the "Warm Intro" first, then phone call, then letter, then LinkedIn, and then Social. We did not include email on the list because it is the least personal, requires the least effort on your part, and is the least effective, but email outreach can work. It's just generally not as effective as the other methods listed above.

The second step is to build some rapport in an initial conversation and schedule the third step: a data gathering conversation. We'll talk about that in the next chapter.

What should you say when sending your messages? First, if you can get a warm introduction from someone in your network, that's by far the best way to start.

If you can't, no problem. Make a phone call. Or if you aren't a phone person, write a letter. Snail-mail can be really strong because almost nobody sends letters anymore. By bucking that trend, you're clearly making an effort and setting yourself apart from the herd.

You can also reach out on LinkedIn. Email is our *last* choice because there's so much spam and you receive the fewest quality responses.

Basically, the key points are these: use their name, tell them that you're an investor, say you're looking to invest, specify the industry, the geographical area, and your acquisition criteria. Then say, "Your company came up in my research." This is so that they don't freak out and say, "My company's not for sale!" It's a *"defreakification"* clause!

In your call to action, say "I'm requesting a connection to see if you might like to chat about the possibility of working together." Don't be overly aggressive or specific. Instead, open up all of the possibilities about how they might want to work with you, as opposed to bluntly saying, "I might want to buy your company." That approach could shut them down completely. You don't know where this is going to go. The important thing is to have a conversation.

If you already own a company, you can say, "I'd like to get into a mutually beneficial referral relationship with you and I'm already in your business." And that encourages them to talk to you because they think maybe they can get some new customers. And maybe they can. Or maybe you can acquire them instead.

Never speak or write in a voice that isn't yours. Rework your scripts until you get them into the language you would use. That's really important. You can't build rapport if you sound like a robot. Be authentic.

Now here's the easiest conversation you've ever started. When you're talking to an owner, just say, "Tell me the story of the business. How did it come about? How did it evolve?"

HOW TO REALLY CONNECT

Use your own PERSONALIZED VOICE

Ask them to tell you the "STORY" of the business

Ask about their ENTREPRENEURIAL JOURNEY
(listen to my Business Lunch podcast interviews)

FIND COMMON TOUCH POINTS you have with them

FUTURE-PACE them by asking "what would you do after you sold the business if you were to sell it"

After that, all you'll have to do is say, "Interesting! Great! Cool!" Trust us—business owners want to tell their stories, and you'll be gathering crucial information and data should you decide to make an offer.

As they talk, find common touch points you have with them. If they say, "I went to school in London," tell them you've always wanted to visit that city—or anything that can help build a bond. Remember, you're talking to a person first and an owner second.

Finally, get them thinking about the future in a nuanced (i.e., not pushy) way. Ask, "What would you do if you ever sold the business? Have you ever thought about selling it?" Your goal is to project their minds into a future in which they've already sold the company.

CHAPTER 3 - FINDING TARGETS TO ACQUIRE

For more case studies, examples, worksheets, checklists, forms, script, and other resources, including quite a few that we simply could not fit in the book itself, we created a resources collection, and all of these resources are available and waiting for you at BusinessWealthWithoutRisk.com/access. Visit the site now and enjoy a huge collection of resources at absolutely no money out of pocket for you!

In the next chapter, we're going to explain how we gather and analyze the data you need to start making deals. You're practically ready to get started!

BusinessWealthWithoutRisk.com/access

Profitable Points

This chapter delved into the crucial aspects of deal-making, from identifying the right targets to crafting compelling pitches. We discussed the concept of CASH-ON-CASH, an effective strategy for acquiring profitable businesses while emphasizing the importance of securing deals at the right multiple or price.

With this knowledge, you're now prepared to turn your insights into actual financial gains. These are practical strategies that you can start implementing immediately. Every word you've read is another step toward acquiring your first business.

As we turn the page to our next chapter, we'll focus on the vital deal analysis process and show you how to gather the necessary data to make informed decisions about potential acquisitions. We'll talk about how to request information in an unthreatening way and make the most out of initial conversations with sellers.

Are you ready to level up your *ACQUIREpreneur* skills and begin dissecting potential deals? Let's proceed to the exciting world of "Deal Analysis."

CHAPTER 4

DEAL ANALYSIS

In this chapter, you'll look at how to gather and analyze the data you need to make a deal.

Once you've completed the initial conversation we described in the last chapter, you need to start asking for information about the company's assets and other financial information.

Tone is crucial here. Typically, we say something like, "To see how we might best work together, I need to learn a little bit about the business." You don't ask for three years of financial statements and tax returns because you don't want the seller immediately on guard, reaching out to their accountants or attorneys and asking you to sign a non-disclosure agreement (NDA).

You just want to have an informal conversation. The goal here is to just get enough information to determine whether you might be interested in actually acquiring this business. As you do more and more deals and start to get the hang of this you will see why this is so important. The fact is that once you have solid deal flow, you will not do MOST of the deals that you see. You will be able to be picky about which businesses you buy and that means that you need to be efficient as you look at all the potential deals that come your way. You need to move through the non-starters quickly, and that means that you won't have time to be signing NDAs and going through middlepeople every time a potential deal comes across your desk.

What Data Will You Need?

Most owners aren't going to have this information at their fingertips, so you may need to set up a separate meeting. In either case, use the Target Analysis Data Sheet form below as a guide to the basic data that you'll need to help you determine if you are interested in acquiring the business and how you might shape your offer to acquire it from the seller.

TARGET ANALYSIS **DATA SHEET**

CASH	$_____	ASK_____, SDE_____, M= _____
ACCT RECEIVABLE	$_____	$_____ Sales, $_____ ARR
NOTES RECEIVABLE	$_____	Excess Owner Comp/Bens $_____
CD/MM/TB	$_____	AP = $_____, RE IP = $_____
SECURITIES	$_____	Def. IP _____
RAW MATERIALS	$_____	Runs _____, shifts @ _____ % capacity
WORK IN PROCESS	$_____	Mkt via _____ Sell via _____
INVENTORY	$_____	CEO SL - COO SL - CFO SL - CMO SL
FF&E	$_____	_____ customers _____ prospects
VEHICLES	$_____	Seller RFL _____
REAL ESTATE	$_____	Seller Wants_____

You can find a digital copy of the Target Analysis Data Sheet and all the other worksheets and resources we share in this book at our book website at BusinessWealthWithoutRisk.com/access along with many additional and free resources that can help you with your **ACQUIREpreneur** journey. Go visit the site now to get a copy of the worksheet so that you can work along with us as we go through the sheet now.

Let's walk through each item:

- **Cash** refers to how much cash the business currently has on hand.

- **Accounts Receivable** or money customers owe but have not yet paid, typically refers to funds you'll receive in 90 days or fewer. These Accounts Receivable or "AR" are very common, and they are created whenever products or services are provided to a customer or client so that they are obligated to pay for those products or services.

  A couple of good examples would be when say a digital marketing agency provides marketing services or an attorney provides legal services or a product seller sells on account with payment due in 10, 15 or 30 days. All these situations create an account receivable for the business that provided those products or services.

- **Notes Receivable** refers to owed money for which the timeline is typically longer than about six months. Usually notes receivable are created for larger amounts than simple product or service provision as is the case with accounts receivable. For example, if a business provided a loan to one of its customers or even one of the business's owners, it is likely that there would be a written promissory note detailing the repayment terms, and that would be considered as a note receivable.

- **CD** stands for *certificate of deposit*, **MM** for *money market*, and **TB** for *treasury bill*—all of which can be turned into cash very quickly. We typically refer to these as "**cash equivalents**." You may include crypto in this category if it is readily exchange-able for cash but the volatility of crypto makes it more difficult to classify or even value.

- **Securities** are stocks, bonds, or similar investments that the entrepreneur has purchased in the name of the company. This might also include NFTs (non-fungible tokens).

- **Raw Materials** are the ingredients or components that get as-sembled into finished goods.

- **Work in Process** is anything that's in the pipeline to become a finished good, where it is no longer identifiable as a raw mate-rial, but not yet identifiable as salable finished inventory.

- **Inventory** is generally some sort of physical asset available for sale.

- **FF&E** stands for *Furniture, Fixtures, and Equipment*—the phys-ical assets necessary to run the business. Some accountants and businesses may refer to this as "PP&E" which stands for *Property, Plant, and Equipment.*

- **Vehicles** refers to the value of any vehicles owned by the business.

- **Real Estate** refers to property owned by the business. We gen-erally don't like to buy real estate as part of an acquisition be-cause it complicates the deal, so we ask about it here to see if the seller intends for it to be part of the sale. Usually, most sellers will want to retain the real estate they own that is used by the business, so that they have the income from rent for retirement. We find it easiest to separate the real estate and deal with it separately, even if you want to acquire it.

- **Ask** refers to the asking price that the seller would like to be paid for their business.

- **SDE (Seller's Discretionary Earnings)** is computed for small to mid-sized businesses. SDEs take earnings and add back interest, taxes, depreciation, and other adjustments to show the full financial benefit received by one full-time owner-operator.[12] SDE gives you a better way to determine how much money you'll make from the business and how it compares to other businesses of similar size. SDE applies to owner-operated businesses. If the business isn't owner-operated, you'll focus instead on EBITDA (i.e., profits). Ultimately, you want to answer two questions: What is the profit? And what is the multiple? You're going to get the latter by dividing the asking price by the EBITDA or SDE.

- **Sales** refers to how much the business is selling right now.

- **MRR/ARR** refers to any annual or monthly recurring revenue.

- **Owner Comp** refers to what the owner is being paid in addition to whatever he or she earns for running the business. If the typical owner of this kind of business earns $100,000 and the current owner is paying themselves twice that amount, we'll need to add that extra $100,000 back to the SDE to get

---

12 For a full discussion of SDE, see Jeffrey Baxter, "Seller's Discretionary Earnings (SDE) Explained with Examples," MidStreet Mergers and Acquisition, or just check our explanation earlier in this book.

to the EBITDA. You can get this information from salary.com, payscale.com, and glassdoor.com. All will give you the typical earnings of a person who's performing a particular job in a particular area for a company at a certain level of sales. Why do you want to know that? So you get a more accurate view of the business's worth since many times the owner or employee earns more than you'll have to pay a replacement.

- **AP** stands for accounts payable, usually short-term bills that are due, but not yet paid. This is basically the inverse side of accounts receivable. In fact, one company's accounts payable (the company that received the products or services and owes the debt) is another company's accounts receivable (the company that provided the goods or services to whom the debt is owed).

- **RE NP** stands for Real Estate Note Payable. On a longer term, like a mortgage or deed of trust, that's basically just debt on a piece of real estate. These are referred to as Notes Payable and, much like accounts receivable and accounts payable, notes receivable and notes payable are counterparts to one another.

- **Def. IP** stands for Defensible Intellectual Property. This could be a trademark, copyright, patent, or a trade secret—all of which give the business a competitive edge. This designation comes from the fact that when you have protected intellectual property, you can prevent others from taking it and using it to their advantage in their businesses. You can literally "defend" your IP from use by others, which provides you with a competitive advantage or "moat" between competitors and your business. Thus, the term "defensible."

- **Runs/Shifts:** If the business that you are considering acquiring is manufacturing something, it is a good idea to find out how many shifts are currently running. This is important to know because it will help you realize how soon you might need to invest in additional equipment and labor to grow the business that you are acquiring. For example, if the business is running only one shift, you know that you can add two more without having to invest in additional equipment.

- **@____% Capacity** means "At what capacity is the business currently operating?" If the company is running two shifts at 67% capacity, you know that you can increase production by about 50%[13] without having to buy more equipment or hire more people. However, if it is already running three shifts at 90% capacity, you know that to achieve any meaningful growth, it will be necessary to invest in additional equipment, labor, and possibly additional space to house operations if you want to grow the business. Sounds messy, right?

- **Mkt via___ Sell via____:** You'll also want to know how the business is currently marketing, getting leads, and closing sales. Maybe they have a sales team and an online cart. This is good to know to help spot opportunities for growth. It's also an important component of your due diligence. If a business has no predictable selling systems then it will have a difficult time scaling. On the other hand, if the business drives most of its customers from some predictable and virtually limitless source like advertising, then it is much more marketable

---

13   Since 50% of 67 is 33.5, which takes us to 100%.

because a new owner can simply ramp up the ad spend and expect a positive result.

- **Current Management. The SL Section:** Next, you want to know what's going to happen to the people who are currently running the company? Who's staying (S)? And who's leaving (L)? So, let's say the CEO is leaving, but the COO, CFO, and CMO are staying. That's great. You now know that you have your core components in operations, finance, and marketing. Obviously, if they're all leaving, you'll need to find replacements, which may make the purchase less than ideal. If you want to operate "above" the business (as we covered in a previous chapter) then you cannot be the person operating the business. Therefore, you will need to find someone who can handle all the important aspects of operations: the manager/leader/CEO/ managing director, etc.; someone who can handle finances and marketing; and so forth. Asking about who is leaving and who is staying for the major operations, financial, and marketing/ sales positions helps give you an idea of whether and how you will be able to acquire the business without also acquiring another job for yourself.

- **RFL** means "Reason for Leaving." Why is the seller selling? When you ask your prospective seller what their reason for leaving the business is, you often learn whether they are a motivated seller or not. If they are motivated, chances are they will give you one of the 10 major reasons that we covered previously. If not, then this may not be the best time to get the best price and on the best terms if you decide to move forward with the acquisition.

- **Seller Wants:** What are the seller's plans post-sale? Sellers have many reasons for leaving (as discussed previously), but once they have gone, it is important for them to have an idea of what they will do after they sell. If you ask them about their plans, you can accomplish two important things.

  First, you help to "future pace" them into a vision of what life looks like after the sale and how much they will be able to enjoy their life once all the challenges of running a business have been left behind. They can visualize themselves on that trip they always wanted to take or pursuing that new opportunity they just have not had time to take advantage of yet. It makes them excited to sell the business and eager to get the deal done, all of which is very helpful to you as the buyer.

  The second great thing about knowing what they want to do post-sale is to help you structure an offer that will be very appealing to them and potentially very favorable for you as well. For example, if you know that they always wanted to buy a boat and that the one they have their eye on costs $200,000, then you know that you can probably make a deal if you can either provide $200,000 at closing, or a down payment for financing on a $200,000 boat, or maybe you could even work to acquire the boat that they want yourself for less than they would have to pay and trade it to them as part of the deal.

Is the Deal Reasonable?

Once you have this data, you need to decide, "Is the asking price reasonable?" For example, their asking price for a small machinery company is $1 million, and there's no real estate involved, and the business EBITDA/profit is $200,000.

To determine the asking multiple, you simply divide $1 million by $200,000, which gives you a multiple of five. Is that a reasonable multiple? You don't know yet, but it is important because you do not want to overpay for the business.

To determine whether the price that the seller is asking is reasonable, you look at comparable sales—what have other buyers actually paid to similar sellers in deals that have already closed previously and recently.

To do this, you'll look at the multiples that businesses are selling for in the real world and adjust those for a smaller company. Typically, you divide the multiple that larger businesses have sold for by four to make that adjustment down for the likely value of a smaller and less marketable business like the ones you are considering acquiring. So, if your research shows that bigger companies are selling at 12x EBITDA to private equity firms, your comparable multiple is 12/4, or three.

EBITDA MULTIPLES BY INDUSTRY

Source: Equidam.com

Industry	Multiple
Advanced Medical Equipment & Tech	24.81
Advertising & Marketing	11.1
Aerospace & Defense	14.69
Agriculture Chemicals	11.48
Airlines	8.16
Airport Operators & Services	8.16
Aluminum	7.57
Apparel & Accessories	12.58
Apparel & Accessories Retailers	10.3
Appliances, Tools, & Houseware	10.36
Auto & Truck Manufacturers	9.81
Auto Vehicles, Parts, & Service Retailers	12.09
Auto, Truck, & Motorcycle Parts	7.08
Banks*	20.56
Biotechnology & Medical Research	16.03
Brewers	15.54
Broadcasting**	8.76
· Other Broadcasting	8.46
· Cable Service Providers	9.66
· Radio Broadcasting	8.46
· Television Broadcasting	8.46
Business Support Services	10.03
· Call Center Services	9.73
· Cleaning Services	9.73
· Commercial Edu. Services	15.17
· Corporate Accounting Services	9.73
· Data Processing Services	9.73
· Exhibition & Conference Services	9.73
· Health, Safety, & Fire Protection Equip.	9.29
· Industrial Design Services	9.73
· Industrial Equip. Rental	9.73
· Legal Services	9.73
· Maintenance & Repair Services	9.73
· Management Consulting Services	9.73
· Office Equip. & Supplies Rental	9.73
· Office Furniture	9.29
· Office Supplies	9.29
· Office Supplies Wholesale	9.29
· Pest Control Services	9.73
· Security Services	9.73
· Testing Laboratories	9.73
· Transaction & Payment Services	9.73
· Translation & Interpretation Services	9.73
· Other Business Support Services	9.73
· Other Business Support Supplies	9.29
Business Support Supplies	11.1
Casinos & Gaming	12.39
Closed End Funds	20.14
Coal	4.53
Commercial Printing Services	10.07
Commercial REITs	7.57
Commodity Chemicals	9.60
Communications & Networking	14.16
Computer & Electronic Retailers	10.30
Computer Hardware	11.76
Construction & Engineering	8.22
Construction Materials	10.75
Construction Supplies & Fixtures	8.55
Consumer Lending*	10.56
Consumer Publishing	10.07
Corporate Financial Services*	20.56
Courier, Postal, & Air Freight Logistics	10.47
Department Stores	11.22
Discount Stores	10.9
Distillers & Wineries	15.54
Diversified Chemicals	8.19
Diversified Industrial Goods Wholesalers	9.69
Diversified Investment Services	20.14
Diversified Mining	7.87
Diversified REITs	7.57
Drug Retailers	10.30
Electric Utilities	12.58
Electronic Components & Equipment	9.29
Electronic Equipment & Parts	10.36
Employment Services	9.73
Entertainment Production	19.03
Environmental Services & Equipment	13.46
Exchange-Traded Funds	20.14
Financial/Commodity Mkt Operators	24.35
Fishing & Farming**	13.69
· Agricultural Biotechnology	13.81
· Agricultural Consultancy Services	13.81
· Agricultural Support Services	13.81
· Animal Breeding	13.81
· Animal Feed	13.81
· Aquaculture	13.81
· Cattle Farming	13.81
· Coffee, Tea, & Cocoa Farming	13.81
· Commercial Fishing	13.81
· Commercial Nurseries	13.81
· Fishing & Farming Wholesale	11.43
· Fur Farming	13.81
· Grain (Crop) Production	13.81
· Hog & Pig Farming	13.81
· Organic Farming	13.81
· Poultry Farming	13.81
· Sheep & Speciality Livestock Farming	13.81
· Sugarcane Farming	13.81
· Vegetable, Fruit, & Nut Farming	13.81
· Other Fishing & Farming	13.81
Food Processing	15.72
Food Retail & Distribution**	9.75
· Beer, Wine, & Liquor Stores	9.47
· Food Markets	9.47
· Food Wholesale	11.43
· Supermarkets & Convenience Stores	9.47
· Tobacco Stores	9.47
· Vending Machine Providers	9.47
· Other Food Retail & Distribution	9.47
Footwear	18.84
Forest & Wood Products	9.42
Gold	11
Ground Freight & Logistics	8.84
Healthcare Facilities & Services	12
Heavy Machinery & Vehicles	12.31
Highways & Rail Tracks	10.91
Home Furnishings	10.93
Home Furnishings Retailers	12.88
Home Improv. Products/Svcs Retailers	12.88
Homebuilding	9.29
Household Electronics	24.35
Household Products	13.81
Industrial Conglomerates	13.81
Industrial Machinery & Equipment	12.21
Insurance Funds	13.81
Integrated Oil & Gas	6.77
Integrated Telecom Services	7.06
Investment Banking & Brokerage Svcs	20.56
Investment Holding Companies	20.14
Investment Management & Fund Ops	20.14
Iron & Steel	5.92
IT Services & Consulting	11.79
Leisure & Recreation**	13.81
· Adventure Sports Facilities & Ski Resort	13.36
· Amusement Parks & Zoos	13.36
· Golf Courses	13.81
· Guided Tour Operators	13.81
· Gyms, Fitness, & Spa Centers	13.36
· Hunting & Fishing	13.36
· Marinas	13.81
· Movie Theaters & Movie Products	13.81
· Museums & Historic Places	13.36
· Professional Sports Venues	13.36
· Public Sports Facilities	13.36
· Theaters & Performing Arts	13.36
· Travel Agents	13.36
· Other Leisure & Recreation	13.36
Life & health Insurance	8.85
Managed Healthcare	11.55
Marine Freight & Logistics	9.58
Marine Port Services	9.58
Medical Equip. Services, & Distribution	21.35
Mining Support Services & Equip.	7.57
Miscellaneous Specialty Retailers	10.30
Multiline Insurance & Brokers	9.05
Multiline Utilities	12.58
Mutual Funds	20.14
Natural Gas Utilities	12.58
Non-Alcoholic Beverages	17.58
Non-Gold Precious Metals & Minerals	11
Non-Paper Containers & Packaging	9.33
Office Equipment	9.29
Oil & Gas Drilling	9.45
Oil & Gas Exploration & Production	5.14
Oil & Gas Refining & Marketing	12.8
Oil & Gas Transportation Services	9.45
Oil Related Services & Equipment	19.63
Online Services **	19.63
· Content & Site Management Services	20.14
· eCommerce & Marketplace Services	19.63
· Internet Gaming	19.63
· Internet Security & Transaction Svcs	19.63
· Search Engines	20.14
· Social Media & Networking	19.63
· Other Online Services	19.63
Paper Packaging	9.33
Paper Products	9.42
Passenger Transportation & Ground	10.47
Pension Funds	20.14
Personal Care Services	13.36
Personal Services **	21.35
Personal Services **	10.34
· Accounting & Tax Preparation	9.73
· Child Care & Family Services	9.73
· Consumer Goods Rental	9.73
· Consumer Repair Services	9.73
· Funeral Services	9.73
· General Education Services	9.73
· Personal Care Services	9.73
· Personal Legal Services	9.73
· Other Personal Services	9.73
Pharmaceuticals	14.5
Phones & Handheld Devices	13.09
Professional Information Services	25.3
Property & Casualty Insurance	10.56
Real Estate Rental, Dev., & Operations	9.45
Real Estate Services	17.02
Recreational Products	13.36
Reinsurance	13.22
Renewable Energy Equip. & Services	11.57
Renewable Fuels	11.57
Residential REITs	23.06
Restaurants & Bars	14.99
Semiconductor Equip. & Testing	17.31
Semiconductors	13.11
Shipbuilding	9.58
Software	24.35
Specialized REITs	23.06
Specialty Chemicals	11.48
Specialty Mining & Metals	7.57
Textiles & Leather Goods	12.58
Tires & Rubber Products	6.63
Tobacco	11.1
Toys & Children's Products	13.36
UK Investment Trusts	20.14
Uranium	9.68
Water & Related Utilities	12.47
Wireless Telecom Services	6.81

EBITDA MULTIPLES BY INDUSTRY

INDUSTRY NAME	Multiple
Advertising	8.86
Aerospace/Defense	12.15
Air Transport	34.43
Apparel	14.69
Auto & Truck	45.73
Auto Parts	10.07
Bank (Money Center)	N/A
Banks (Regional)	N/A
Beverage (Alcoholic)	17.61
Beverage (Soft)	20.74
Broadcasting	7.84
Brokerage & Investment Banking	N/A
Building Materials	13.27
Business & Consumer Services	17.40
Cable TV	11.11
Chemical (Basic)	10.01
Chemical (Diversified)	13.38
Chemical (Specialty)	15.56
Coal & Related Energy	5.79
Computer Services	10.70
Computers/Peripherals	24.76
Construction Supplies	15.23
Diversified	11.37
Drugs (Biotechnology)	14.40
Drugs (Pharmaceutical)	14.32
Education	14.43
Electrical Equipment	15.96
Electronics (Consumer & Office)	18.96
Electronics (General)	17.52
Engineering/Construction	10.85
Entertainment	36.26
Environmental & Waste Services	14.98
Farming/Agriculture	14.71
Financial Svcs. (Non-Bank & Insurance)	N/A
Food Processing	12.88
Food Wholesalers	15.87
Green & Renewable Energy	22.94
Healthcare Products	28.53
Healthcare Support Services	10.36
Healthcare Information & Technology	29.32
Homebuilding	9.54
Hospitals/Healthcare Facilities	8.97
Hotel/Gaming	38.32
Household Products	17.60
Information Services	31.70
Insurance (General)	9.99
Insurance (Life)	12.51
Insurance (Prop/Cas.)	9.69
Investments & Asset Management	26.17
Machinery	16.70
Metals & Mining	13.90
Office Equipment & Services	8.82
Oil/Gas (Integrated)	10.77
Oil/Gas (Production & Exploration)	6.39
Oil/Gas Distribution	9.12
Oilfield Services/Equipment	11.35
Packaging & Container	10.34
Paper/Forest Products	7.71
Power	11.89
Precious Metals	36.26
Publishing & Newspapers	9.77
R.E.I.T.	22.72
Real Estate (Development)	47.57
Real Estate (General/Diversified)	25.25
Real Estate (Operations & Services)	14.82
Recreation	22.59
Reinsurance	12.92
Restaurant/Dining	23.53
Retail (Automotive)	11.56
Retail (Building Supply)	12.59
Retail (Distributors)	13.88
Retail (General)	12.29
Retail (Grocery & Food)	5.75
Retail (Online)	33.19
Retail (Special Lines)	11.40
Rubber & Tires	9.84
Semiconductor	18.04
Semiconductor Equipment	18.69
Shipbuilding & Marine	10.67
Shoe	35.83
Software (Entertainment)	25.09
Software (Internet)	19.21
Software (System & Application)	30.42
Steel	9.74
Telecom (Wireless)	10.14
Telecom Equipment	13.92
Telecom Services	6.76
Tobacco	10.48
Transportation	12.96
Transportation (Railroads)	15.46
Trucking	10.06
Utility (General)	12.15
Utility (Water)	20.92
Total Market	20.02
Total Market (W/O Financial)	16.52

Industry Determines Valuation

What Business Are You In?

What Valuation?

Source: Stern.NYU.edu

The two tables above give you the sales multiples for several types of businesses as determined by Equidam and Stern School of Business at NYU, respectively. These multiples charts can serve as a reasonable guideline for determining what multiples are reasonable for you to consider paying when acquiring the same types of companies listed in the tables.

We provide you with both of these tables so that you can see that multiples vary depending on what source you look to for that data. This is because multiples are based on the average selling price for a cohort (or group) of different companies that actually recently sold, and those cohorts invariably comprise different groups of companies, depending on who is putting the table together.

The tables above give you the average EBITDA multiple for companies in various industries. For our machinery company, the average is 16.7x. Keep in mind that this figure includes companies much larger than the one in our example.

So, you divide 16.7 by four and get 4.175. This means that the asking multiple of five is a little higher than you would want it to be. But you might be willing to still go for it if they give great terms. Why do you divide by four? It is definitely not a scientifically determined number. It's just the number that we have found to be reasonable and workable to translate the multiples that very large companies sell at and which are reported in tables like those we share with you above. If you use the multiples provided in those tables for smaller companies, you will end up paying too much. So, divide by four as a rule of thumb, and get something closer to what you should actually pay. Not scientific, but workable.

IS _x EBITDA **PRICE REASONABLE?**

ASKING	$_____
REAL ESTATE	($_____)
NET ASK	$_____
/EBITDA	$_____

ASK MULTIPLE _____ **INDUSTRY/4** _____

You can use the calculator above to determine whether the seller's asking price is reasonable for any company that you are considering acquiring. Write the seller's asking price in the space to the right of the word "Asking." If there is any real estate, write the value allocated to that real estate on the next line, and then subtract the value of that real estate from the seller's asking price to determine the Net Ask. Next, divide that Net Ask by the business's EBITDA (profit) to determine the "Ask Multiple." Write the Ask Multiple down next to "Ask Multiple" and then take the industry multiple you found using the industry multiple tables and divide that by four, then write that number down in the "Industry/4" space. If the Ask Multiple is greater than the Industry/4 Multiple, then the seller is likely asking too much for the business. If the Ask Multiple is less than or equal to the Industry/4 Multiple, then you likely have a fair and reasonable price being asked by the seller.

The next table provides some additional guidelines for adjusting your multiple across all industries for owner-operated companies (remember for owner-operated businesses you use SDE or Seller Discretionary Earnings and for professionally managed businesses you use EBITDA or Earnings Before Interest, Taxes, Depreciation, and Amortization) based on SME size.

If the business profit (SDE) is $1 million per year, it's typically going to sell for a multiple of 3.35 to 4.25. On the other hand, if it's making $100,000, it's going to sell for 2 to 2.7. So, you'll be looking at a figure between $200,000 and $270,000. Notice that the smaller the business, the smaller the multiple.

AVERAGE SDE MULTIPLES BY SIZE

SDE	MULTIPLE	BUSINESS VALUE
$50,000	1.0 - 1.25	$50,000 - $62,000
$75,000	1.1 - 1.8	$82,500 - $135,000
$100,000	2.0 - 2.7	$200,000 - $270,000
$200,000	2.5 - 3.0	$500,000 - $600,000
$500,000	3.0 - 4.0	$1,500,000 - $2,000,000
$1,000,000	3.25 - 4.25	$3,250,000 - $4,250,000

This provides an often-overlooked opportunity. First, you can acquire a business that has growth potential that has a lower SDE and then, as you grow, it quickly increases its value because multiples for higher profit businesses are higher than those for lower profit businesses.

But an even bigger opportunity with much less work exists by acquiring four or five smaller similar businesses and aggregating them (or merging them together). Let's say that you acquire six businesses with

$90,000 in SDE. If you combine those businesses into a single business, you will have one business earning 6 x $90,000 or $540,000. Each of the $90,000 businesses would be acquired at a multiple of around 1.5x SDE (based on the chart above).

So, you would have paid a total of $810,000 to acquire all six businesses. Keep in mind that later in this book you will learn how to do this with no money out of pocket, so don't worry if you don't have or don't want to part with $810,000 in cash.

Once you have combined those six businesses into a single business, you would then have one business that was generating $540,000 in SDE, and looking at the chart above, you can see that a business with $500,000 of SDE would sell for a multiple between 3x and 4x SDE.

Let's pick a multiple in the middle of that range and say that you could sell the business for a 3.5 multiple. That means you should be able to sell this combined business for 3.5x the SDE of $540,000, which equals $1,890,000!

By simply combining them into a single business, the value increases by over $1 million. The businesses you paid $810,000 for are now worth $1,890,000, which creates a built-in profit for you of $1,080,000. That's the power of understanding how multiples work.

For a software as a service company, the story differs a bit. In general, if a SaaS business's annual recurring revenue (ARR) is greater than $1 million and it is privately owned, it is typically going to sell for about 70% of public SaaS valuations.

Thus, if its ARR exceeds $1 million and public companies with that ARR are currently selling for a multiple of 15.5x ARR right now, the multiple for the privately owned business would be about 10.9x ARR which is 70% of the 15.5 multiple. For companies with an ARR of less than $1 million, you're typically looking at a of multiple 3x to 10x the

TTM as of this writing, although these numbers can vary wildly as SaaS comes in and out of fashion with Private Equity, Growth Capital, Venture Capital, and Family Office investment funds.

Listing Analysis: Case 1

Although very few deals come from listing sites, those sites are good for practice. When we look at the listing below, for example, we see 10 key bits of information, which we've listed in the left-hand margin.

10 Keys:

1. **Broker Listing**: We can see from the broker image and blurb in the bottom right-hand corner that this listing is represented by a business broker. This is a negative because, as we explained, that's often a sign that we're not working with a motivated seller, but someone willing to hold out for the best possible offer.

Working with a broker typically adds cost and complexity. For us, a *broker* is very often a *deal breaker!* The job of a business broker is to create an auction situation where multiple buyers are bidding to pay the highest price for a business and the competition among competing bidders drives up the price to get the seller the maximum price possible in the sale. This is the exact opposite of what we want to do. We are looking for motivated sellers eager to sell quickly and willing to discount their price, not those who are patiently waiting to receive the highest price possible.

2. **Location Match:** This is a positive because we want a business in the San Diego area. When searching for businesses on a business listing site, make sure you filter out businesses beyond your target geographic area.

3. **Seller Financing:** This is a positive because we typically get better terms (e.g., interest rates and down payments) from a motivated seller than from a bank. Traditional business loans must go through multiple layers of approval, which can take many months to complete. Motivated sellers want to keep the financing process moving forward. The fact that the listing includes the option of seller financing indicates a seller who is somewhat flexible with respect to terms and who may be willing to come down on price.

4. **CF not EBITDA:** This means we need more information here. They've listed cash flow but not EBITDA, which is not the same thing. EBITDA, remember, is earnings before interest, taxes, depreciation, and amortization and is a useful metric for gauging a company's overall health and profitability.

5. **The Multiple:** This is another case where we need more information. At first glance it seems positive since it's less than four: $1,400,000/$404,731 = 3.46. Note, however, that we prefer to make this calculation with EBITDA rather than cash flow, so we'll want to recheck this approximation when we verify the former figure.

6. **The 34% Operating Margin:** This is a positive. To calculate this figure, we divide cash flow by gross revenue: 404,731/1,190,352 = .34 or 34%. We generally like that number to be above 15% and this one qualifies quite well in that regard.

7. **The 41-year History:** This is another positive. They've proven their mettle and clearly aren't just a flash in the pan. We know that 90% of businesses fail within the first 10 years of existence. This business has beaten the odds and only has about a 10% chance of failure at this point, which means that our risk of failure is dramatically less than if we were acquiring a business that had only existed for, say, three to five years.

8. **FFE** (furniture, fixtures, and equipment): This is included, so that's a positive: $192,000. Remember, FF&E is also sometimes referred to as PP&E (property, plant and equipment) and includes computers, desks, machines, etc.

9. **Leased Space:** This isn't included, so we need to find out about that: What's the payment? How long does it last? What are the terms? How much space do they have? Is there a renewal option? Is there an opportunity to expand? How much of the actual space are they using in the business currently?

10. **No Inventory:** This is a negative. How is that possible for a manufacturer? They should have raw materials, work in

progress, and finished goods. So, we need to dig in and understand what's going on here.

If you had a color copy of the listing we are analyzing here, you would be able to see that we mark the positives in green (as in greenlight the acquisition), the negatives in red (things that could dissuade us from completing the acquisition) and things for which we need more information in yellow (caution light color). But, because you are likely NOT looking at these charts in color, suffice to say that we usually color code them so that we can quickly tally the number of greens and reds and calculate what we like to refer to as the Acquisition Quotient or AQ Score. This score provides a quick guide for our assistants who vet deals and determine which ones merit bringing to us for further consideration.

For this listing, we have two minuses, five pluses, and three cases where we need more information. That gives us a plus three (i.e., five green lights minus two red lights) on what we call our Acquisition Quotient (AQ). We'll see why this tally is important in a moment.

First, however, let's evaluate the pluses and minuses on the business's description page shown below. We consider the "New Listing!" a negative despite their enthusiastic exclamation point. When owners first list their business, they typically want the most money because they haven't yet received lower offers or no offers. We prefer a listing that's been up for at least six months, so the seller has experienced the reality that they are not likely to get the high number they usually believe that their business is worth. A bit of frustration is a great motivator for a seller.

Business Description

-4 + +6 = +2 AQ SCORE

New Listing!

This custom plastics manufacturer has been established over 40 years and services a variety of industries including automotive, electronics, packaging and more. Long list of repeat clients and extremely consistent revenue and profitability. Operating out of a convenient North San Diego County location featuring an 8,357 sf facility owned by the Sellers (not included) in the $1.4M asking price). Sellers are willing to sign a new favorable lease with the next owner and are negotiable on the length of term and option to extend. Asking price includes all required equipment on site. Owners are looking to retire and have successfully navigated multiple recessions and this most recent Pandemic with minimal financial impact. Owner is active in the business in a sales and management role and the company has an experienced staff at 5 Full Time employees. Call Listing Agent Sean today for more details on this exciting opportunity!

"Over 40 years" in business is a positive, as are "repeat clients" and "extremely consistent revenue and profitability." The sellers own the facility, but it's not included in the asking price; that's a negative because it just means we're going to have to work out this real estate issue with them. At the same time, it's a good sign that they're "willing to sign a new favorable lease." The asking price includes the equipment. That's good. The owner wants to retire. Fantastic. That signals a motivated seller. The company was minimally affected by the pandemic—another plus.

Now a couple of negatives: the retiring owner has been active in the business. That's bad because we're going to have to replace them. Ideally, we want the owner to stay. That's how we work *above* the business. Why would owners sell and stay? Because they don't want the hassles of ownership, the risks of being an entrepreneur. They may want to work *in* the business and still operate it, but not have to deal with all the risks and headaches. There are a million reasons the owner might stay.

So, here's one of our first questions to ask the owner when we talk about acquiring their company: "Is this something that you want to stay in as an operator, even after the sale?" And they might or might not. If they do, we don't have to find somebody to operate it. If they don't, we're going to ask about the current manager, the person directly under the owner. We would definitely consider giving that person the opportunity to run the company because he or she is already managing day-to-day details.

The next place we would look would be the leadership team—typically the head of marketing, the head of accounting, the head of operations, the head of manufacturing, or the head of technology. Are any of them good candidates to run the company?

If not, we look at any key employees who might be viable leaders. If we aren't satisfied with those options, we would reach out to our networks and ask, "Does anybody know or want to run a machine manufacturing company?" And then our last option would be a job search or a recruiter.

The Detailed Information in the figure below provides additional data we would want when evaluating a prospective acquisition. First, the building has 8,000 square feet. But we need some context before we can give that a plus or a minus. How much space do they need? Is there enough room for us to expand if we're successful? A definite plus, however, is their willingness to offer four weeks of support and training.

Detailed Information	-0 + +1 = +1 AQ SCORE
LOCATION:	San Diego County, CA
REAL ESTATE:	Leased
BUILDING SF:	8,347
LEASE EXPIRATION:	N/A
EMPLOYEES:	5
FURNITURE, FIXTURES, & EQUIPMENT (FF&E):	Included in asking price
FINANCING:	$1,200,000 Down, Balance Seller Carry Note
SUPPORT & TRAINING:	4 Weeks
REASON FOR SELLING:	Retirement

Notice that each of the previous three figures has an AQ score in the upper right-hand corner. We derive this by simply adding the positives and negatives. Actually, we have a virtual assistant that does this for us, but you can also do it yourself, which is a good idea at first as you're learning to evaluate this information. If the combined score of the three evaluations is lower than two, we're not interested. You may set a different number, but we don't want to do turnarounds of flailing companies; we want a majority of positive qualities. As we've said, we seek a profitable business so we can work above it.

The method we're working through here is a rough way for you to screen these deals and separate the sheep from the goats. If we add all three AQ scores above, we have six negatives and 12 positives. So, the deal is a solid +6, 3x our minimum. This is definitely a deal we would take a look at. Our point in running through this exercise is to give you some practice in identifying the key variables. Now you know how to look at a business the way we do!

The Gap

Before you start thinking about structuring the financing and your ultimate offers for a deal, you have to consider what we call **the gap**. The difference between the seller's price and what we have available to pay is "the gap." To make it really simple, the gap is the difference between the price the seller wants and the price you want to pay.

WHAT IS THE GAP?

The gap is the amount of money that stands between what you want to pay ($0) and the amount the seller wants in cash for the business. So if a seller is selling the business for $1M and you have $500 that you are willing to pay, then the gap is $100k.

Of course, you could just write a check for the sale price, or obtain financing for the sale price, but when we are making deals, our goal is to use creative financing to fill the gap from $0 all the way up to what we have to pay the seller for the business. We'll be talking a lot more about this later but having this concept in mind is helpful for the discussion that follows.

In order to help you understand the gap a bit better, we'll show you an example. The table below provides a detailed analysis of a company that's purchase price is $1.4 million. (Which means that if you want to pay $0 out of pocket, then the gap is $1.4 million.) Now let's say that the owner is volunteering to provide $200,000 in seller financing, which fills in $200,000 of that gap. Now you only need another $1.2 million to be able to acquire the business.

CHAPTER 4 - DEAL ANALYSIS

In the scenario above, there's still $1.2 million to find in order to acquire the business. Most people who have not read this book would probably seek to secure some type of financing. In the United States, they might go to a lender and ask to do an SBA loan (a loan from the Small Business Administration). Or, in other countries they might seek out similar programs offered from time-to-time by the governments in those countries. Other would-be business buyers might seek out a loan or some other bank financing from commercial banks or credit unions. And this would be fine. But it's not the only way to do it, and considering the fact that you're reading this book, you probably aren't interested in going that route either.

Since we want to do our best to fill the gap completely– so that we are literally paying $0 out of pocket, then we have to do some creative financing to close the rest of the gap. What's more, if you're anything like us, you want to do your best to not acquire debt that would require your personal guaranty. No smart business owner wants financing that requires their personal credit and assets to secure the loan—after all, if things didn't work out with the business, you don't want to risk your personal or other business assets to have to repay the loan.

Back to the example at hand, you have $1.2M left to close in the gap. For calculation purposes, we recommend you start by running an analysis based on what a normal loan would cost to determine how much profit an investment in the business would generate under a "traditional" financing scenario. Keep in mind, we are going to target a $0 out of pocket acquisition, so your return would in effect actually be infinite, because you will be acquiring with no money. But, until you learn our creative financing strategies later in the book, we'll have you do it this way for simplicity.

168

Based on traditional financing scenarios, this is approximately what it would cost to acquire this company:

ANALYSIS LISTING #1

PURCHASE PRICE	$1,400,000	ROI
SELLER FINANCING	($200,000)	124.5%
SBA 7(a) @ 75% LTV	($1,050,000)	
DOWN PAYMENT ("Gap")	$150,000	Install $84k
CURRENT CASH FLOW	$404,731	Manager
1st YEAR LOAN PAYMENTS	($217,987)*	
FREE CASH	$186,744	ROI w/Manager
MONTHLY FREE CASH	$15,562	68.5%

Combined payments on SBA 7A loan of $1,050,000 6% 7 Yr = $15,259.10/month x 12 = $183,109.20/year
plus Seller Financing of $200k 6% 7 Yr = $2,906.50/month x 12 = $34,878/year

If you look at the asterisk at the bottom of the table, you see that in the US, the SBA would make a loan like this at around 6% over seven years, so we're going to assume that's what we can get from other sources using the creative financing strategies that we will teach you a bit later in the book. In the above scenario, the buyer gets $200,000 from the seller and another $1,050,000 (75%) from alternative, creative financing sources. That leaves $150,000 gap left to fill.

We did the math for you, but if you're curious how we did it, we calculated the difference between the $1.4 million purchase price, the $200,000 in seller financing, and the $1.05 million financing—since 75% is the most we can get on the loan-to-financing ratio (1.4 x .75 = 1.05). This left us $150,000 short of the purchase price.

Later in this book, we'll show you some creative strategies that can get that $150,000 gap closed down to $0, but for now, from a cash flow standpoint, you can assume an investment of $150,000 cash.

So, the question is: Would this make sense to purchase under this scenario? Let's say that the current cash flow is $404,000 a year on this business. Your first-year payments would be $217,000. That means even after you make those payments, you still have $186,000 in cash left—which is $15,000 a month. Not too bad.

Our point is this: If you see a $1M gap and you don't have $1M to spend, don't automatically give up on the deal. Gaps are made for closing! If you're not used to doing financials for businesses, we recommend that you read through this case a few times. It'll start to make sense, we promise! And do the math on paper because it gets easier when you work through each step yourself.

You don't need to be an expert on creative financing to make this happen—you just need to be willing to look at the numbers in the gap and figure out how you can make them all fit together.

INSTALLING PROFESSIONAL MANAGEMENT

As you think about how to close the gap to $0, one strategy that almost always proves effective is to install professional management. When the seller is leaving, they leave a management hole but often they are paying themselves from profits as opposed to deducting a salary. That means that the profit of the business is artificially high because whoever we put in there to run the business is going to want to get paid. Installing professional management often has an ROI of 68.5% or higher.

You need to account for installing management as you consider how you close your gap. In the scenario we just talked about, you would get 124% on your money the first year, without that expense, because you would be spending $150,000 as the down payment that you couldn't get financed, meaning you could recover 100% of your out-of-pocket investment of $150,000 and still actually be ahead 25% on your initial investment out-of-pocket the first year.

By adding a manager, you install someone to manage the company and oversee things. Look at payscale.com, glassdoor.com, and salary.com to see what a business manager salary is in your area for a similar type and size of business. For example, in San Diego where we live, a new hire will cost about $84,000 a year. You take $84,000 out of this $186,000 return on investment to determine the real return after adding that cost.

After making that change to our return on investment calculation, we conclude that our ROI is going to be about 68.5%, which is still pretty great. So we like the deal and it makes good financial sense, assuming the rest of our due diligence checks out and everything else in the business looks okay.

Listing Analysis: Case 2

The second listing is a medical spa. Again, there's a broker here—good old Jerry Diza down in the bottom right corner. That's a negative, not because we don't like Jerry! It's because, as we mentioned earlier, we generally don't get the best deals when business brokers are actively involved in a current listing.

The listing is located in San Diego County. So that's good. But, there's no seller financing. That's another negative. The multiple is very low: 1.3. So that's good. And the 54% operating margin is fantastic. So, this is starting off as a mixed bag. The listing doesn't say when the business was founded—and we're going to need that information. We're looking for at least three years. As we said earlier, the longer the business has been around, the lower the chance of its failure. SBA data shows that 90% of businesses fail in the first ten years, so longevity suggests a lower risk of failure.

Also, notice that the EBITDA ($2.08 million) and cash flow ($1.14 million) differ significantly. What's going on with that $900,000 difference? We need to understand that. We don't understand how a spa could have no furniture, fixtures, and equipment! This seems impossible! Surely, they have those special chairs, the goop they're putting on people's faces, towels, and so on. It's a negative that these aren't included.

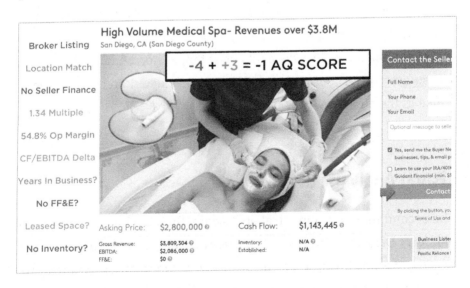

Is it a leased space? We don't know. That's another question we're going to have to ask. And there's no inventory. That makes no sense. So, our AQ here is negative one (i.e., four negatives and three positives).

The business description below answers some of our questions. There are two high-volume locations. The business has been around since 2012. It's a top ranked medical spa with experienced staff. So that's all great. Our AQ score here is four positives and zero negatives. That's why we have to dig into these a little bit.

Business Description $\boxed{-0 + {+4} = +4 \text{ AQ SCORE}}$

HIGH VOLUME MEDICAL SPA

2 high volume locations. Upscale Medical Spa proudly serving the northern San Diego area since 2012. As a top ranked medical spa, their core beliefs include: customer satisfaction, safety and training. Since 2012, the med spas have continually grown their team and services over 5,000 happy clients and 10,000 treatments performed.

Med Spa Services Include:
? Lip fillers: Injectables | Botox | Juvederm | Restylane Lyft | Dysport | Xeomin | Kybella | Trusculpt | Laser Treatments Face & Body | Laser Hair Removal | Vascular Treatments | IPL (Photofacial) | Body Sculpting Trusculpt | Chemical Peels | Dermaplaning
The highly trained staff has over 30 years of experience in medical aesthetics and skin care industry.

But if we dig even further, everything gets confusing. These are the kind of issues we're training you to spot. Look at the "consistent revenues" in the next figure. In the upper right, the business claims to have earned $3.7 million in 2019, $3.4 million in 2018, and $2.6 million in 2017.

But then at the bottom of the figure, the numbers for these years are completely different—by large margins. And these differ from those in the previous figures where gross revenue was $3.8 million and cash flow was $1.1 million.

This is very messy—and we prefer to avoid messes. On the other hand, messes can be great deals! If a listing presents challenges like these, causing other **ACQUIREpreneurs** to give it a pass, this could be something special for you—a great opportunity to secure a great deal with less competition from other potential buyers. If you have the time and a greater tolerance for "mess" (risk, in other words), don't pass up this kind of deal.

Another negative: this broker says you "must show proof of financial capability," but the ad doesn't say how much that is. Brokers often ask you to prove that you have the money to buy a company sitting in a bank account somewhere. We don't know many wealthy people who just have their money sitting in the bank doing nothing. But, much more importantly, why would we share our financial information with someone we don't know before we even know if we are interested in the deal?

We need more information before we can determine if we want to make an offer on this. So, we would just tell them we are happy to provide proof of funds at the appropriate time when we are ready to make an offer and we know what the offer is going to be. If that is not good enough for them, we hit them with those famous words from Shark Tank: "I'm out!" There are innumerable other listings we can peruse.

That's one reason we deal with motivated sellers and not with brokers. As an aside, it doesn't matter if you don't have the money in the bank to buy a company. Most buyers don't. Most private equity companies don't. How do they make deals happen without the cold, hard cash? They use commitments from other people and creative financing to make things happen. You'll learn how to do that in the next chapter.

So, this isn't a deal we would consider. Overall, the three figures give me an AQ score of plus one, and we don't act unless the number is two or higher. On the other hand, this could be a great opportunity if you're willing to unravel the inconsistencies. Not us—we're out.

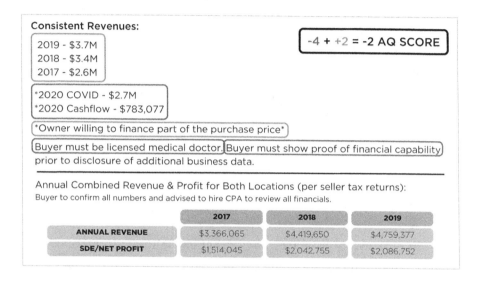

	2017	2018	2019
ANNUAL REVENUE	$3,366,065	$4,419,650	$4,759,377
SDE/NET PROFIT	$1,514,045	$2,042,755	$2,086,752

Let's work through the analysis below the same way we did in Case1. Seller financing is at 20% of $2.8 million (i.e., $560,000). Our 75% loan would be worth $2.1 million, which means we'd have to come up with $140,000 in cash. That's our down payment gap.

The cash flow could be $1.1 million, but as we mentioned, the company has listed three different numbers, so we have a lot of uncertainty here. We simply don't know how much money the company is making. If we assume that their first number is correct, our year-one loan payments would be $463,877. That would leave free cash flow at $679,000, which amounts to over $56,000 per month. And we don't need to adjust that downward because the company already has a manager—unlike the situation in Case 1. So that high return is pretty solid, and thus this deal could be interesting for someone willing to examine and then confirm an accurate set of numbers.

ANALYSIS LISTING #2

PURCHASE PRICE	$2,800,000	ROI
SELLER FINANCING	($560,000)	485.4%
SBA 7(a) @ 75% LTV	($2,100,000)	
DOWN PAYMENT ("Gap")	$140,000	Already Has F/T
CURRENT CASH FLOW	$1,143,445	Manager
1st YEAR LOAN PAYMENTS	($463,877)*	
FREE CASH	$679,568	
MONTHLY FREE CASH	$56,631	

Combined payments on SBA 7A loan of $2,100,000 6% 7 Yr = $30,518.21/month x 12 = $366,218.52/year plus Seller Financing of $560k 6% 7 Yr = $8,138.19/month x 12 = $97,658.28/year

In part two of this book, we will show you how to increase the value of companies exponentially. We also have value-increasing resources you can check out at scalable.co. But our focus here is how to buy a business for no money out of pocket. That's because *you need to own a business before you can start increasing its value.*

At this point, you know which companies interest you and what data you need. You also know how to reach out to the owner, collect key data, and analyze it. In the next chapter, we're going to go into specific strategies for creative financing that will enable you to buy a company with no money out of pocket. So, if you're already eyeing deals and collecting data from companies, fill out the *Target Analysis Data Sheet* we included at the beginning of this chapter.

We're about to have some fun!

For more case studies, examples, worksheets, checklists, forms, scripts, and other resources, including quite a few that we simply could not fit in the book itself, we created a resources collection and all of these resources are available and waiting for you at BusinessWealthWithoutRisk.com/access. Visit the site now and enjoy a huge collection of resources at absolutely no money out of pocket for you!

BusinessWealthWithoutRisk.com/access

Golden Nuggets

This chapter was all about deal-making, the data, and asking those initial, casual questions that pave the way for solid business opportunities. Without any formalities or NDAs, you've learned to uncover crucial information about a potential acquisition.

Take a moment to acknowledge this new skill set. You've gained the know-how to efficiently sift through many deals, honing in on the promising ones. Remember, the key to success here isn't the volume of deals you encounter but selecting those with true potential. And now you know how to do just that.

Next, we'll step into the exhilarating world of financing.

The upcoming chapter will explore the "deal stack"—an arsenal of ten creative strategies to acquire a business without spending a dime of your own money. Our mission is to provide you with more options than anyone else. We're not just talking about making acquisitions possible here.

We promise this game-changer will show you how to acquire businesses with zero money out of pocket!

FUNDING THE DEAL

The Deal Stack

We call this the "deal stack" component because we're going to show you 10 methods you can combine (i.e., "stack") until you get the amount you need to purchase a business with no money out of pocket. Why is it called a "stack"? Because the various no money out of pocket funding strategies are like Lego blocks, where we start with a target—the purchase price, and we have $0 towards that.

The difference between the target acquisition price (or the price the seller is asking for the business) and the amount of funding you have to meet that price is "the gap." Your goal is to get from your $0 starting point to the acquisition price by piecing together several different creative financing strategies to completely close "the gap" to $0 and be able to acquire the business.

CHAPTER 5 - FUNDING THE DEAL

Each creative financing strategy stands on its own, but together they combine to form a complete "deal stack" that can help you acquire almost any business, very often with little or no money out of your own pocket. This is where things get really, seriously fun!

In military battles, the winning general isn't always the one with the most soldiers, but the one with the most and best options or tactics. That happens in sports as well: you'll see underdog teams win because they have plays that the other team didn't anticipate. Our goal is to provide you with more and better options than anyone else looking to acquire the same business. That gives you options. It puts otherwise unaffordable businesses within reach. It is a total game changer.

Let's say that you're trying to acquire a $1 million business. And you have $0, meaning you aren't going to put up any of your own money to make the purchase. Chances are you won't get the whole $1 million from a single method. But by combining funds from multiple sources, you can raise the entire sum without reaching into your own pocket. The key here is the *cumulative impact* of your sources, with each whittling down the amount you need until you reach your goal. You just have to consolidate—to stack—enough different strategies into your deal stack to completely close the gap.

Roland has identified over 220 different methods for creatively financing any deal, but we're going to focus on 10 of the most common and most applicable for our purposes here. (That way, we don't have to double the length of this book and strain your attention span!) Anyone interested in learning all 220 methods should consider enrolling in Roland's EPIC M&A courses or EPIC Elite programs. We'll provide information about how to do that at the end of this chapter, but the primary focus right now is getting you super valuable information to be able to do deals with little to no money out of pocket.

You can also learn more about the 220+ financing strategies and access a wide array of valuable information that we couldn't fit in this book or that we developed after this book was published by visiting the website for the book at BusinessWealthWithoutRisk.com/access.

10 Ways to Acquire a Business with Zero Money Out of Pocket

Before we dive into the various creative financing strategies, it's important to note that some of these strategies can be used before you close the deal and own the business, and others aren't available until you complete the acquisition and own the business assets. Accordingly, we will identify whether a particular strategy is a pre-closing or post-closing strategy.

Note that pre-closing strategies are typically specified as part of your letter of intent (LOI). The LOI is the term sheet that you sign with the seller laying out the deal points for your acquisition transaction. You will have to work with the seller to discuss, present, and agree on the pre-closing strategies for your deal stack and then include them in your LOI.

However, the post-closing financing strategies by definition do not take place until after you already own the business. You do not typically discuss these strategies with the seller because they will only complicate your negotiations, and the seller likely will not have thought about most of these strategies in operating their business, and if you make the seller aware of these strategies, they may very well decide to keep the business simply because they resent the idea of you being able to acquire their business for no money out of pocket by using the assets of the business itself to pay for it.

So, post-closing strategies are not in the LOI and you don't talk to the seller about them. Pre-closing strategies are in the LOI and you *do* need seller agreement to use them in your deal stack.

Now let's examine the strategies.

Carve Out

This is relevant whenever a business has assets that you don't want or need to run the operation—and that's true more often than you may suppose.

For example, you want to acquire a company that makes car parts. The asking price is $1 million, but the person who owns the company had always wanted to expand into the candy business, so she bought these confection manufacturing machines, but never really used them.

Well, if your focus is strictly car parts, you don't want to pay for candy manufacturing machines you're never going to use. And the value of those machines is $300,000. You could basically just do a $300,000 carve-out, removing the candy making equipment from the deal and correspondingly lowering the purchase price and then you would only owe $700,000. You've just reduced your price tag by 30%.

Or let's say that you want to buy a roofing manufacturer. They make roofing materials, and several years back they also started a roofing installation business. If you are only interested in the roofing manufacturing business and don't want to buy the service installation operation, then just remove those parts of the business from your offer. Just offer to acquire the manufacturing part and reduce the purchase price by the value of the installation business.

What you are doing here is cherry-picking the best parts of the business while simultaneously reducing the purchase price.

Similarly, you may find as you get into the asset list for the business that the seller has personal assets that they bought using the business to help them reduce income taxes. Maybe they have their personal automobile owned by the business. Maybe the business has a stock and investments account. Maybe the owners invested in art for their personal collection, but they ran the expenses through the business to write those purchases off. There are quite a few purchases that may have been run through the business for assets that are not essential for the business to operate and earn a profit. The more of these you can identify and remove using the carveout strategy, the lower the purchase price will be. Also, you will close the gap more quickly between available funding and the amount you'll need to close the deal.

Carve outs are a pre-close strategy, and you'll get the seller to agree to them as part of your negotiation and you will specify them in your letter of intent (LOI).

Supplier Loan

This is great because when you're acquiring a business, you're frequently inheriting some sort of suppliers or contractors. Maybe you are working to acquire an auto parts business. Someone has been providing the company with raw materials.

You can approach that company and say, "Hey, I'm working on acquiring this business and we'd like to keep buying from you. Would you be willing to make a loan to the company so that we can acquire it? If so, we'll agree that you'll continue to be our supplier for the next 24 or 36 months."

When you do a deal like this you need to agree on pricing for the committed term as well. It is very important that you agree on pricing because you don't want to be locked into a long-term purchase/supplier commitment and then have the supplier raise prices on you. Ideally, you lock in the prices you are already receiving or get an even more favorable price. But if you can't get the supplier to agree on price locks, the next best thing is to use something called "*favored nations pricing*," meaning that whatever pricing the suppliers offer to their best customers—the lowest price that they offer to anyone else—is the price that you will pay. Effectively, even if prices go up or materials cost change, you will always be guaranteed to receive the best price from that supplier.

People often ask me, "Why would a supplier do that?" The answer is simple: to keep your business. Train yourself to look at these deals from the perspective of the other party. From their point of view, a new owner may well opt for a new supplier—and then they're out of luck. It's in their interest to do what they can to keep you as a customer. That gives you some leverage.

Roland was involved in a real estate business that rehabbed houses, and his partner's family did about 1,100 rehabs every year. So, we were thinking, "Hey, we buy about $60 million in supplies from Home Depot every year. What if we cut them out and set up our own supply business? We could call it "Rehabbers' Warehouse."

We don't know if Home Depot caught wind of this, but the timing sure was convenient, as they approached us and said, "Hey, listen, we'd like to reward you for buying from us, and we want you to continue to do so. How about if you take a $2 million check from us right now? You don't have to give any of it back. It's not a loan. And at the end of two years, as long as you've continued to buy from us at the same level, we'll give you another $2 million."

Leverage can be worth a lot of money!

Suppose, for our car parts case, you were able to get a supplier loan of $100,000. Add that to your carve out of $300,000 that we talked about earlier in the last section, and you've now reduced your gap from $1 million to $600,000. This would be something you'd do post-closing, and it would not be in your LOI, although you might have the conversations with the suppliers about this before you agreed to the deal with the seller.

A great way to find a significant amount of money using this strategy is to ask the seller for a list of their top 20 suppliers and approach each of those 20 suppliers asking about the possibility of a supplier loan.

As a backup to asking for a loan where the supplier actually cuts you a check, you could also just ask for better payment terms. If you approached suppliers and were able to negotiate terms for payment of your bills with them from a cash payment up front basis to a 90-day credit term, you would effectively secure a one-time cash windfall equal to 120 days of your total supplier purchases.

This happens because the business currently pays immediately for items from those suppliers. That means there are zero days of credit being extended by the suppliers. If instead you have 90 days to repay, you save the immediate payment, the payment for the next purchase that would have been made 30 days after that initial purchase, the payment for the purchase that would have been made 60 days later, and the purchase that would have been made 90 days later.

If total supply purchases average $25,000 per month, then that means you will free up $100,000 of cash over the next 90 days as a result of negotiating this deal. If supply purchases are $100,000 per month, you free up $400,000. This is money that can be used to pay the seller cash without negatively impacting the cash flow of the business you are acquiring at all. It's a one-time, free-money strategy that gives you cash to buy the business.

Accounts Receivable Factoring

Accounts receivable is the short-term trade credit that businesses extend to their customers, who have to pay them back, typically within 30 to 90 days. Consider this: there are businesses (called *factors*) that will either lend you the money you're waiting to collect or buy the accounts receivable outright at a little bit of a discount. Typically, you can expect to receive 75% to 85% of the total accounts receivable in good standing that a business has on its books when you factor in accounts receivable. Essentially, you're just speeding up the process of getting the money your customers owe you. This would be done post-closing, and it would not show up in your LOI.

Let's say the company you're acquiring has $200,000 in the accounts receivable pipeline. You can usually get 80% of that from a factor business. In this case, that amounts to $160,000. Add that to the deal stack of the two methods described above, and you now have a deal stack equal to $560,000 and a gap of only $440,000. You're now just $440,000 away from having all the funding you need to make a deal.

Revenue-based Financing

A number of lenders will look at the cash flow of the business and say, "Hey, your business makes a profit of $100,000 a month. We're willing to lend you 80% of what you take in for six months—or $480,000 (i.e., $80,000 x 6)." This is called RBF or revenue-based financing.

Why would they do this? Because they know that the business has a productive history, and capital sitting idly erodes, so there is a motivation to deploy it (e.g., by loaning it to earn interest). One reason we emphasized checking the businesses founding date in the last chapter is that businesses with a track record of stable and predictable consistent income can very often get this kind of financing. Lighter Capital is a good source here, but you can research *revenue-based financing* or *revenue-based lenders* on Google to find many others.

How do you secure this money? Simply go to the lender and say, "Take a look at our cash flow. We'd like to get a revenue-based financing loan on it." Then you pay off the loan from part of your future revenue.

Let's say that you could get $140,000 from revenue-based financing. Now your stack is growing (currently with this strategy added the deal stack stands at $700,000 and the gap is only $300,000). You're only $300,000 away from acquiring this auto parts company with no money out of pocket. By the way, revenue-based financing is done post-close, and it's not included in the LOI.

Owner Carry

This involves asking the seller to give us a loan for part of the purchase price. We typically ask for an 80% seller carry to start, but we're willing to negotiate down from that. We're often able to get the 80% on a five- to ten-year loan at very low or no interest. In our $1 million auto parts case, 80% of the $1 million purchase price would be $800,000 in seller financing, but you don't need that much because of the earlier creative financing strategies that you used in your deal stack.

For the deal in this example, you'll only ask for 10% owner carry, also called *seller financing*, which is $1 million x 10% or $100,000. Now your deal stack stands at $800,000 and the gap is only $200,000. You're only $200,000 away from your goal. You negotiate an owner carry pre-close and you include it in your LOI.

Integrator Equity

"Integrator" refers to the people who are working in the business. In Chapter 1, we emphasized that we want to work *above* the business, not *in* it. One way we do that is to have the owner (or a member of the leadership team) stay to take care of day-to-day operations. We can make this proposition more attractive by giving that person an opportunity to acquire part of the business with us.

Very often the employee will jump at this offer, saying "Oh my gosh, I never even knew that was possible!" And they may have many ways to come up with the cash: home equity, stocks, investments, savings, or loans from friends and family.

You'd be amazed at how many times the people who were working in the business are elated to be offered an ownership interest. What's especially attractive about this approach is that the employee now has skin in the game, which means he or she is more likely to stay and perform well.

It's a win-win situation.

In our hypothetical auto parts case, you could offer the employee a 10% interest in the company. That gets you another $100,000, which puts your deal stack at $900,000, and the gap at $100,000. You're now just $100,000 away from your goal. Integrator equity is typically done pre-close, but it does *not* go in the LOI. The seller can know about it but doesn't have to.

Also, don't be afraid to give up a bit of equity if doing so allows you to work above the business. For the record, we don't own 100% of any of our businesses. We have partners that are doing the things that we don't like to do or that aren't part of our superpowers. On the other hand, we don't like to give up too much equity. As a rule of thumb, if you're in the 5% to 20% range for team members, that's a good place to be.

Inventory Consignment

In this case, you can say, "Okay, Mr. or Mrs. Seller, you've got about $50,000 in inventory in the business. I'd like to pay you for that as it sells." Remember, inventory typically sells at a significant markup. So, let's say you have inventory in this business that you could go out to the market and sell for $50,000. And you're in a "keystone" model where you mark it up 100%. So, $50,000 of inventory would have cost you half of that to actually own.

That means making a profit of $25,000. So, you're going to say, "Mr. and Mrs. Seller, I want you to consign that $25,000 worth of inventory, and as it sells, I'll pay you back." What's cool about that is that it requires the seller to show you that he or she has confidence that you can succeed with the business after the closing when the seller may no longer be there to run the business. Inventory consignment is done pre-close, and it goes in the LOI. So now the deal stack stands at $925,000 and the gap is only $75,000. You're now just $75,000 short of your $1 million goal. Exciting, isn't it? We're sure you feel that way! We certainly do!

Private Placement Memorandum (PPM)

Another option you have is to raise money. You could go to third-party investors and say, "Hey, would you be interested in investing in this company?" Now, you'd have to give up equity for that, but it's a great way to raise money. It's very common, but it's a bit expensive, and there are also securities laws to think about at the state and federal levels in the United States, and in many other countries as well. You have to pay an attorney to prepare the documents and then you have to figure out how to find investors.

So you're not going to use that in your hypothetical stack to reach $1 million. But be aware that it's very easy to do so. It's also probably the most common thing that happens when private equity, family offices, or those types of companies are looking for money to buy a business. Consider the fact that people think, "I need money, so I need investors." The truth is that you very often can create a deal stack and completely fund the gap *without ever having to speak to even a single investor.*

This is something you'd usually do pre-close if you needed the funding for the deal, but it is also often done post-close to raise money for growth or to pay off debt that you incurred to complete the acquisition. Typically, it is not in the LOI. Why? Because it isn't something you need to talk about with the seller. It's something you do on your own. However, sometimes financing may be a contingency of closing the deal and if you want to make closing contingent on obtaining financing from investors (or even from a bank for that matter), you would want to build that financing contingency into the LOI.

Earnout

In this case, you're going to say "Hey, listen, Mr. and Mrs. Seller, I'm willing to give you the $1 million for the business, but I want to be sure that it's going to continue to perform at the current level. So I want to hold back $75,000 in the form of an earnout. As long as the business continues to perform consistently over the next two years and either earns the same profit that it has, or that you say it will, or generates the same level of sales that it has, or that you say it will, I'll pay you that earnout amount." This is done pre-close because you need the seller to agree to it, and it goes in the LOI.

So, in your hypothetical deal here, $75,000 brings you to your $1 million goal with a deal stack of $1 million and a $0 gap, all without having to use any money out of pocket. You've asked only for $75,000 because that's all you needed. But it's not uncommon to obtain an earnout equal to 10% to 40% of the asking price with a one- to four-year term, which in this case, would have been as much as $400,000 ($1 million x 40%). The earnout can be a key part of your deal stack. It is a wonderful tool to use to close the gap between what the seller is asking and what you feel comfortable paying as well. In those cases, you offer to pay the amount you are comfortable paying. Then if the business hits the earnings and sales levels that the seller believes it will, but of which you have some doubt, then the seller gets a "bonus," and you reduce your risk.

Deferred Down Payment

You might be wondering, "Well, but wait, what do we do about these strategies that require ownership to do the financing?" That's a chicken

193

and egg thing: You need to own the business to do them, but you can't own the business until you do them.

Don't worry. Roland came up with a magical tactic a few years ago in the context of a deal and then gradually applied it to businesses. It's called the deferred down payment (DDP). Here's how it works: You tell the seller, "Listen, I need to do some financing to pay you. And I need the business title to complete some of that. So, I'm asking you to take part of the money shortly *after closing.*"

In essence, this is a short-term loan—much shorter than the five to ten years you'd seek for the owner carry/seller financing that we discussed above. This is going to be 30 to 90 days—and never more than 180 days. But it allows you to close the deal and then employ the post-closing tactics we just mentioned. In our hypothetical case, you need the title to complete three strategies.

1. The supplier loan for $100,000.
2. Accounts receivable factoring for $160,000.
3. Revenue-based financing for $140,000.

That amounts to 40% of the deal (i.e., $400,000). So you're asking for that amount in DDP. We'd give ourselves 90 days to complete this funding. You could probably get it all done in 30 days, but this way you build in some extra time in case you run into any issues. You negotiate that DDP pre-close and it goes in the LOI.

Collaboration is Crucial

The ideal negotiating strategy involves collaboration between the buyer and seller. If the seller says, "I want $1 million for the business," you say, "Great, let's get together and talk about that and work together to collaborate to get you the price that you want." So before submitting the LOI, you'll have gone over most of the important points. You'll know if the seller is open to an earnout, a DDP, a carve out, and the other strategies we discussed above. Don't spring these ideas in the LOI unless you know the owner will agree to them. Instead, make your best case for each of your strategies in conversational negotiations. Then the LOI just confirms what you've already agreed on. Don't waste your time asking for options the seller has already nixed.

Whenever possible, we deliver the LOI in person so we can walk the seller through it. Or we arrange a phone conversation in which we say, "Before we send you the LOI, let's get on a call so we can go over it with you." That way you reduce the possibility of unpleasant surprises or conflicts. The owner knows what's coming and is on board with it. You aren't throwing him or her a curveball.

The big advantage here is that you get live feedback as you're talking. Normally, we'd have a conversation, and the owner would think about our proposal for 24 hours and say, "Yes," "No," or "Here's our counteroffer." Then we would wait 24 hours before we came back again, so the process is relatively quick. Sometimes it's two or three days. It depends on the cadence of the negotiation and the deal. We tend to match the seller's pace on these things, so we don't seem overeager. In other words, if they take two or three days to respond, we're going to take two or three days, even if we could get back to them in five minutes. We want a motivated seller, but we never want to appear to be an excessively motivated buyer.

Also, physical positioning matters a lot when you are collaborating. Show the seller that you are literally on their side by sitting next to them, not across a table or desk when negotiating. Let them feel that you are really trying to get them the price that they want and take advantage of the law of price and terms.

The law of price and terms dictates that if the seller gets the price they want then they have to agree to your purchase terms, which for us includes several of the deal stack strategies discussed above. If the seller wants all cash, then they will not get their price, they will have to reduce to the price you agree to. You don't get to have your cake and eat it, too. Either you get your price that you want and agree to the purchaser's terms, or you reduce your price to get the all-cash ideal terms that you as a seller would like to receive.

Using the law of price and terms when negotiating provides a huge collaboration tool. Of course, you typically have movement on both sides of price and terms, but stating the law at the outset can really help move things along as you negotiate.

Your First Deal: How Big?

We're often asked if we can recommend a dollar threshold for a first deal. Unfortunately, we can't give a blanket recommendation. A lot depends on your level of experience, your comfort level, and your goals. One of the people who took Roland's advanced course started with a $90 million deal and another secured a $100 million private equity funding. So, big deals are possible right out of the gate. But each of these people are what we would call sophisticated businesspersons or experienced entrepreneurs, people with big dreams, a thirst for knowledge, and a passionate dedication to achieving the high goals that they set for themselves. If that sounds like you, by all means, go big, but for most people a small deal to get their feet wet followed by a few medium-sized deals is the best path to take.

But if you really pushed us and insisted that we pick a number for a typical reader of this book, we'd say start with a deal under $5 million. If you're looking to do something super simple, we'd recommend buying a Facebook group or a podcast, a social account, or some other bit of media. Those are easy deals to find and close quickly.

Deals like that will help you gain confidence and refine your skills, and you'll go on from there to more complex and larger deals. If you decide that you'd like to have somebody work with you on a regular basis and give you guidance along your journey to doing no money out of pocket deals (or any kinds of deals for that matter), we have two programs that can provide you with essential mentorship and coaching so that you can quickly move up the ladder to bigger and bigger deals.

To get your wheels turning a bit, consider the following three case studies based on deals we've engineered.

Case Study #1: Acquiring a Facebook Group

This acquisition involved somebody asking $125,000 for a 53,000-member real estate agents group on Facebook. At the time, it was the second largest such group—although we've grown it a lot since then.

We were able to negotiate the price down to $75,000. This was a group that had not made any money. It was a passion project of the person who started it. But, because we owned a real estate brokerage, we knew that even getting just a couple of agents from that group to join our brokerage firm was going to generate a huge win and a good continuing stream of cash flow for us. That's how the real estate brokerage business works. The more agents you have out there selling homes for you, the more money you can make.

We used revenue-based financing to make the deal. In negotiating, we said, "Hey, listen, you're not making anything right now, but we have a great plan to generate cash from the group, so we're going to pay you $70,000 of the purchase price from the first money we make." The owner said yes, and we had a deal.

$125k FB GROUP FOR $0 OOP

$125k Ask 53k Member FB Group

$75k Purchase Price Agreed

$70k RBF First Funds In From Cash Flow

$50k 1-Year Sponsorship MB

$20k 1-Year Sponsorship Training

$5k Split Energy + CC Cash Advance

We then went out and sold a sponsorship. This, by the way, is an 11th strategy for your deal stack. You can sell sponsorships as opposed to having an investor come in. The advantage is that sponsors pay every single year to continue their sponsorship, while an investor invests one single time and then is a co-owner of your business forever.

We knew that we could get sponsors for this group. The owner of the group had not explored any monetization opportunities, so this group represented a blue ocean for whoever got in there to share opportunities with the agent members.

So, we approached a mortgage broker and said, "Would you like to have access to 53,000 real estate agents to provide content and hopefully get mortgage business?" And the broker said, "Absolutely! We'll do that $50,000 in a heartbeat." So, within a week, we had a sponsorship deal that brought in 67% of the purchase price. Not only did we not come out of pocket to get it, we also did not give up any equity and we created an annual cash generating recurring stream of revenue.

We then did a $20,000 sponsorship deal with a training company for real estate agents. That covered $70,000 of the $75,000.

For the remaining 5%, we did a split-equity deal. That's strategy number 12 for you. The person who brought us the deal just wanted to say they were in business with us. So we had them invest $2,500. Then we employed strategy number 13: a cash advance on a credit card for the final $2,500.

Now, we did not need to do the credit card financing to close the deal, but it is an excellent example of how when you make a game out of it, almost anything can be fun. In this case, we made a game out of not having to come out of pocket one cent, and using the strategies shared above, we were able to do just that. Sometimes the very best ideas are born of necessity. Gamifying the process as we did on this deal can very often generate powerful new ideas on how to do business.

All in all, our financing strategies generated $75,000 and allowed us to acquire the group for no money out of pocket.

Case Study #2: Acquiring a SaaS (Software as a Service) Company

Our business partners had been wanting to add a software as a service to one of our businesses, but there was a big problem. None of us had ever built a software development team before.

We knew that there were a lot of great software dev teams out there already working for other businesses, so we decided to try the "acquihire" strategy of acquiring a business with a functional team in place. In an acquihire situation, you acquire a company or a division of a company primarily for the purpose of acquiring the *team* that is working there. That way, we could quickly deploy a skilled dev team for one of our businesses rather than painstakingly assembling a team ourselves.

This SaaS company had an asking price of $300,000. We were already using the software at one of our companies, DigitalMarketer, and everyone loved it. One of our employees told us, "Hey, these guys are interested in selling. Are you interested in acquiring the company?" We set up a call with the owner and were able to reduce the purchase price to $100,000 after going back and forth a couple of times and after engaging in the collaborative process we just shared with you previously.

$300k SaaS FOR $0 OOP

$300k 3-Year-Old Software As A Service (SaaS)
[Vender to One of Our Companies]
$100k Purchase Price

$90k - $10k Month Owner Carry for 9-Months

$10k DDP Funded In 1-Week From 1st Email

We financed $90,000 of the total $100,000 purchase price as an owner carry—$10,000 a month for nine months. We designated the remaining $10,000 as a deferred down payment, which we funded in seven days with an email saying, "Hey, we just acquired this company, and we're going to give you guys a great package of services." So the DDP worked really well and we were able to pay this off almost immediately.

When the dust settled, we had a new asset: an experienced cohesive software development team. That team went on to develop several projects before we ultimately exited the company to another business a few years later.

Case Study #3: Acquiring a Publisher

In this case, we wanted to buy a $3 million publishing house with an asking price of $3.9 million. The EBITDA of the business was about $1.3 million, so they were asking for a purchase price equal to about 3x annual profit. We ultimately negotiated a $2 million acquisition price with an owner carry of 80% (i.e., $1.6 million)—and no interest over three years, with the full payment not required until the end of the term. That's about a 1.5x EBITDA valuation on this deal, which seemed like a very fair price.

We had a deal now, but we still had to come up with $400,000 to cover the difference between the $2 million purchase price and the $1.6 million of seller financing. We decided to accomplish this through a DDP. (Remember that a DDP is a deferred down payment. The DDP allows you to time-shift title from the seller to yourself without having to come up with cash out of pocket to bridge the time between making a deal and closing the transaction.) Roland approached a neighbor who had expressed interest in getting in on one of his deals. Roland told him about what we were considering, and he agreed to loan Roland's company (remember, always use an SPV!) the money at 10% interest on a three-year balloon. And that's how that deal was made.

A balloon payment is a single payment that must be paid at the end of a loan instead of in amortized monthly payments over the full term of the loan. Balloon payments can be very helpful in financing the acquisition of businesses because they give the buyer great flexibility and keep cash flow freed up to use for growth.

When we are negotiating a payment over time, we almost always start out asking for a multi-year balloon payment at no interest. We don't always get the seller to agree to that, but it is where we start...and very often they say yes!

$3M PUBLISHER $3.9M ASKING

$3M Publishing House ($1.3M EBITDA)

$2M Acquisition Price (1.5x EBITDA)

$1.6M 80% Owner Carry - 3-Year Balloon **@ 0%**

$400k 20% DDP (30-Days)

$400k 3PL **3-Year 10% Interest Only No Warrants**

$800k Integrator Equity Sale **20% (3x Valuation)**

Own 80% for $0 OOP + $360k Cash

We had to arrange that initial $400,000 loan quickly because we only had 30 days to get that money based on the deal that we cut with the seller. Now that we had that in place from Roland's neighbor, we had time to find less expensive and longer term financing for that $400,000 part of the deal.

So, we now approached two people whom Roland had known for years, both of whom told him that they really wanted him to find a deal that they could do together. One of these people was Roland's private banker at his local bank, and the second was an accountant who had been asking for some time to get in on one of these deals. Roland told them, "I've got a deal right now. If you would like to invest, I can let you in at a 3x valuation."

Notice the difference: we're selling this interest at 3x, and we paid 1.5x, so we're doubling our money. But we have no qualms about that. Why? Because we're the one who put the deal together. We're the one on the hook to make it work. We're giving the potential investors an opportunity that they can take or leave: they can each buy 10% of the company, and they each pay $400,000, which is a fair price for a company like this. Just because you can put the deal together for less does not mean that you have to feel bad about selling it at a higher price to investors who come along later.

In fact, this is done all the time, both with respect to the sale of businesses and with the sale of real estate. Very often, an investor will find a real estate property and purchase it from a motivated seller at a very low price and then turn around and sell it through a real estate agent at a significant profit, even without doing any rehab work on the property.

In this case, we sold 10% of the company to Roland's private banker and 10% of the company to his accountant for a total of $800,000 (20% of a $4 million company valued at 3x annual profits of $1.3 million). We had paid only $400,000 for that 20% though because we bought the entire company for $2 million. 20% of that $2 million payment price equals $400,000. That means we made a $400,000 profit on something that cost $400,000, thereby doubling our money.

Very seldom does anyone ever ask, "Well, what did you pay for it?" They either like the terms or they don't. Quite frankly, the market value is the market value, regardless of what you acquired it for. If the market value was less than what you paid for it, do you think anyone would pay you more than market value just because you paid more? It just doesn't work that way. Things sell based on market value, not based on what you paid for them. In this case, Roland's banker and accountant both liked the deal and agreed to the terms.

Using this $800,000 in cash from his banker and accountant, we were able to pay back Roland's neighbor the $400,000 loan, plus a full year of interest ($400,000 x 10% interest = $40,000). Better still, Roland did not have to pay him the full year because Roland only had his money for a very short period of time before paying it back. He wanted to create a lot of goodwill and have him tell everyone at their country club how great it was to do a deal with him! So, Roland paid him a full year's interest and his neighbor was ecstatic.

Roland lives on a golf course in a country club community, and so now the neighbor is going to tell everybody in the club, "Roland's a great deal maker! He gave me my money back in a month with 12 months' interest!" How many of those people, including him, do you think are going to want to come back and do business with Roland in the future? We are playing a long game here. The more goodwill and the happier the investors we have, the more they will tell other people and our ability to fund deals just keeps on getting better and better.

If you're doing the math, even after selling 20% of the company to his banker and accountant, we still own 80% of the company. We've spent zero money out of our pocket, and we made $360,000 cash in our pocket in the process (i.e., the $800,000 from the two buyers minus the $440,000 to the neighbor).

Can you start to see why we love this business? We are absolutely certain that you're going to love it too!

Would You Like Even More Advanced Training and Support?

Obviously, over the course of five short chapters, we can't convey everything we know about deal-making that we have learned over our collective decades of doing this or the thousands of deals we've done. We've given you a solid foundation though, and the basic skills to get started, and that may be all that you need to move forward on your EPIC deal-doing journey.

However, if you are someone who wants to fully commit to an investment career, to living the **ACQUIREpreneur** lifestyle of unlimited wealth creation or to seriously pursue the world of entrepreneurial investing, then you may want to consider participating in Roland's EPIC Board mastermind and network, or enrolling in one of Roland's more advanced workshops on **ACQUIREpreneurial** investing.

The *EPIC Accelerator* program (EpicNetwork.com) provides hundreds of videos, including a core training on the EPIC acquisitions principles that every **ACQUIREpreneur** should know, as well as over two hundred videos providing training on every topic you can imagine in the acquisitions space. Roland has interviewed dozens of business owners that he completed EPIC acquisition or consulting for equity deals with so that you can see from both Roland's and the selling entrepreneurs' perspectives how those deals came together, how they were negotiated, why the sellers decided to move forward with the deals, how the deals turned out, and what additional deals Roland and the selling entrepreneurs went on to do together AFTER the deals were closed.

Roland's advanced training will help you absorb the knowledge that he has distilled down to the essentials—information that will set you apart from other investors. He will guide you past the common mistakes using insights that he learned the hard way through trial and error, and he also has the time and video format to deeply detail the over 220 different funding strategies he uses to help him close his acquisitions with little or no money out of his own pocket.

Roland's program also provides live mentorship group calls with experienced deal experts who have completed and mastered the training. These are people from Roland's team who, along with Roland himself, will coach you through the deals you're making. So, you'll never be stuck thinking, "What do I do next?"

Keep in mind that you have everything you need to start doing EPIC deals on your own from the material in this book, so this training is not necessary for you to take what you are learning in this book to start doing deals. The training is simply a supplement and deep dive for those who would like the help and coaching in a live feedback format, where you can get extra help, mentorship, coaching, and guidance as you move forward to do deals.

You can find out more information about the different levels of EPIC training, from the free materials that supplement this book, all the way up to the year-long EPIC Board which is a deals mastermind of like-minded **ACQUIREpreneurs** working together, sharing deals, and supporting one another in their **ACQUIREpreneurs** journey, all available at EpicNetwork.com.

One of the greatest resources we make available to you at BusinessWealthWithoutRisk.com/access is access to Roland's FREE 5-day business acquisitions challenge called the EPIC Challenge. That challenge provides an immersive experience in the material covered so far in this book and is an excellent resource for gaining a deeper understanding of all the things you've learned so far. You can join our next 5 day challenge at GetEpicChallenge.com.

To date we have identified almost two hundred different deal sources—along with business-buying checklists, agreements, letters of intent, scripts for conversations, models, and checklists to provide you with the tools you need at the precise moment you need them. We also have a total of over 220 creative funding and finance strategies, which we're constantly updating. As you move forward in your own EPIC journey, we are confident that you will uncover even more sourcing, funding, and acquisition strategies and we welcome your feedback and sharing with us, as we are all always learning new ways to do deals.

When you complete your acquisitions and are ready to exit, you will find everything you need in part three of this book where we talk about getting exit ready.

As you pursue your EPIC journey, remember that one of the best ways to stay the course, continue to be motivated, and do more deals is to partner with others who can help you along the way, or those who have different skill sets, or enjoy doing different aspects of acquisitions that you may not be as strongly skilled in or that you just might not really enjoy doing as much as other aspects.

To help you and us with this, we have built an EPIC community of over two thousand investors, where we collaborate with people whose superpowers complement our own. A community like this allows you to instantly go from having no network to having a huge network of people you can work with. That is one of the greatest benefits of getting involved in our EPIC community. You can find details of how to become a part of that community at EpicNetwork.com.

One other resource that Roland created to help people do more deals, more quickly, on the best terms possible, is his DealDone.io software. This software will do all of the calculations for you, suggest different possibilities for funding, calculate the results of different options, and help you structure the best and most favorable deal possible when you are negotiating with potential sellers.

This ability to do these EPIC deals and acquire as many companies as you like with little or no money out of pocket is absolutely magical when you understand it—a skill you can take with you to any country, any place in the world. You don't ever have to go into an office again.

You can do deals. You'll know that your financial future is solid because you've mastered this skill. And we'll walk you through everything.

We hope that you'll decide to join us on the journey and make your investment career a reality rather than a mere pipe dream. Think about what an extra supplemental income would mean to you. How would a significant increase in your personal net worth from buying a single company at an under-market acquisition price change your quality of life? Those dreams are within reach if you take action based on what you've learned so far in this book.

For more case studies, examples, worksheets, checklists, forms, scripts, and other resources, including quite a few that we simply could not fit in the book itself, we created a resources collection, and all of these resources are available and waiting for you at BusinessWealthWithoutRisk.com/access. Visit the site now and enjoy a huge collection of resources at absolutely no money out of pocket for you!

In part two of this book, we will shift the focus to deals orchestrated by Jay, along with some updates and additional tools from Roland, as we build on the ideas we've discussed above by talking about how—once you own a business for no money out of pocket—you can exponentially increase its profit.

BusinessWealthWithoutRisk.com/access

Wealth Wisdom Wrap-Up

Over this chapter, we've built your "deal stack," demystifying the process of combining numerous strategies to raise funds for acquiring a business with little to no money out of your pocket. We've bridged the gap between the acquisition price and your starting point using creative financing strategies.

But the journey doesn't stop at acquisition. Remember, buying the business is just the beginning. The real fun begins when you start growing it! The next section will unveil a thorough and actionable distillation of our life's work.

In Part Two of our journey, you'll learn about "The Profit Explosion Formula."

Here, we'll help you grow exponentially in the business you've created, built, or bought. We'll start with our next chapter, "Moonshot: Achieving Maximum Growth." Whether you're a new business owner or an established entrepreneur, get ready to learn proprietary strategies and tactics that can lead to truly astonishing growth.

We'll go beyond the ordinary and introduce you to concepts that require virtually no major upfront investment or risk but can produce outsized revenue and profit. Get ready to learn from our cumulative century of experience empowering companies to transform and maximize growth.

This part of your journey, dear reader, is about building on your success and moving toward the entrepreneurial stratosphere. Let's jump in.

PART TWO

The Profit Explosion Formula:

**Creating Exponential Growth in
The Business You Create, Build, or Buy**

CHAPTER 6

MOONSHOT: ACHIEVING MAXIMUM GROWTH

Achieving Maximum Growth

Okay, so you've acquired a business, or maybe you skipped the first part of this book because you already own a business and would like to find out how to grow it... **quickly, powerfully, exponentially.** That's what this second section of the book is all about. We're now going to share with you the mindset and a wide array of our proprietary strategies and tactics to create truly astonishing growth. You'll learn how to earn profits that we call *"beyond exponential."* Why settle for linear growth? Why not grow the business intelligently, rapidly, and powerfully? Best of all, the concepts we'll share require virtually no major upfront investment or risk to produce outsized revenue and profit explosion. That's what you'll discover right now. So, let's jump in.

Between the two of us, we have spent nearly a century, collectively, doing disparate things in different industries; a pattern of undertaking a new pursuit, succeeding in it, and moving on to the next challenge, continuously expanding into new entrepreneurial frontiers, continuously growing not only our own businesses, but those of others, and attaining worldwide achievements few others have accomplished. And we've examined hundreds of strategies, business models, and value propositions across a staggering number of fields, serving well over ten thousand clients in more than one thousand industries, and over 7,200 sub-industries worldwide, empowering struggling companies to turn things around and maximize growth, and competent businesses to become industry standouts.

The following chapters are a thoroughly actionable distillation of our life's work. We've organized these concepts in order of universal importance, meaning that you should focus on the earlier topics to a greater extent and then move forward to the remaining suggestions. Our intent is not to write exhaustively about every topic, but to awaken you to a taste of the rich ideas that we've shared with thousands of private entrepreneurs we've served or guided, so that you can apply what suits your own needs and business goals. We've got more than 90 core strategies that we've taught, but it's simply impossible to teach 90 strategies in depth in one book, even in a book of this length. Just get going and see how these ideas can transform your business and your bottom line. You'll find the list—there are 97 core strategies listed—in the back of the book in the Appendix. We've estimated that these strategies have created more than $30 billion (with a B!) in profit growth for our clients and students. Now it's your turn to implement them.

You will find in this section a powerful mélange of both theory and practice: actionable insights backed by rigorous thought and application. That is a formula we've been perfecting for decades, and it works. By the way, we have identified over 90 separate categories for exploding profit performance in a business no matter the size, type, scope. Few, if any, require additional investment or risk. Each category offers from 5 to 25 different impact levers you can profitably pull.

The pace of information in this book will be fast, turbo-charged, and exhilarating. Prepare to explode the performance of every business you ever own or acquire by orders of magnitude. Open-mindedness is not precisely what we're seeking here. Rather, it's about developing a possibility mindset that lets you tell yourself that working smarter, not working harder, is the master key to riches.

If there is one common thread uniting the diverse topics we will cover, it is this: we will challenge you to go deep and deconstruct your idea of what is possible for your newly acquired business. Only then can you achieve exponential growth that will revolutionize your business and change your life. We will encourage you to question the status quo, tear down routine and convention, and journey through *terra incognita*.

Your competitors fear the unknown, so your competitive advantage will lie in demystifying the unknown, invisible, and unexplored to discover the opportunities that others are missing. But you must possess a prejudice towards action, be a monster of execution, refuse to be wedded to tradition.

You are about to learn how to out-think, out-market, out-sell, out-perform, and greatly out-earn anyone else you compete against. We'll show you how.

For more case studies, examples, worksheets, checklists, forms, scripts, and other resources, including quite a few that we simply could not fit in the book itself, we created a resources collection, and all of these resources are available and waiting for you at BusinessWealthWithoutRisk.com/access. Visit the site now and enjoy a huge collection of resources at absolutely no money out of pocket for you!

The Mind-Stein Effect

Our techniques work best when they're accompanied by a *mindset shift* through which you look at your individual capabilities, your company, your industry, and the world at large in a completely new light. Only then can you unveil the bounty of untapped opportunities waiting for you.

We want you to emulate the mind of Einstein—the "Mind-Stein Effect" as we like to call it. Now, we know we are not the first to tout Einstein as the paragon of achievement. But most other folks who speak glowingly of Einstein miss the point entirely. It wasn't simply Einstein's *intellect* that was the linchpin of his unnatural success. Yes, he was a preternatural genius, perhaps the greatest one of the twenty-first century. But what really dazzles us about Einstein—and what you should seek to imitate—was his whole worldview, his mindset. And why is this essential? Because to our way of thinking, *range is power.*

That mindset was the fuel that, powered by his unparalleled intellect, allowed him to burn so bright and so hot. Keep that in mind as you read. You will get the most out of this book not merely by memorizing our techniques but by understanding them at a deeper level and integrating their ideas with your own. As Einstein himself said, "Education is not the learning of facts, it's the training of the mind to think."

So what exactly is the Mind-Stein Effect?

First, Einstein was *unimaginably inquisitive*. He possessed an insatiable thirst for knowledge of every kind. We share that trait with him, and, for a large part, our inquisitiveness accounts for our own outsized success, at the risk of sounding braggadocious for a moment. He was tenaciously focused on solving problems and was driven by a keen, pragmatic, logical intelligence, and sharp intuition. He sought to understand what drove outcomes, impact, and results. We love finding correlations where others see only disparate events. We also love applying approaches from one industry or vertical, where they are commonplace, to other industries or verticals, where they are completely unknown and therefore shockingly powerful. We love untangling seemingly Gordian knots because they frequently hold the answers to enormous business jackpots. The broader your understanding of this approach to business, the greater your ability to create outstanding and even delightful profit results.

Einstein was also passionate about trying new things and testing new ideas, and he understood failure is part of the road to success. You can control failure in ways that make it almost irrelevant as we will show you in specific case studies throughout this book. And, importantly, he had an unfailingly optimistic attitude which imbued him with the confidence that no problem, no matter how big or vexing or intractable, was too big to overcome.

The progenitor of the theory of relativity was also famous for his sense of humor and his humanity. This is not ancillary to his cognitive power but part and parcel of it, for Einstein understood that problem solving, whether you're decrypting the great astrophysical puzzles of the universe or trying to figure out why your marketing isn't generating growth, especially where explosive growth can be found, should be a joyous act.

We, Roland and Jay, both love trying to smash open performance and we enjoy the process as much as the rewards. We always have enormous fun as we grapple with these questions and create business success for ourselves and our clients. It's not just about the money you'll make. It's about the pleasure and enjoyment you'll experience along the way, instead of having what our friend Tony Robbins calls a J.O.B. (which stands for Just Over Broke!).

When you combine a spirit of playful creativity with an embrace of humanity at large, good and surprising things happen. When we travel to Asia, which we do frequently, we relish the pleasure of sitting in the lobby and smiling at people who are shy or put off by our directness. They start very stiff and do not smile back—until they do.

Then they beam and share an ephemeral but powerful moment of human connection. Try doing this on an elevator, too, beaming at strangers until they let their guard down and you have both shared a laugh. The effect is profound because you can see their body language instantly change, and they just open up and their mood shifts.

The lesson there is that if you "get comfortable with being uncomfortable," try new approaches, shed your fear of failure, and make connections and perform actions no one else is, you will, like Einstein, thrive. You've heard of shape-shifting, right? Well, that's exactly what we are talking about!

This book will teach you how to buck convention and defy norms and, in doing so, break through to a new way of engaging with the world and connecting the dots in ways few others do. That is what will give you enormous wealth creating business advantage. As our friend Tony says, if you do what everyone else does in your field, but you do it just a little bit better, after a while, you'll have a massive advantage over everyone else.

To that end, we presume you've got your version of your "business bucket list bonanza," in your head or written on a piece of paper next to your desk. Probably it shares a few goals, aspirations, and outcomes with the bucket lists of like-minded entrepreneurs. *I want to develop substantial passive income. I want to travel the world first-class, staying in the most extraordinary lodgings, and dining in the best restaurants. I want to fund a lavish lifestyle. I want to undertake work that is fulfilling and allows me to thrive and bring all my talents and vision to bear. I want to distinguish myself as an expert or a thought leader. I want to be a benefactor or philanthropist.*

All worthwhile goals, to be sure...but now toss them out! We challenge you to replace that list with one much more audacious, bolder, and more daring. One might say to "dream the impossible," but we wouldn't phrase it that way, because in the next pages, you'll see that what we are offering is firmly in the realm of possibility. Nothing is "impossible." Impossible just means you haven't yet figured out how to achieve it. One of our good friends, Dr. Alan Barnard, the world's leading expert on the Theory of Constraints, first enunciated by his mentor, Eli Goldratt, teaches that everything is impossible...until you add the word "Unless." So all of this may sound impossible, unless you know how. And in these pages, you will discover exactly how to make this seemingly impossible goal come true in your own business and in your own life.

For more case studies, examples, worksheets, checklists, forms, scripts, and other resources, including quite a few that we simply could not fit in the book itself, we created a resources collection and all of these resources are available and waiting for you at BusinessWealthWithoutRisk.com/access. Visit the site now and enjoy a huge collection of resources at absolutely no money out of pocket for you!

Rocket-Fueled Recap

In this chapter, we unveiled our proprietary strategies for astronomical growth and setting your sight beyond mere linear progress. We shared wisdom garnered from our vast and varied experiences, honing in on strategies that allow for intelligent, rapid, and powerful growth without excessive risk. This is the essence of our shared century of wisdom and experience in entrepreneurship, dedicated to helping you take your enterprise to the next level.

As we continue our journey, the next chapter, "Mental Models for Thinking Better," will add another crucial tool to your arsenal. It's not merely a method; it's an entirely different way of thinking, which reveals correlations and relationships that others often miss. This skill gives you a tremendous advantage, enabling you to identify hidden assets, overlooked opportunities, and underperforming revenue activities—the raw material for exponential growth.

We'll explore why many businesses overlook these opportunities and help you break free from the industry norms and conventions. We'll dive into the science of variability, revealing how simple tweaks can yield powerful outcomes.

Our ultimate goal is to transform you into a "Human Hedge Fund," capable of continuous and stunning growth in every business you acquire. Get ready to shift your perspective and start thinking better!

MENTAL MODELS FOR THINKING BETTER

While neither of the authors of this book may be Einstein, we do both possess one talent that has accounted for our success, and we've multiplied this success many times over by teaching others the same thing. It's not a method per se, *it's a totally different way of thinking.* That talent is the ability to see correlations, implications, quantifications, anomalies, relationships that few others perceive, including you and, in all likelihood, your competitors.

Learning how to spot unseen opportunities gives you a monumental advantage, leading you to finding hidden assets, overlooked opportunities, underperforming revenue activities, under-monetizing resources, and underdeveloped relationships. The raw material of exponential growth.

CHAPTER 7 - MENTAL MODELS FOR THINKING BETTER

At the outset of our careers, each of us had an epiphany. People in a given industry tend to all do things the same way. This is true of any area of business. There is a certain myopia that sets in. Even clever CEOs tend to cleave their thinking around the norms or conventions of their field. "Business as usual" becomes just that, *usual*.

Consequently, they overlook opportunities to *optimize*, to market, sell, strategize, attract, convert, remonetize, position, etc. Not because they're not trying but because their frame of reference is narrow: it's everything they've done or witnessed, and it's confined by the "bucket" of their industry. Monkey see monkey do. The herd follows the herd.

Both of us have been extensively trained in the science of variability. Do something one way and it produces X. Yet do it another way and it produces 2x; do it yet another way and it produces 3x; and so on. By the way, none of these other ways require any additional time, resources, money, or risk. We obsessed on what those ultimate performance factors were and how anyone could harness them. That reflection birthed methodologies like RSO (Reverse System Optimization), and PEQ (the Perfect Enhancement Quotient) to capitalize on those variable possibilities. We came to realize that if you tweak just one or two little things of strategic value, it gives you an edge. And that little edge multiplies many times over to become a big edge, as everything we do in business has the capacity to grow exponentially. Exponential growth is, of course, one of the pillars of our teaching, and the value proposition we offer to you in this section of this book. We believe you can have continuous and stunning growth in every business you acquire.

You Are a "Human Hedge Fund"

In a hedge fund, investors pool their assets in the hopes of earning an outsized return beyond "alpha," alpha being the expected rate of return of a corresponding benchmark. A well-managed hedge fund can make a lot of money for its investors, but alpha is difficult, and it can only be done with shrewd decision making and a careful allocation of assets.

Each reader of this book is a "human hedge fund," whether you know it or not. Your "portfolio" consists of various aspects of your life: your business, your career, your family, your ambitions. These are all separate "asset classes" into which you are pouring resources (time, effort, opportunity cost, human capital, intellectual capital). You likely don't even know what each asset class allocation is returning to you or the minimum return that you should accept on that asset class as terms of a percentage of your hedge fund.

Nor do you know what kind of yield you're getting. One asset might be 40% risk and 3% yield. The other might be 3% risk and 40% yield—and you don't even know it. As manager of your own human hedge fund, you don't even know what alpha would be or how to measure it, what the "norm" is to determine it, or how well you are performing.

If that were a real-life hedge fund, it would be a miracle if it was able to beat the market. If you were an investor in that fund, you'd pull your money out post haste!

Our intention with this analogy is to encourage you to judge yourself and look at how you are investing, mis-investing, or underinvesting your time, effort, money, and resources, so you will challenge yourself to adjust your allocations, your yield, and your risk. Only then can you thrive financially and live the life you desire.

Tunnel Vision vs. Funnel Vision

The pattern of ossified thinking that keeps business owners "stuck" is what we have dubbed "tunnel vision": doing what everyone else does (and what you perhaps have been doing), just because it's the status quo or the norm in your field. Funnel vision, in contrast, is widening the scope of your vision beyond the confines of what is familiar, traditional, accepted, or standard operating procedure in your industry.

One of the most powerful ways to evolve from tunnel vision to funnel vision is to borrow successful approaches from outside your industry. This comes back to the concept of endless curiosity we discussed earlier, the thing that makes you most like Albert Einstein (even if you don't "get" physics!). Don't just observe what your competitors are up to and try to adapt that. Study what companies that have absolutely nothing in common with your own industry have done to succeed. You'll find that other industries are a gold mine of fresh ideas.

Jay started with Icy Hot, a company that produces pain relief creams, and helped grow it 20,000% in one year. How? He used an advertising model that had never been used in that industry. He approached magazines, mail-order advertising agencies, radio, and television stations that had unsold air time or print space with the unusual proposition of running ads for Icy Hot.

He promised they could keep whatever money people sent them, plus a fixed amount per unit, which meant that he would be paying them 115% of its full sale price, incurring a small loss on Jay's part. Until Jay did that, no one had ever paid or offered to pay someone more than the full selling price in exchange for assuming all the selling risk.

Within a year, this strategy ballooned to more than one thousand separate arrangements with magazines, newspapers, television stations, radio stations, and catalog companies, which garnered him five thousand to ten thousand Icy Hot orders from first-time customers each day. This led to an eight-figure exit in just 15 months! This was Jay's first exposure to the power of the approach we are teaching you now.

Roland did this in the product launch space. One year he was traveling in France and Italy with his wife and just as they reached the end of their trip, a volcano in Iceland erupted, closing all air space across most of Europe and stranding Roland and his wife in Napoli, Italy.

As they were at the end of their trip, Roland asked his wife if she would mind him testing his hand at selling something as an affiliate online while she relaxed and read books as they waited for the all-clear to fly home to the States. She agreed, and Roland searched online for a product to sell as an affiliate.

He soon found what he was looking for, a $3,000 product that was about to be launched in the online marketing space that included online training and a software component. Roland signed up as an affiliate and set about generating sales. The only problem was, he had no list to market the product to as he was brand new to the online marketing space. Sounds like a big problem for Roland, right? Of course not, because he was operating from a funnel vision, not a tunnel vision, perspective.

Without missing a beat, he set about forming strategic partnerships with other much more experienced online marketers who already had large mailing lists. He simply reached out to them via email and asked if they were planning to promote the $3,000 product, and if they said they weren't, he asked if they would be interested in letting him handle all the work of creating emails and generating marketing materials and other inducements to purchase, and then they would split the profits from the sale 50/50. Several of them said yes, and before he knew it, Roland had well over a dozen marketing partners, each of whom controlled a very large email list.

No one had ever thought to be the center of an affiliate-based launch and aggregate other marketers to combine forces into a single mega-affiliate before. Over the course of the next six days, Roland and his group set a record at the time for total sales during a launch, tripling the previous record and generating $1.3 million in sales and commissions of $650,000. However, in addition to the base commissions of 50%, Roland took the #1 spot in the promotion which added another 15% commissions to total sales, thereby generating an extra $195,000 in commissions for a total of $845,000 from six days of work. Not a bad payday for a bold new way of thinking implemented quickly, all while stuck in a foreign country at the end of a big trip.

PayPal is another example of Mind-stein-like thinking. It was originally established to sell security software for handheld devices like the then-popular Blackberry. That venture failed, and subsequently the founders switched their focus to a digital wallet and then after a merger with Elon Musk's X.com company in 2000, became hyper focused on an electronic payments system, eventually becoming PayPal in 2001. Today it's a Fortune 500 firm and one of the biggest players in the tech and online payments space.

Brian Chesky and Joe Gebbia thought differently when they came up with the idea of putting an air mattress in their living room and renting it out as a bed and breakfast, an idea that changed the way people vacation and completely disrupted the hotel business. Their company, originally founded as AirBedAndBreakfast.com—now AirBnB.com—is worth about $110 billion.

We could provide you with stories like this all day long and fill dozens of books with them because the truth of the matter is that original thinking has created virtually all of the most important products, services, and businesses in our lives today.

Industry "best practices" are, in fact, anything but, because **they keep you mired in the status quo.** And you can't succeed if you're simply imitating what your competitors, which may be much larger, more efficient, and vastly more resource-rich, are doing. The greatest breakthroughs will invariably come from outside, not from inside, your industry.

Tunnel vision is the death of innovation. Funnel vision opens up a new vista of innovative possibilities. People tend to identify "innovation" with "technological improvement." Technology may be part of it, but the most profit-maximizing forms of innovation may have nothing to do with technology at all. Rather, innovation is coming up with new ways of adding value whose benefits are immediately self-evident to the market you serve.

Interestingly, some of the most notable (and profitable) commercial breakthroughs, including some brands and products that are now multibillion dollar household names, came from outside their industry. Fiber optics came from aerospace, rather than telecommunication. The invention of Viagra was a happy accident that came about while Pfizer was trying to develop a new heart medication. Minoxidil (brand name Rogaine) was first created to treat ulcers, then utilized for its capacity as a vasodilator to treat hypertension, but the function for which it generates billions of dollars a year is reversing hair loss. Ballpoint pens gave birth to roll-on deodorant, and the most successful baby carriage uses the collapsible wheel technology from airline landing gears.

Many of these products would likely not exist if an entrepreneur had not innovated by looking beyond the contours of their industry. Traverse the wilds of the business world, venture to far-flung fields that may have no apparent relevance to your own, and there you will find riches hidden where no one else is looking. Borrow liberally and adapt to your business's needs.

Again, think like Einstein. Your brain is designed by evolution to solve problems and create opportunities, but it can't if it doesn't know what its job is. You must have an inexhaustible thirst for knowledge within your field *and outside your field*. Hopeless, bottomless, relentless curiosity will lead you to breakthroughs because your mind will be constantly searching, consciously and unconsciously, for solutions.

Your competitors may have deeper expertise in your particular industry than you, but the weapon you wield over them is a deeper, broader knowledge in other areas, including fields that may only be tangentially related to your day-to-day business. Different sources and realms of knowledge interact and react, like alchemy, and catalyze into novel and innovative ways of doing business that others do not see, for they are working in a blind spot that does not inhibit you. Be the one-eyed man in the land of the blind.

There are many cases to be made for eschewing the modern trend toward hyper-focused specialization. One of the best is that made by former *Sports Illustrated* writer, David Epstein, whose excellent book, *Range*, makes the case for generalists, those who have a broad competence in many areas rather than an extreme mastery of one very narrow niche. Having knowledge and skills, information, tools, and data from many different perspectives, industries, and sources can be a fountainhead of world-changing, dynasty building ideas.

Start asking yourself, "What preconceptions about my life or business currently hold me back?"

"What factual assumptions am I making that may not be actual facts?"

"What language patterns am I using to frame potential solutions that may lead me to make incorrect assumptions?"

In the chapters and models that follow, you will learn to think and operate your business with an exponential growth mindset that shatters self-limiting cognitive habits.

Inversion Thinking

Think about and plan for the opposite of what you want to happen. Carl Jacobi said, "*Man muss immer umhehren*" – "You must always turn back."

Charlie Munger said, "It is remarkable how much long-term advantage people like us have gotten by trying to be consistently not stupid, instead of trying to be very intelligent...Invert, always invert. Turn a situation or problem upside down. Look at it backward. What happens if all our plans go wrong? Where don't we want to go, and how do you get THERE? Tell me where I'm going to die so I don't go there."

Consider the following example of inversion thinking:

1. **Goal:** What do you want to happen? E.g., get more new customers for your product or service business.

2. **Inversion:** What is the opposite of what you want? E.g., how can you prevent the business from getting new customers? Answer, don't send out any mail, don't hire salespeople, don't run ads.

3. **Preventative solutions:** How can you ensure that the marketing gets done on time? Create a mail calendar and assign dual responsibility and reporting.

Inversion Thinking Exercise:

1. **Goal:** What is your biggest priority goal between now and the end of the year?

2. **Inversion:** What is the opposite of what you want? E.g., how can you prevent the business from getting what you want?

3. **Preventative solutions:** How can you ensure the outcome that you do not want, never happens?

The following chapters will show how you can practically apply this type of thinking to excavate opportunities for exponential growth.

For more case studies, examples, worksheets, checklists, forms, scripts, and other resources, including quite a few that we simply could not fit in the book itself, we created a resources collection and all of these resources are available and waiting for you at BusinessWealthWithoutRisk.com/access. Visit the site now and enjoy a huge collection of resources at absolutely no money out of pocket for you!

BusinessWealthWithoutRisk.com/access

Business Breakdown

In Chapter 7, we focused on changing your thinking process and teaching you to see correlations and implications that are typically invisible to others. We shared insights about the often-overlooked opportunities to optimize, market, sell, strategize, and remonetize. With the methodologies like RSO and PEQ, you learned how small tweaks can create big outcomes without demanding any additional time, resources, money, or risk.

As we continue into Chapter 8, "Optimization, Levers, and Fulcrums," we will take a significant leap in the journey. Incremental growth might have you reaching for the sky, but we want you to rocket beyond the stratosphere into exponential growth. Here, we're not merely concerned with growth but with an accelerating rate of growth, a trajectory that curves confidently upward. It's about explosive and sustained profitability.

We'll delve into "optimization" and explore how to maximize profits while minimizing resource expenditure and risk. You'll learn about the potential for asymmetric returns and how scaling up requires relentless curiosity, learning new things, and stepping far beyond your intellectual and professional comfort zones. You'll discover that there's no limit to what you can improve and how these improvements can exponentially grow your business.

Get ready to accelerate and optimize!

CHAPTER 8

OPTIMIZATION, LEVERS, AND FULCRUMS

If incremental growth is reaching for the sky, geometric growth means rocketing up into and beyond the stratosphere, that outer boundary of the earth where you're breaking free from the pull of gravity.

We seek exponential (geometric[14]) growth as opposed to incremental growth. Incremental growth proceeds at a fixed rate of change. With exponential growth, not only does growth occur but the rate of growth occurs; it increasingly accelerates. If graphed, it would look like

---

14 Technically, in math, exponential and geometric growth are not equivalent, but what matters is that the growth rate *accelerates*, leading to massive profits, as opposed to incremental growth, which is merely linear (increasing at a constant rate).

a parabola rising confidently upward. Virtually limitless. That is explosive business growth and profitability in a nutshell.

Exponential growth happens when you find ways to maximize profit while maintaining or minimizing expenditure of resources and risk.

Optimization: Asymmetric Returns

Scaling up requires *optimization:* the *highest and best use* of time, effort, resources, access to markets, capital (intellectual, monetary, human), IP, etc. Exploring, being relentlessly curious, learning new things, and venturing far beyond your intellectual and professional comfort zones will lead you to new opportunities for optimization.

And there is no limit to what you can improve. You can optimize how an ad performs, you can optimize the media you use, you can optimize the offers you make. You can optimize the way that you convert them, etc. You can optimize how a sales force sells.

Among the many prestigious companies we have counseled was W. Edwards Deming's organization. Deming was the father of process improvement and an optimization wizard. He would, for example, visit a factory where one hundred people were doing the same thing. Most consultants would look at the factory floor activity and say, "These hundred workers, that's a process." Deming would identify it as an *event*, and then examine the micro-processes underlying it, breaking it down to throughput, downtime time, time it took for preventative maintenance, variation, and so forth.

Then he'd apply the Pareto principle, also known as the 80/20 rule. Of these hundred factory workers, who are the 20% who generate 80% of throughput, who are the 20% who excel at minimizing downtime, etc.? What are they doing differently? How are they doing it? What's their mindset? What's their methodology?

By applying this heuristic to eight or ten processes going on in the factory's production, he would boost output by 10% here and 10% there. These "ten percents" would then compound through those eight to ten processes to generate much bigger numbers: 10x10x10 equals 1000. That's a textbook definition of exponential growth. And that's how Deming took the previously poor-quality Toyotas, the Hyundais, the Nissans, the Sonys, and the Mitsubishis of the world and made them production dynamos.

This kind of optimization can be applied to virtually any business and to any mission-critical aspect of that business. Say you have a team of five salespeople all doing the same thing. There's no variation or differentiation in their work. This is a highly inefficient method. Instead, examine who is best at what. Break down your salespeople's activities into microprocesses. Maybe someone is adroit at opening accounts, someone else sells at full margin extremely well, another salesperson is brilliant at repeat sales, another one is best at working with distributors.

Now you can optimize your workforce to skyrocket growth, because if you have one salesperson who excels at X, another at Y, and another at Z, you now make them specialists in their respective areas of expertise (rather than squandering them by having them work on tasks they underperform at.) And now that you have turned an inefficient team of generalists into an optimized team of specialists, you've crowned them as the expert in their particular microprocess who can teach fifty others how to do it just as well. So now you have 150 specialists who earn their keep by concentrating on a single, profitable activity that they do best.

CHAPTER 8 - OPTIMIZATION, LEVERS, AND FULCRUMS

The changes you implement need not be dramatic. It's remarkable how a simple tweak can yield exponential rewards. For example, in our work with the number one Honda Acura dealer in the country, we advised the owner to go under the hood and quantify the performance of his finance managers. He found that the guy who was working the night shift, where there was notably less traffic, was nevertheless out-earning the day manager by a factor of two. So he switched them, placing his most productive manager on the high-traffic shift where he'd generate the most revenue, and profits jumped significantly as a result.

Everyone knows the brand Toyota, but few appreciate that one of the things that made the car manufacturer into a household name worldwide was its innovative, ultra-efficient approach to manufacturing. Its "lean manufacturing system," also called "Just-in-Time" production, is so essential to Toyota's business that the company describes it not just as a manufacturing process but as part of its *philosophy:* "a production system based on the philosophy of achieving the complete elimination of all waste in pursuit of the most efficient methods."[15]

It emerged as Toyota's engineers sought to improve the cumbersome and somewhat clunky method of making cars that was standard at the time. The Toyota Production System (TPS) is founded on two concepts: "jidoka" ("automation with a human touch"), whereby any problem on the assembly line triggers an immediate shutdown to prevent defective products from being produced; and the "Just-in-Time" concept, in which each process yields only what is necessary for the *next* process, avoiding waste, duplication, excess inventory, and bottlenecks.

---

15   "Toyota Production System." Toyota Motor Corporation, n.d., global.toyota/en/company/vision-and-philosophy/production-system

These techniques were so effective that they've been imitated many times over, all over the world and across multiple industries, so it's easy to underestimate how innovative the TPS was (and still is). It's a shining example of optimization in practice.

Beyond Exponential: Levers and Fulcrums

Throughout our careers, virtually every year we create new categories of geometric growth, some of which we'll talk about later: sticking point solutions, the Power Parthenon, key ways to grow a business, among others. And we started thinking, what's *beyond* exponential? What's "geometry times geometry times geometry"?

We found this answer:

Mathematically there are five gradients of performance above and beyond exponentiation. Mathematicians define this as "hyper-operational:" one of a sequence of operations for compounding numbers that increase in growth iteratively. Tetration, pentation, hexation, heptation, and octation are what lie beyond exponentiation.

This is not just abstraction for abstraction's sake. Consider it a kind of thought experiment that serves to radically expand your conception of what is feasible. Thinking in hyper-exponential terms expands the realm of possibilities that you can achieve in your business. It's not enough to merely read about these techniques and apply them. You must shift your whole mindset.

In lay terms, there is far higher performance possibility in a vast number of areas of a business revenue system beyond even exponential. The revenue system includes how you attract and target prospects, how to convert them to buyers, what to do at the point of sale, what to do after the sale, and how to deal with them after the sale.

CHAPTER 8 - OPTIMIZATION, LEVERS, AND FULCRUMS

The means to achieve exponential or even hyper-exponential growth is via *levers* and *fulcrums*. A lever is a bar or beam that allows one to move large amounts of weight on one end by applying pressure to the other end. The fulcrum allows the lever to function by serving as the pivot point.

As Archimedes, Ancient Greek thinker and mathematician, said, "Give me a lever long enough, and a fulcrum on which to place it, and I shall move the world." They are so ubiquitous because they enable *more work while minimizing effort*. We use levers and fulcrums every day: scissors, screwdrivers, car jacks, pop-top cans, chopsticks, wheelbarrows, crowbars, cranks on your window, and push buttons on your car. In business, they function much the same way, by making vast outputs of work easier and allowing you to do *much more* with *much less*.

It is easier to leverage profit strategies and grow your bottom line than your top. Multiplying the bottom line rather than the top means you can grow without adding to top line expenses (expanding, opening new locations, hiring new people, etc.).

When you triple the profit you make, you have more revenue to build your top line. Profit begets profit; success begets success. It creates a feedback loop that accelerates at an ever-greater rate, producing parabolic growth.

How can you create small changes that yield a disproportionate impact? What can you do to dramatically boost profits without a concomitant increase in costs or risk?

We've encountered this problem thousands of times in our career; it is in fact one of the things we do best. Here is one example: modify the headline/greeting/subject line in your email marketing. Make it more eye-catching, irresistible, click-worthy, or eloquent. In "effort cost," this action is negligible; it would take you one minute of intellectual labor to dream up a new and better email subject line. The benefit, however, is multiplied many times over, by the hundreds or thousands or tens of thousands or millions, depending on how many people your email campaign reaches.

Or, you can leverage *reach:* implement a referral strategy where your referrals (like a lever) do all the heavy lifting. Almost every business we look at gets 10% to 100% of sales from referrals or word of mouth, yet not one in a hundred have in place a formalized, systematized, referral generating system. Obviously, this is a wasted opportunity. Referrals are warm leads. There's an implicit trust built in when a client or colleague or acquaintance refers you to someone else; they vouch for you, free of charge. A well-functioning referral system is self-perpetuating (referrals beget referrals which beget other referrals), allowing you to expand your reach beyond your circle of influence (and into the "referees'" circle of influence.) If a business has no referral system, by adding just two or three formalized ones, you can double, redouble, and redouble again the number of no cost referral buyers that business generates and blow up the bottom line.

Another area that benefits from levers is *process.* So many of our technological advances serve to simplify processes in some way. Take a simple online scheduling system, like Calendly. Calendly allows clients to view available meeting times and schedule a meeting without ever interacting with the company. It also has a reminder function that will automatically remind the client about the meeting.

Without a scheduling technology like this, logistics and scheduling can consume a huge amount of human capital and time. Especially for companies that deal with clients in different time zones, the effort to schedule meetings or calls can be daunting. The result? Not only do you need more staff hours tied up in the process of scheduling, but your company becomes difficult for clients to work with, which is a sure way to turn them away. Introduce a simple technological lever, and all of these problems disappear. Logistics become seamless, customers are happy, and staff can focus on what's important instead of getting bogged down by a calendar.

Customer Management Systems (CMS) that let you easily track detailed contact information, and Customer Relationship Management systems (CRMs) that let you easily track and manage your client interactions, can have a similarly outsized impact on a company. By bringing information together and organizing it in one place, it becomes easy for individuals in an organization to access and act on it. This can save a huge amount of time, while uncovering data that can directly impact your bottom line.

There is no industry where this technique cannot revolutionize some aspect, great or small, of how business is conducted. We have changed the script of a greeter at a furniture store and tripled sales. We've changed the opening paragraph of a sales letter and doubled the response rate. We've changed the headline in an ad selling gold bullion and quintupled the number of sales while tripling the size of the average sale. We've changed the call to action, we've changed the positioning, we've changed the risk reversal, we've changed the credibility factors, the proof, and each one of those has an impact on your operational efficiency.

There are over 50 ways to make yourself and your team more productive and efficient. None of those ways requires major effort. No one can possibly apply all 50, but if you just picked three or five and dedicated yourself to making the most of them, your results will be off the charts. Often, the most underutilized asset of a newly acquired business is its intellectual capital—the way its leaders think.

Three Ways to Grow a Business

Allow us to share with you now a deceptively simple yet overwhelmingly powerful concept relating to the growth of the business you are now operating, whether it is one that you started or one that you have purchased using the guidance in the first section of this book.

The concept is that there are three primary ways to grow a business: sell more people; sell more each time; and sell the same people more often.

If you have ever attended Tony Robbins' Business Mastery seminar, then you will be aware that Tony devotes two or three hours to teaching this core idea, because it is so powerful and because its application is so broad. Let's go over briefly the ideas the concept represents because when you master them in your business, your income will skyrocket.

1. *Sell more people.* It sounds obvious, and of course, it's extremely straightforward: make more sales. There are myriad ways to do that. In addition to increasing your marketing or advertising, as we discussed elsewhere in these pages, you can seek joint ventures. You can see who has a pipeline and could offer your products to their list. You can use any of the countless tools in this section of the book to increase the number of sales you make in a month, in a quarter, or in a year.

2. *Increase the size of each sale.* We are hardly reinventing the wheel when we suggest that you respectfully offer your buyers upsells and cross-sells at checkout time. Chances are that if a person needs one of the things you produce or provide, that person also needs several other things you sell. Why limit their

options by failing to offer them, again in a respectful and credible manner, the goods or services they would find extremely helpful? You can also offer volume discounts. You can combine offers. You can offer a buy two, get one free. The options are limitless, and the result is that the average size of your sales increases on a consistent and systematic basis.

3. *Sell more often.* Most businesspeople, no matter how long they have been in business, make the rookie mistake of waiting for customers to reorder, instead of offering the opportunity to reorder on a regular basis. Your customer list is solid gold, yet most businesspeople are far more interested in the chase for new customers instead of the proven method of going back to current customers and asking for additional sales.

In any given year, your customers need far more than they are going to purchase from you in an initial sale. Of course, you want to look for new customers. That's the first part of this triad of approaches to increase your income. At the same time, let's not neglect those current (and past!) customers, virtually all of whom are probably extremely happy with you and what you offer. Go back to them on a regular basis and offer to sell them again. Better still, put them on a recurring purchase program so that every month, or every two months, or at whatever rate is appropriate, they reorder automatically. If you sell them once, you can sell them many times. Why not do just that?

Those are the three ways to increase the size of virtually any business. And here's the even more exciting news: you only have to increase on a percentage basis each of these three methodologies to enjoy amazingly exponential growth! You don't have to double the number of people you sell to, or how much they buy, or how often they buy. Instead, if you can increase each of these three areas by even a small percentage amount, over a period of a year, your revenues will skyrocket. That's what's so beautiful about this "three ways to grow a business" approach and that's why we are sharing these ideas with you. We would now like to show you in visual form just how robust growth can be even with a relatively small percentage increase in each of the areas we are discussing. Please review the following charts which demonstrate the sales optimization we are proposing for you and your business.

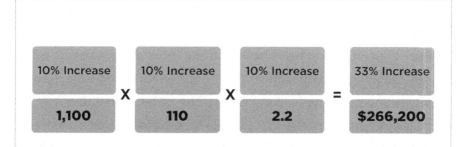

A 10% increase in each of the three areas
equals a 33% increase in revenue.

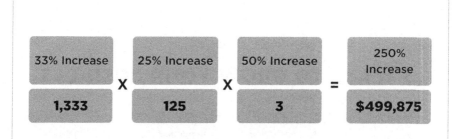

Look what happens now...
The results are exponential?

Optimization - 3 Ways to Grow Your Business

If you were to 2X (Double) Each of the 3 Ways to Grow a Business....

Increase Clients	Increase $ Per Sale	Increase Repurchase Frequency	Total
1000	100	2	$200,000
2X	2X	2X	2X
2000	200	4	$1,600,000

A 2X Strategy per "way" gives an 8X (800%) Outcome

10 x 10 x 10

The "10x10x10" paradigm, illustrated in the previous charts, demonstrates how increasing growth in several areas has a compounding effect to produce exponential growth. As an example, imagine you increase your number of annual clients by a thousand, the average dollars per sale by $100, and the repurchase frequency by a factor of two. 1,000 x 100 x 2 = $200,000.

Now bump each of those numbers up by 10% (achievable through optimization), and do the math. That's $266,000 in revenue, a 33% increase resulting from a meager 10% uptick.

Double those numbers now, and you get $1,600,000, an 8x increase resulting from a 2x change, or 2^3—literally, exponential growth. When you hear stories about entrepreneurs who enlarged the size of their firms with dazzling speed, and wonder by what magic they achieved it, now you know what they did!

We have since added three additional "advanced ways" of growing a business to the original three: 1) penetrate new markets each year, 2) introduce new products and services each year, and 3) purchase your competitors' businesses or assets each year. Since you read the part of the book where we talked about acquisitions, we presume you're already envisioning how you can do exactly that, since this strategy intersects in many ways with the EPIC process.

The idea, of course, is not necessarily to fire on all these cylinders, but the more categories you can expand into (the more 10% "boosts" you can achieve on the micro level), the more those 10% increments will multiply on the macro level.

Power Parthenon Strategy: One of The Ultimate Profit Prescriptions

First, consider what we call "the diving board theory." Most businesses have just one primary driver of revenue. That's their "diving board." A diving board is helpful in that its springiness can propel you upwards, but it's also supporting the entire weight of your body. Applying the metaphor to business, your diving board may be profitable, but it constitutes an all-your-eggs-in-one-basket risk: if that board snaps, you're tumbling into the water at an awkward and probably painful angle.

In business terms, any number of things could transpire that jeopardize your primary revenue source. For example, your best salesperson leaves or starts selling the same product or service for less.

Consequently, we encourage our clients to add multiple "support pillars," which combines the age-old stratagem of diversification with the methodology of optimization to create a durable foundation. The Parthenon of Ancient Greece was an architectural marvel for many reasons, and one reason it's still standing 2500 years after its construction is that its roof is not supported by a single pillar but by a legion of formidable marble columns six and a half feet in width.

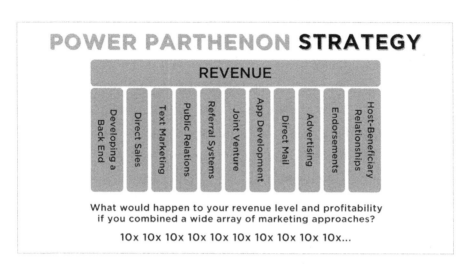

An example of a modern-day Power Parthenon is Disney. Disney started off as a cartoon studio, but today, their revenue comes from a diverse range of products: TV streaming services, movie production, theme parks, resorts, a cruise line, live entertainment shows, not to mention merchandising, which is why even if a pandemic comes along and Disney's theme parks and resorts suffer, the company as a whole can still get by. We can comfortably expect Disney's Parthenon to keep standing for decades.

Military theorists call this the "force multiplier effect," which refers to a factor or factors that provide much greater effectiveness (without a concomitant increase in size) than they would have without it. The force "multiplies" as the advantage compounds throughout the military operation. Examples abound: precision-guided munitions are one, and aircraft carriers are another.

The way combat is also conducted can be a force multiplier. For example, an invading army would probably try to knock out the enemy's infrastructure and communications first, an effect that would reverberate and *multiply* many times over in the ensuing battles and put their adversary at an immediate disadvantage. Force multipliers provide an asymmetric benefit by allowing a numerically inferior fighting force to even the playing field with a larger and better equipped army.

What are the additional pillars that you can add to your own business to increase diversification of revenue and decrease labor dependencies? What additional source of revenue can you envision for your business and how can you diversify your labor allocations to reduce the risk that the business suffers in the event a key person leaves its employ?

Power Pivots: Small Moves, Massive Profit Increases

Pivots are essential for exploding the bottom line. The growth they produce is staggering, and the effort required to create those results is minimal.

To pivot means to turn around a point, and it's an apt phrase, because if you break it down, "pivoting" really has two parts: the central point or anchor and the movement. (Levers and fulcrums also operate by pivoting). Pivoting essentially means you stay rooted in place, cemented to the ground with what is working, while shifting and moving into new territory.

We've identified several pivots that can energize your business.

1. **Marketing pivot:** What you say, to whom, and how. New marketing channels and avenues. Possibilities are endless here. WeddingWire, a tech company that connects engaged couples with vendors and wedding planning ideas, pivoted their marketing by creating a more tailored email campaign to boost their app, and increased adoption by 74%.

2. **Strategy pivot:** Change your strategy to change your results. Most businesses actually have no strategy whatsoever. They are purely tactical.

3. **Product/service portfolio pivot:** Create more enticing versions of existing product offerings and expand into altogether new product lines. Borrow from other industries. See what your competitors are doing and do it better, or value-add to it.

4. **Supply chain pivot:** Find new suppliers or tap existing suppliers to finance new ventures. (In the first half of the book, we discussed leveraging suppliers as a low-risk source of financing.) We've had suppliers pay for marketing and hire salespeople. It sounds too good to be true, but it makes sense: your suppliers thrive when *you* thrive, and they too are looking for promising partnerships and additional streams of income.

5. **Preeminence pivot:** This is big enough to warrant its own chapter, in the penultimate chapter of the book, but we'll mention it here, too, as it is a type of power pivot. Achieving preeminence means you cultivate a reputation for doing what you do better than anyone else, in a spirit of service. You shift your focus from falling in love with your company, industry, or product

line to falling in love with *the people you serve* and seeing how your products and services make a difference in their lives.

Years ago, Jay was advising a billion-dollar home building company. "What is it you provide?" Jay asked. They answered, prosaically, "We build houses." "No," Jay said, "You provide the means to get people out of a substandard living situation and into a home where they can excel. You're the catalyst for the growth of new communities, new friendships, new relation-ships. You're allowing people to generate wealth, security, and longevity." Reframing how you look at what you do is a preem-inence pivot.

6. **Target market re-focusing pivot:** Most people just throw mud at the wall and see what sticks. They utilize an imprecise "macro" approach, not a precise, specialized "micro" approach.

7. **Positioning pivot:** a strategic shift in how a company or prod-uct is presented or perceived in the market. This often in-volves redefining the target customer, the context in which the product is used, or the key benefits and features that are em-phasized. It's important to note that a positioning pivot doesn't necessarily involve a change in the product itself, but rather a change in how the product is marketed and perceived.

8. **Business model pivot:** A fundamental change in how a com-pany creates value and generates revenue. This could involve changing the product or service, the target market, or the method of monetization. It could also mean changing the way the product is delivered to customers or how customers are charged for the product or service.

9. **Branding and messaging pivot**: Changing how you're seen in the marketplace. This commonly involves redefining the company's identity and the way it communicates with its audience. This type of pivot can sometimes include changes to the company's name, logo, tagline, visual identity, tone of voice, and overall messaging.

10. **SEO pivot**: A good friend of ours is the leading authority on SEO and uses 36 SEO levers. Most businesses use one (if any at all). Visit our resources page at BusinessWealthWithoutRisk.com/access to see these.

11. **Social media pivot**: A core change in a company's social media strategy. This could include changes in the social media platforms used, the type of content shared, the tone and style of communication, the frequency of posts, or the way the company interacts with its audience on social media.

12. **Competitive intelligence pivot**: Most businesses are woefully ignorant about their competition. When someone hires us, we ask at the start, "Tell me about other companies in your market. What are their marketing strategies? What's their big positioning advantage? What's their value proposition? Strengths and weaknesses?" These are fundamental evaluative questions, but the typical response is, "Well, I don't know." How can you achieve geometric growth if you don't even know what you're up against?

13. **Lead generation pivot**: There are countless ways to start a relationship with prospects. Some people do it with a book, some people do it with an experience, some people do it with a questionnaire. Airstream, the recreational vehicle manufacturer,

needed to generate more, higher quality leads at costs that were similar to previous marketing campaigns. So they began to publish genuinely useful information for customers across a buyer's journey, targeting prospects who lived near Airstream dealerships. The strategy allowed them to generate 78% more leads, while decreasing the cost of each lead by 44%.

14. **Try something new and evaluate if it's working:** If not, try something else.

15. **Partnering/joint venture/strategic alliance pivot:** A strategic change in a company's strategy used to determine who it forms partnerships with or creates operational or strategic alignment with. This can involve actions such as cross-promotion, offer collaboration, product creation, operational alliance, financial agreements, or pooling resources, sharing risk, and leveraging each other for a mutual benefit. This is often seen when a company goes from in-house operations to partnering with other companies for certain functions, like manufacturing, distribution, marketing, or product development.

16. **R&D pivot:** Research and development related to product, marketing, hiring, managing, value creation, strategy, and expanding into new markets, learning about the operational nuances of your own business, market research. The sky is the limit.

Sticking Point Solutions

Most business owners are stuck, and the majority of them don't even know it. They can even be "profitably stuck"—they're making money but they don't realize how much more money they could be making. Even business owners who take to heart the mantra "grow or die" struggle to achieve sustainable growth. They run out of ideas and don't know how to keep the momentum going. Being stuck is a miserable state to be in— an emotional as well as financial drain—as you struggle to get un-stuck while seeing your profits stagnate or decline and your competitors eat into your market share.

Such moments are when owners need to broaden their horizons, tear down their comfort zone, and locate those covert opportunities we've talked about. However, most business owners who find themselves stuck do just the opposite, double down and retreat further into what they've been doing. Familiarity creates comfort, and change is scary, so they cling to the status quo. But as the oft-quoted expression (usually attributed to Einstein though he probably didn't actually say it) goes, "The definition of insanity is doing the same thing over and over and expecting different results."

Try something different, and you'll be able to pull yourself out of the quicksand. Every business can use the following powerful profit levers to get unstuck. Here is a list of ways in which businesses may be stuck. Ask yourself these questions and don't be afraid to tell yourself the truth!

1. Are you stuck losing out to the competition?

Just because a competitor is outperforming you does not mean they're better; they probably just have a shrewder positioning, marketing, or selling strategy. Change your strategy to change your results. Ask the tough questions of yourself to determine what is working and what isn't. Iterate new approaches, and when you find one that works, *scale up*: leverage it to its maximum effect.

Understand the difference between, and utility of, optimization and innovation. Finding the highest and best use is *optimization*: taking what's working and making it work to the nth degree; or, fixing or replacing what's not working. *Innovation* is engineering breakthroughs, taking controlled risks, and looking outside the industry for new ideas.

2. Are you stuck not selling enough?

Your sales team is the vanguard, your strike team, your first line of offense. Reorient your sales strategy around a more consultative, client-centric paradigm. "Consultative selling" is like a doctor helping a patient find a cure for a disease: a salesperson's job is not merely "to close" but to provide solutions to the client in a way that benefits both parties. People buy from salespeople whom they trust, who they know have their best interests at heart.

Meanwhile, leverage your advertising. As we said before, leveraging small changes (in ad copy, in email subject lines, in headlines, etc.) can generate exponential returns. Invest in advertising that focuses on your target audience.

Sell more through inventive relationships and associations. If you're lacking resources, joint-venture with those who aren't.

3. Are you stuck with erratic business volume?

Volatile cash flow month-to-month is anathema to strategizing (which is your chief task as owner and CEO) because if you can't count on a certain amount of money coming in, it's difficult to project income and expenses, know what resources you can leverage where, and formulate medium- and long-term plans. Each month you're winging it and grinding through the days on a wing and a prayer.

Focus on the 20% of clients who generate 80% of the impact (and cut loose the few who cause an outsized drain on resources). Then create a system for maintaining these clients to smooth out erratic business volume while winning new clients like them.

4. Are you stuck failing to strategize?

Most businesses are not sufficiently strategic, analytical, and systematic. They're *tactical*: a little of this, a little of that, and let's hope it all adds up to something sustainable. Tactics without a big-picture strategy is throwing mud at the wall and seeing what sticks. You can only find the blind spots, the ones that provide the best opportunity for rapid growth, by having a panoptic, strategic outlook.

Strategy emerges from four key questions: Who are your best potential clients? What do they need, want, or expect? Is there a demand for your product/service? Who are your competitors? This is Business 101, yet you wouldn't believe how many entrepreneurs fail to answer these fundamental questions.

Strategy is not merely rational/logical/cognitive; there's an emotional component too. The best strategists are driven by a mission they love, and they are confident in the knowledge their venture is improving lives. Above all, know your purpose, and love your business and your market with passion.

5. Are you stuck still doing what's not working?

This concept is central to everything we teach: *Following the herd is fatal to long-term growth.* Replicating what everyone else does, or merely repeating the way you've done business since forever, means you can never differentiate from others.

Identify business constraints and eliminate them. Turn your sales team into a specialized assembly line, where each member is equipped to leverage what he or she excels at; then scale that system up by bringing on additional specialists. Study what other companies and industries, including those completely different from your own, are doing and adapt their techniques or processes.

6. Are you stuck being marginalized by the marketplace?

If you don't stand out among the crowd, you'll be marginalized by the marketplace. How can you expect to compete with bigger, more established firms when you're doing and saying the same things they are, just at a much smaller scale?

Cultivate preeminence in your field. Be recognized as an expert in a class of his or her own and as a better investment than anyone else. That doesn't just mean excelling at your job; it means epitomizing empathy and a desire to serve and give, not merely sell and take. Preempt your clients' concerns and predict their objections to doing business with you.

7. Are you stuck insisting that "I can do it all myself?"

We celebrate the spirit of the intrepid business owner at the top of the pyramid. But entrepreneurism is a collective effort. A "go it alone" mindset is a liability, not an asset, particularly when you need help getting unstuck. Approach the problem with the goal of helping other people get what they want so they'll help you get what you want.

The fastest thing anybody can do to become more productive is extricate themselves from the things they're doing themselves.

First, figure out the three most important activities you engage in for your business. Then break them into sub-processes and identify which ones are the most relevant, which ones you are the most competent at, and which ones you are the most passionate about.

If you're spending time and effort on sub-processes you're minimally interested in or mediocre at, delegate them to someone else. If you are not competent and you are trying to do something to just get to an incremental level, don't do it. You want to operate in the exponential zone. Stop burning energy on activities that don't excite you. Give it to someone who does it better.

Consider undertaking a joint venture, even a small one. This permits you to continue working on your own business while expanding into new territory. Joint ventures pool risk, boost sales, provide access to new markets, offer added value to clients, expand your own access to partners' knowledge and experience, and offer you more flexibility. Chapter 11 on relational capital expands on this subject.

For more case studies, examples, worksheets, checklists, forms, scripts, and other resources, including quite a few that we simply could not fit in the book itself, we created a resources collection and all of these resources are available and waiting for you at BusinessWealthWithoutRisk.com/access. Visit the site now and enjoy a huge collection of resources at absolutely no money out of pocket for you!

Visionary Viewpoints

Now that we've journeyed through the realms of exponential growth and debunked the traditional norms of incremental growth, we hope you've discovered the boundless opportunities that geometric growth offers through the critical concept of optimization. There are few things we enjoy more than curbing the expenditure of resources.

Looking ahead, we'll focus on unearthing the primary drivers that can rocket a business's growth beyond imaginable limits. If anything we've shared so far might seem overwhelming, this next part will help clarify your path.

So get ready to embrace the pressure because it's under the most immense pressure that the most brilliant diamonds are formed!

BusinessWealthWithoutRisk.com/access

CHAPTER 9

PRESSURE MAKES DIAMONDS

DRIVERS OF EXPONENTIAL GROWTH

Throughout decades of helping businesses expand to staggering heights, we've identified nine primary drivers of achieving growth beyond what their owners ever thought possible. If you feel overwhelmed by the abundance of options or techniques in this book, or are unsure where to begin, this chapter will clarify some of the paths you can take.

But first, a story from Jay. Call it a "Tale Of Two Friends." One of these friends was a brilliant copywriter, more tactical than strategic. The other was not quite as gifted a copywriter, but he was an unparalleled strategist. Both these friends got excited about the possible business opportunities created by the advent of a new industry: artificial diamonds (cubic zirconia). Cubic zirconia had been around for a while, but it wasn't until the 1970s that breakthroughs in production allowed their mass production. These stones were and are an appealing and inexpensive way to wear a little bit of flash and to display a little bit of glamour. Diamonds, after all, have been coveted for centuries, and most people can't distinguish between cubic zirconia and the real thing.

Friend #1 (the tactical copywriter) started a company with the fun and snappy name "Beverley Hills Diamond Company." He paid $25,000 to run a full-page ad in *The New York Times* in which he advertised his artificial diamonds for about $40. The ad generated quite a few sales, and he walked away from that campaign with $7,000 in profit. Not bad, but it wasn't enough to convince him to persist. Thinking tactically, he surmised he could keep running the same ad and would probably keep netting a few thousand bucks, but the margin wasn't enough to justify the risk.

The more strategic friend, **Friend #2**, also started a company in the same niche. He also ran a full-page ad (in the *LA Times*) at around the same cost. But his ad copy wasn't quite as sharp, or perhaps the readers of the *LA Times* just weren't as enthralled by fake diamonds as their East Coast counterparts. In any event, **Friend #2** ended up *losing* a few thousand bucks when sales failed to recoup the cost of the pricey ad.

Friend #1 was excellent at some things, but again, he did not approach his new venture *strategically*. There was no all-encompassing idea about brand identity, value proposition, or target market. It was just "here's this new product, it's nice, maybe I can sell it." Consequently, his approach lacked attention to presentation and design.

The whole value proposition of a cubic zirconia is that it possesses the same luminosity and appearance of luxury as a diamond at a fraction of the cost. But he didn't *treat* his own product as such. So instead of shipping it in a nice velvet box like you would a diamond, he just kind of threw it in a loose bag and put it in the mail.

Friend #2, the strategist, would place the loose stone in a beautiful wood box in a velveteen jeweler's bag and ship it in a padded envelope accompanied by two documents. The first document was a letter from him, the CEO of the company, thanking the recipient for entrusting the company with their business and emphasizing that in their hands was something dazzling, brilliant, and captivating unlike anything they'd ever seen—the miracle of a diamond made by a machine!

He went on to say how so many of his customers would go to their jewelers and ask them to set the loose stone in a necklace or bracelet or ring, and the jewelers would charge an arm and a leg for that, but his company would do it at a fair price.

"And," the note said, "we guarantee that your jeweler will charge twice as much. If he doesn't, we'll refund your purchase price."

Moreover, he offered this irresistible offer: "We will not consider your purchase binding on your part until you have both worn the item for at least 45 days and gotten compliments galore from all your friends and people you don't know. And finally, in grateful appreciation for you having trusted us in the first place, in the event you decide to send your stone back to us, we'll refund double what you paid for it. We've also included a postage-paid envelope."

The other enclosed document, by the way, was a catalog.

In this way, he won their trust and their confidence, and not only was the product legit, but he *believed* in it, which encouraged customers to make additional purchases. How could they not? The catalog was right there in front of them.

So, in the end, while **Friend #1** walked away with seven grand, **Friend #2**, who initially lost $5000 in a pricey ad campaign, finished out the year with $25 million in sales.

Savvy readers will identify in this story the application of several of the drivers of growth below. One is strategy. Another is changing your business model (if selling single stones in an envelope wasn't cutting it, change the presentation and up-sell them on supplementary products). A third relates to changing your marketing (if an ad doesn't convey the value proposition, find another way to do so).

Don't just stand there. Bob and weave. Be agile. Act. Innovate. Strategize. And grow rich, using the nine drivers of exponential growth below.

1. Change Your Marketing

As a lever of geometric growth, marketing has a special advantage: you can dramatically ramp up results without a corresponding increase in costs. In many cases, the most effective marketing techniques have a fixed or semi-fixed cost, but strategic iterations can make that cost a much more effective investment.

You could get higher quality prospects or buyers, with larger size purchases, and larger profits per purchase. Case in point: you have a single salesperson on the team. They're in the office from nine to five each day, and they're drawing a fixed salary, whether they land two prospects, five, ten, or zero. Likewise, if those prospects turn into customers, the salesperson's salary remains the same whether those customers purchase $10, $100, or $10,000 units of sale.

Or, say you rent a booth in a sales convention for a thousand dollars a day. You're spending that thousand whether you win zero new clients or a hundred. The cost may be fixed, but the upside is virtually limitless.

So how do you turbocharge the upside while keeping costs steady? The first step to overhauling marketing is to *audit* your current strategy. Here, we're talking about both processes and personnel. Which marketing processes deliver the most bang for the buck? Which salespeople and other employees are delivering the goods? *Quantify* it. Later in this chapter we'll discuss how to use testing to measure the effectiveness of different marketing techniques to get precise, granular data on *what works*, then concentrate your resources on that and blow up the bottom line.

Supplement the internal audit with an external look across the wide vista of the business world. Not just competitors in your field, but enterprises (both similar and dissimilar) in far-flung industries you may or may not know anything about. As we discussed earlier, some of the best ideas lie in the least likely places.

2. Change Your Strategy

Strategy is the brain and nerve center of a business. Without a carefully considered strategy, you're just an automaton, going through the motions. They might be the right motions, but eventually your lack of strategic thinking and vision will catch up with you and you'll stumble.

Strategy is the master purpose at the heart of your business. It's often conflated with, though not the same as, your business model. Strategy is the articulation and realization of the entire operating approach, the integration of each little element, one with another and with the whole entity, in the service of a big-picture, long-term vision.

To change your strategy, first understand that strategy is proactive, not reactive. If you have any strategy at all now, you'll probably find that it is reactive. You win at chess through foresight: thinking three moves ahead and also anticipating your opponent's moves three moves ahead. You don't win by waiting for him to slide his knight into an attacking position and fork your king and rook, then take a shot in the dark at how to counter. That is being reactive, and it's a fast way to lose the game.

One way of clarifying your strategy is by considering the following: *what big operating approach will provide the greatest outcome in the fastest period of time on the most sustainable and enduring basis?* Only until you have answered this question can you drill down and examine which *tactics* (which moves and maneuvers across the chess board) will facilitate that strategic vision.

With strategy, as with all elements that lead to hyper-exponential growth, don't be shortsighted. Open your mind to new, disparate, and unfamiliar perspectives. Study the strategies of other companies in other industries. What works for them? What elements would similarly work for you? Think big here. Don't just examine three or four; learn about a *hundred* other firms' strategies. It's a lot of work but it will give you a comprehensive picture of business strategy (and an ample pool of strategies to choose from) and simultaneously sharpen your own strategic-analytic skills.

3. Change Your Use of Capital

Here we are considering not only financial capital but also human and intellectual capital.

Training is one form of investing a little to reap outsized gains. An incremental increase in performance in each of ten sales reps will produce a disproportionately large return, as each rep's improvement multiplies.

Remember that your job as business leader is not merely to "sell"; it's to *educate*. Allocate some capital for marketing materials that demonstrate your products' superior value in the market. One of Jay's clients is the owner of a large gourmet delicatessen. His prices are 30% higher than his competitors down the road, and definitely higher than the large supermarket next door. But his business really took off when the deli started publishing a brochure entitled, "Discovering Manor Table Cheeses." Not only was it interesting, but it established the deli and its owner as the go-to local authority on cheeses. The message was, "We know our product. Now, you can too." The owner gained a competitive edge not through cost-cutting, but through investing in educational marketing materials that set him apart from the rest.

4. Change Your Business Model

There is a subtle but important distinction between business model, strategy, and tactics. They're related, and they all dynamically interact and affect each other, but the business model is best understood as the means you use to affect your strategy, as the whole integrated approach to carry it out.

For example, in the early days of the internet, many upstart dot-coms relied on "first-mover-advantage" and reaching a critical mass of followers before later figuring out how to "monetize" what they were doing later. (Of course, some of these pioneering companies were more successful than others.) The common *strategy* for early dotcoms was to develop back-end sales, repurchases, and advertising dollars. An example of *tactics* was to underprice products to entice customers excited about and new to the prospect of online shopping, and then build a more profitable relationship from there.

Kevin Systrom and Mike Kreiger, the founders of a check-in site called Bourbn, reimagined their business when it became clear that it was too similar to competitor FourSquare. They took a data-based approach and found that there were three features of their app that users liked the most, and they chose to focus on just one of them, a feature that allowed users to share photos. They renamed the app Instagram (a portmanteau of "instant camera", "telegram" and created an app that grew to be purchased by Facebook for $1 billion and that now boasts over 1 billion users.

If your business model does not allow any room for back-end sales, you're missing an opportunity for growth. "Marginal net worth" is the term we use to quantify a customer's lifetime value after accounting for the costs of luring in that customer initially. Just by adding one more step for each customer—one more back-end, transaction addition, upsell, cross-sell, one little add-on to the package—you can explode your profits.

If you have a seasonal product you sell once every June, and you figure out how to entice people to buy it also in March and September, you've tripled your profits. If your average customer makes a purchase twice a year but you elevate that to five times, you're on the way to exponential growth. These are incremental advances which, *when multiplied over time, frequency, volume, number of customers*, and so forth, yield exponential results (the 10% x 10% x 10% principle with which you are now familiar). And it starts by selecting a business model that allows for such changes.

A business model that is 1) more effective on the acquisition side while 2) encouraging residual income or solidifying a long-term relationship on the client side is optimal.

5. Change (Leverage) Your Relationships

Relationships are often the gold mine that business owners don't know they are sitting on top of. A company that is resource-poor but relationship-rich is still primed for growth. Over the years we've worked with struggling, cash-strapped firms whose owners fretted that they had little wiggle room and were basically out of options. But relationships allow you to leverage your and your collaborators' labor, time, capital, and other precious resources together, thus complementing each other's strengths and mitigating each other's weaknesses.

Consider also the relationship you have with existing customers, even those who have fallen by the wayside and no longer purchase from you regularly. It may not be "active," but as long as you left that relationship intact, they are still a source of referrals, of personnel (perhaps you're in the market for a new sales rep and they know of an ideal candidate), or of opportunities (for example, *their* contacts are looking for distribution channels for a product that you sell on a wholesale basis).

Relationships really are a powerful source of leverage that tend to be hidden in plain sight. They're so important beyond exponential growth that we dedicate a whole chapter, Chapter 11, to leveraging your relational capital.

6. Change Your Distribution Channels

Distribution channels are another hugely underutilized asset. The sky is the limit. You can create deals with supplier networks. You can utilize your clients' clients as a distribution channel. You can sell other people's products. There are many areas of distribution within reach that you probably aren't even aware of.

Let's say you're selling a high-end brand of dog food which you distribute through a hundred retailers on the West Coast. You only manufacture this one product, but you have relationships (see #5) with other manufacturers of pet supplies that are in need of distributors. So, because you have great rapport with the buyers at these one hundred retailers, and you're connected with manufacturers in need of a retail outlet, you can leverage your privileged position as middle-man and organize a deal in which you secure the rights to sell other manufacturers' products at the retailers you have been doing business with.

It sounds too good to be true, but if you take advantage of such situations, you can make more money selling other companies' products than your own. We know, since we've helped countless businesses do it themselves.

Jay recalls one such deal. He was consulting with a struggling company that produced athletic apparel. They were pulling in about $500,000 in profit annually, but sales had slowed down. They needed a breakthrough idea, something to resuscitate their flagging numbers. When Jay took a good look at their business, he saw their most valuable asset was not its limited line of sportswear but the fact that they had accounts with five thousand retailers nationwide, including big-name companies like Nordstrom's, Target, and Kohl's.

Jay advised them that instead of trying to squeeze water from a stone by focusing on their own poorly selling clothing line, they would be better served by securing the rights to sell *other* companies' athletic apparel. Those companies would receive a royalty, and Jay's client would leverage their vast distribution network and solid working relationships with the retailers, and together they'd make a fortune. The struggling company boosted their profit by about 10x as a result, and they didn't even have to increase sales of their own product to achieve it.

7. Find New Markets for Your Products and Services

This driver complements #6. Are there other channels, markets, niches, etc. where your products or services would sell? Or can you package your products and services with others to reach new or untapped customer bases? Could you tweak, modify, or extend your current offerings to synthesize "new" products? Just by adding one or two or five different components you can create an entirely new product and penetrate new market niches.

The best medium for market research is right in front of you: your own customers. Are they clamoring for a different version of a product/service you offer that you don't yet carry (or perhaps no one carries)? Listen to them and deliver what they're asking for.

Don't be afraid to think big. Lego has always been a children's toy brand, but realized that the product was also good for stressed out adults who want to unwind. They've gradually introduced more and more adult sets featuring famous buildings like the Eiffel tower, or iconic movie or TV sets like the $800 Millennium Falcon. And guess what? Adults are buying them.

8. Change Your Processes, Procedures, and Systems

Recall our earlier discussion of Deming, a visionary who revolutionized the Japanese automobile industry by making a science of process improvement. The totality of business activity in a firm is constituted by a series of discrete processes—dozens, hundreds, even thousands in a complex organization. If you can make incremental changes to a large number of processes, those changes compound in exponential fashion. Doing a sales call, tallying inventory, manufacturing parts, resolving customer complaints, taking orders—virtually any process is ripe for improvement.

The key to process improvement, as with so many things, is testing, monitoring, measurement, and analysis. Granularly (at a very fine and detailed level) examine what works well and what doesn't. Amplify the former and minimize or cut out the latter.

Process improvement provides a parallel opportunity for leverage, in addition to its bottom-line boost for your own business: you can sell or teach your methodology to larger firms that will pay vast sums of money to adapt it to their own production.

Jay recalls how one client's simple process improvement yielded million-dollar results. George Culp, part-owner of the H.W. Culp Lumber Company, attended one of Jay's weeklong training seminars, during which he learned about the value of a special kind of relationship: licensing.

George had developed an innovative kiln-drying technique for his lumber; he was a trusted source for his clients; and he was truly preeminent in his field. However, lumber is so heavy that even if George wanted to give his product away free to somebody three thousand miles away, the cost of shipping was prohibitively expensive. That put a cap on his growth because he was limited to selling it locally.

However, instead of making the lumber himself, George partnered with lumber yards as he could, teaching and selling licenses for his proprietary kiln-drying methods which pulled in $2 million a year.

Our careers abound with such examples, like the car wash owner who developed a technique to get people to buy a hot wax upgrade and trained two thousand other car wash owners to do the same, or the dry cleaner whose killer ads were licensed to five thousand competitors. It may seem in this case like these entrepreneurs were giving away something that gave them a competitive advantage, but that is myopic, incremental (not hyper-exponential) thinking. Savvy business strategists recognize the leverage opportunities that lie hidden beyond the most obvious application.

9. Change Your Ideology

Success in business—impressive, chart-busting, beyond-exponential success—is about more than dollars and cents, more, in fact, than the bottom line. You must be animated by a greater purpose, driven by a quest to build something long-lasting or create something grand or make a large number of people's lives better. Einstein, surely, was motivated not by the desire for prestigious physics prizes or the adulation of his peers (and certainly not a salary), but by a thirst for knowledge and a desire to unlock the cosmic mysteries of the universe, and thus bring all of humanity closer to greatness.

If your ideology is "I like what I like" or "My business is just my job" or "I don't trust others, everyone else is out to get me," you will likely lack the motivation to roam outside your comfort zone, talk to others, learn new things, and embrace novel philosophies—all the things essential for breaking out of your rigid, ossified mold. Beliefs drive behaviors, and behaviors drive results!

Testing, 1, 2, 3!

Testing is one of the most overlooked powers at your disposal. Taking action and implementing new tactics is good, but most people stumble when they act without any self-evaluation, any analysis. Running out and trying things without scrutinizing their impact is self-defeating.

Testing—trying things different ways and then measuring their impact—is how you winnow down the panoply of strategies to what works best. We've tested headline changes in ads and enjoyed 500% (not a typo!) increases in results. We've tested 33 different ways to greet customers as they enter a store to find the most effective approach—and when we found the right greeting sales skyrocketed (and "Just looking around" plummeted).

We've A/B tested pairs of mailings. We've tested different bonuses. We've tested different methods of risk-reversal. We've helped litigators test different ways of presenting to juries. *Any business in any industry is ripe for testing.* How else can you compare X with Y and see what works better? The most (seemingly) inconsequential tweaks can produce massive results. Each variable tested creates an improvement in results. Taken together, the lessons learned from a series of tests are accretive—you get benefit on top of benefit on top of benefit, and it all flows to the bottom line. That's the enormous power of testing. That upside variation that makes being in business very exciting, wouldn't you agree?

Don't get overwhelmed. Use a simple A/B test: two variables of the same thing. For example, you supply two different ads, "A" and "B," which are the same size. The ads are circulated amongst audiences of comparable demographics, and because the ads take up the same position in the newspaper and are read by similar audiences, you can fairly compare their results. A/B splits allow you to save money on losing ads and on pre-testing in inexpensive, smaller-circulation, regional editions.

Here's another example: the clothing site *Hanna Andersson* was combining a toddler line of clothing with a children's line for the first time. Their default images for their products were of children's sizes, but the company thought they might get better conversions if the images on the site matched the product purchased—toddler size images for toddler clothing purchased, and children's size images for children's clothing purchased.

They hired an A/B testing agency to test both images to see which converted better. They found that the images which reflected size led to a 22% increase in purchase rates on those items. Do they know that this is the way to go from now on? They do. But only because they bothered to test it.

Every transaction, buyer, lead, and client is worth a different amount. Until you quantify the differential, you're either overpaying or undervaluing.

Even if something has appeared to work for you for years, there's no reason why you shouldn't test it. As we've already stressed in this book, most businesspeople are not operating anywhere near their potential. Testing is the only way to make sure that your existing practices are optimized.

CHAPTER 9 - PRESSURE MAKES DIAMONDS

Even if you've got an I.Q. of 160, you can't predict the future. Nor will you have the aptitude for knowing intuitively what will work better than what you're doing now. That's where testing comes in. So test, re-test, and keep testing. The sure-fire way to look like a genius every time is to test. The marketplace will always reveal to you the optimal way to go. We still have to test our assumptions because different techniques work differently in different markets, and the only way to be sure is by applying tests.

You can never establish in advance what will be in demand in your market or what the best pricing, advertising, or packaging will be, so you must ascertain the answers to these things by going to your clients and prospects and seeing what they think and how they vote—with their credit cards.

You can have a significant increase in inquiries, clients, and sales (without increasing your expenditures) by testing copy, different ways to say the same thing, the appeal of one magazine compared to another, one mailing list against another, one radio time slot against another, one offer against another, one guarantee against another, one sales presentation against another, one direct-mail package against an-other...the list is endless. Sales thrusts, prices, ad concepts, headlines, commercials, follow-ups, and on and on. Keep experimenting to find new controls. A small shift can produce big results. That is the nature of profit-exploding beyond exponential growth.

If you're testing different ads or sales pitches, one way to "test small" is to rent a list of the subscribers to your target publication. Find a list of 5,000 to 25,000 people that imitates your target audience and rent part of it. Ask the list manager to split the names in half for you and send your "A" ad to half of the list and your "B" ad to the other half. Then, record the results and compare them.

If you're not testing now, it's likely that you are relying on the wrong approaches to pretty much everything that you're doing, from the way your salespeople greet people in your stores to the ads you're running, from the bonuses you offer to the method of risk-reversal you offer, and, because of all this, your business is underperforming.

We advise that you test only one variable at a time. This is the scientific principle of control, which means isolating the variable so you are sure of the source of different results.

Moreover, it is *essential* to keep track of your responses and their results, as well as every other bit of necessary marketing information, with painstaking fastidiousness. You must be able to attribute each response to the appropriate variable or experiential approach you're testing, and you can accomplish this by employing various methods. You can use a differently coded coupon for each version of your ad, tell respondents to give a specific department number when they contact you (you don't actually need to have the departments), ask respondents to tell you how they heard about you in order to receive a discount or bonus, include a code on the mailing label returned with the order that will distinguish different versions of the ad, have different phone numbers that people can call for each offer, or make different package tests and keep track of which bonuses or prices prospects ask for.

Once your testing methods become more refined, you want to take quality of response into account, not just quantity. Testing every aspect of your proposal is vital. For instance, if you create an ad or sales approach that generates double the amount of starter clients as another, don't automatically toss the other ad. Many lead-producing or prospect-generating marketers do not consider convertibility in their overall marketing analysis, but later on, you may realize that the ad you chose not to run drew in more profitable clients who repeated buying 10 times longer than the better pulling ad. That is why you must test and continuously keep track of your data, such as which ad, sales process, or approach by a salesperson brought in the sale, how many orders each of those processes generates, how much money they stimulate or lose, how much the average order is worth, how much upfront profit or yield was generated, how much a client or order costs, and how much or how many times the client reorders.

With this information, you'll be able to determine the number of prospects who convert into buyers, the average dollar a first-time client is worth, how many times a year a client repurchases, and how much each purchase is worth in gross and net dollars.

PEQ Optimization

PEQ stands for Performance Enhancement Quotient. It's a methodology for optimally leveraging the top drivers of your success. Every business operates with a finite number of "drivers," the primary activities that generate revenue. An organization's fate rests on how effectively or in-effectively they can maximize their total performance in each driver.

This is elementary enough, but when it's time to wade into the tactical details, business owners get lost in the morass of options and paths to take. Do I invest in sales or marketing? (This is actually a false dichotomy, but that's another story). Which driver do I optimize first? How do I deal with the multitude of moving parts in an organization such that one driver impacts another?

The PEQ process is a system for dramatically ramping up performance, capabilities, and results throughout a company's en-tire selling system, without a corresponding increase in effort or resource expenditures.

One of the foundational concepts of PEQ is one you are familiar with by now: every company possesses underperforming assets, overlooked opportunities, underutilized activities, underrecognized relationships, underperforming distribution channels, and capital and human capital that can be more productively and profitably deployed—each of them is a gold mine hidden in plain sight.

How does one cut through the underbrush that blocks the entrance to this untapped gold mine? By identifying all the strategically critical activities *and*, in particular, the people performing those activities. Assess the performance capability of each person in those areas.

The list of activities may be bountiful—30 to 90 impact points or performance levers even for a small and relatively uncomplex organization. Look for themes in that list. Normally, within each "macro activity" are between two and ten critical sequential processes that need to happen together strategically for maximum results to occur.

Think of each process as a lever. It can be of high pitched, low pitched, or no pitched advantage. The steepness and angularity of the pitch determines its bottom-line impact.

Any revenue-generating process that's allowed to function at suboptimal performance levels causes the entire selling system to underperform. Just as outperformance compounds, yielding exponential impact, substandard performance can also compound, reducing efficiency and productivity to the lowest common denominator. A chain is only as strong as the weakest link.

The PEQ is fundamentally about the intersection of human capital with processes. If there are 30 people performing the same sales activity, the variation in their respective efficacy will be significant, upwards of 2000% or beyond. This is another way of applying the Pareto principle: your top performers will be few in number but end up driving the bulk of your profit-generating activity. Their underperform-ing counterparts will, conversely, account for a disproportionate drag. Optimizing in light of the realities of Pareto asymmetry requires that you concentrate your resources on the 20% of inputs (top performing employees, in this case) who generate 80% of output, while cutting loose the 80% inputs that yield a paltry 20% output.

For instance, imagine you employ 40 account executives. Ac-cording to the 80/20 rule, it wouldn't be surprising that eight of these 40 account for 80% or more of your active, large direct accounts. Give those eight the resources they need to thrive and to multiply those gains—in-cluding training others to work as adroitly as they do—and cut loose or internally rotate the other 32 where their skills and potential are more effectively leveraged.

We are practitioners of high-level geometric process improve-ment, which we perfected from our work with W. Edward Deming's organization. We discussed Deming a few times already. Deming was a visionary in the way he—much like Einstein, really—took a complex concept and broke it down in a simple reconceptualization that was, despite its simplicity, revolutionary. (We reference Einstein here be-cause what is so elegantly simple, and at the same time so stagger-ingly complex, not to mention ground-breaking, as "$E=mc^2$," the famous relativity formula?)

Each top performer's methods and mindsets can be measured, quantified, codified, and taught to everyone else doing that process (not to mention new recruits who will further drive exponential growth when they come on board).

Remember that one of the recurring themes of our strategy for hyper-exponential growth is stacking improvement upon improve-ment upon improvement such that they compound. A 10% boost is nice, but 10% x 10% x 10% is a 1000% increase. Therein lies the simple mathematical wizardry of parabolic growth. In our work, there are a dizzying array of 10% to 100%—or even 500%—improvements that are possible. So, buckle up!

Therefore, in keeping with the PEQ, when you combine performance enhancement (P.E.) and process improvement (P.I.), not only do you reap the rewards of each, but they *compound* each other to produce staggeringly large gains that each could not deliver on its own. To understand how this might look in practice, imagine that a team of salespeople boost their respective output by 3, 5, 10, or 20% per process activity. That isn't much on its face, but consider that these percentage gains are happening across 30-40 segments. That's geometric progress. 3% x 5% x 8% x 10% x 5% x 2% x 10% equals exponential gains.

Therein lies the relevance of testing, which we just discussed. You have to iterate and measure to dig deep and find out what is working and what isn't. Get very granular—that's something Deming was an expert at, identifying not just the processes but the processes within the processes within the processes. You can likely identify 30 high upside leverage improvement processes or factors that each and every sales rep (or assembly worker, or customer service agent, or other team member) is transacting and then determine who excels in what, and what factors that success can be attributed to. Then optimize by "universalizing" their methods throughout the organization.

Sometimes this analysis is quantitative (comparing sales figures across months, quarters, years, etc.); other times it's qualitative (open-ended interviews); or often, a combination of both. We're proponents of open, continuous Socratic interviews of the 20% of top performers in each process category in front of all the rest of the sales reps. It is painstaking, but if you can invest eight hours of this, depending on the size of your team, you'll be able to "power through" the key 25-30 high impact points or processes. Recording and transcribing the interviews makes the data even more robust and primed for analysis, and also constitutes a valuable resource for training and development. Not only employees who were present during the interviews can benefit, but future team members can also consult these reports. This in and of itself is an excellent example of how minimal input of time/labor can be harvested over and over at scale, for years to come.

More recently, Jay has put forth another concept he calls "revenue system optimization" or RSO, which takes up to 61 impact leverage points in a company's revenue system and systematically questions how each of them is conducted, looking for incremental improvements in each one. The synthesis of multiple incremental improvements compounds and combines to give you *geometric improvements* in the system as a whole, thus exploding profits to unimaginable heights. For the full list of 61 RSO items, visit the resources page for this book at BusinessWealthWithoutRisk.com/access.

In summary, break down your operations into the top 30 to 40 revenue-generating processes in your selling systems. Determine who are the four or five best performers in each category. Reverse-engineer what it is that makes them so good at those tasks, and then translate that insight into systematic, actionable behaviors that their colleagues can adapt as well. The gains will multiply across each performer operating in each process and in no time, you'll see your bottom line grow exponentially. Five employees and 30 processes equal 150 success-boosting applications. It's not magic. It's just math.

Power Performance: How to Plug Into an Unlimited Source of High Performance Growth Opportunity

Imagine that you could tap into millions or even hundreds of millions of dollars of other companies' access to the same buyer prospects you want to sell. Their credibility becomes yours. Their hard won and massive investment and effort in gaining the trust of the marketplace becomes *your* trust and credibility with their clients, subscribers, members, and users.

Sounds good? It's actually great. Power Partnering allows your company to use the endorsement, sales force, email access, distributors, buyer base, or franchisees of another company and leverage them for your products or services. You don't invest or risk anything until highly profitable sales are generated. Then you only pay out to the company with whom you partnered a share of all that new-found, heretofore unavailable sales.

Think it's hard to do well? An interesting data point is that nearly 40% of revenues of Fortune 1000 companies have come from partners. But you don't have to be a Fortune 1000 company to benefit. Jay took a brokerage company from $300,000 in profits to $500 million in under two years. How? Just by structuring endorsement deals for that brokerage company with a group of investment newsletters who recommended the firm to their subscribers. Jay generated a further $250 million in combined sales, products, and services in less than three years by partnering with Tony Robbins as well as *Success* and *Entrepreneur* Magazines. All partnered with Jay to promote Jay's offerings to their audiences in exchange for a share of the revenues those efforts generated.

Colonial Penn Insurance created a huge increase in insurance sales when they partnered with the AARP. Similarly, Carnival Cruise

Lines generated hundreds of millions of dollars of cruise sales when they partnered with large numbers of radio and TV stations. Grocery stores partner with banks. Truck stops partner with fast food brands. Disney partners with McDonald's. Any size, type, or scope of business can usually find all sorts of other companies who have the same profile buyer that the original business wants to reach. Then it's just working out the revenue or profit sharing deal...and you're off to the races (and the bank!).

You can also make your product or service an add-on that other companies can combine with their basic products or services. Or they can make your offering an entry-level product or service that feeds more profitable sales. Once again, everybody wins.

It works the opposite way, too. You can go to any companies who sell complementary products or services and structure profit-sharing deals to offer their products or services to your buyers, *even to your unsold prospects*. The possibilities are boundless. It's all about the mindset, the Mind-stein way of looking at profit opportunities that none of your competitors even consider (or understand!).

Now, let's look at the flipside—what we call the "unlimited business checkbook." This is possibly the most liberating concept of all of the ideas we will discuss in this section. Why? Because by understanding and accessing this concept, your newly acquired business never needs to be resource-impaired or limited in any way, ever again. Here's the secret: no matter the resource you need, be it sales, operations, technology, facilities, or expertise, someone else already possesses that resource...and in excess capacity. Just figure out who they are and what it takes to get them to make that excess capacity resource available to you, always on a result-achieved basis.

Many times, we collaborate with other companies who provide accounts receivable, payroll, customer service, or other needs. Think about Amazon, which created cloud storage for itself and then turned that into a huge business to serve other companies. How many ways will you devise to mine the "unlimited checkbook?"

Now that you have a context for clear understanding of what's possible, let's explore a truly delightful and fascinating topic, which we call Relational Capital.

For more case studies, examples, worksheets, checklists, forms, scripts, and other resources, including quite a few that we simply could not fit in the book itself, we created a resources collection and all of these resources are available and waiting for you at BusinessWealthWithoutRisk.com/access. Visit the site now and enjoy a huge collection of resources at absolutely no money out of pocket for you!

BusinessWealthWithoutRisk.com/access

Riskless Recap

After turning up the pressure into the drivers of exponential growth, we ventured through the avenues that businesses can explore to achieve unimaginable growth. Hopefully, this has helped clarify your path.

As we journey ahead, we'll navigate the often-overlooked realm of "Relational Capital." Our exploration will underscore the potency of other businesses' resources—a bounty that often lies untapped yet brimming with potential. Instead of striving to construct everything you need from scratch, you'll learn to spot opportunities in the richness that other businesses have already cultivated.

You're also about to learn perhaps the entrepreneur's most underestimated shortcut—the potential of partnership and collaboration. This will show you how to double your business revenues by harnessing the "relational capital" accumulated by people, influencers, media, indirect competitors, and complementary competitors.

And what's even more enticing?

The upcoming chapter will introduce you to joint ventures, strategic alliances, and other forms of collaboration that can be set up and utilized with zero upfront cost. This is where we flip the traditional investment concept on its head and charge ahead, ready to turbocharge your business. So let's journey forth and unlock the immense potential that lies in the realm of relational capital!

RELATIONAL CAPITAL

Often, your most underutilized asset is not, in fact, "yours" at all. Rather, it is the bounty of resources that other businesses possess which sit idle. You have a lack, they have an abundance—like a negative and positive charge, these conditions attract each other.

Instead of trying to build what you need from scratch, other businesses have already painstakingly cultivated what you need, and if you approach them with a mutually beneficial offer of a partnership or collaboration, then they will be more than willing to share in that bounty with you. It's the entrepreneur's most overlooked shortcut. We have been able to double business revenues again and again by finding these unseen opportunities. People, influencers, media, indirect competitors, complementary competitors who have built up the goodwill and trust and connections provide the "relational capital" needed to turbocharge your business.

CHAPTER 10 - PRESSURE MAKES DIAMONDS

What is especially powerful about joint ventures, strategic alliances, and other forms of cross-collaboration is that you can set them up and harness other business' resources with *zero upfront cost*.

Technology companies are particularly fertile ground for partnerships. Digital technology by nature is uniquely scalable, and subscription services enjoy the benefit of a high customer lifetime value, since often, they sustain client relationships for years and years. This also presents an opportunity on the front-end to acquire the buyer through a strategic relationship with a prospective partner offering complementary services. Strategic alignment can be profitable for both parties.

Consider one of Apple's biggest moves. Though we tend to forget this today, in the '90s, the company was on the brink of collapse. Apple had gone through years of financial loss, and Steve Jobs was brought back on board to revive it.

One of the first major catalysts of Apple's comeback was not a revolutionary product, but a revolutionary partnership—with Microsoft. The two companies set up a five-year contract promising an updated Mac version of Microsoft Office and a $150 million Microsoft investment in Apple.

Though it seemed like Apple drew outsized benefits from the partnership, in truth, both companies benefited. Apple introduced Internet Explorer, Microsoft's browser, to Mac and dropped a long-running lawsuit against Microsoft for allegedly copying Mac's look and feel. Microsoft's move also made it appear less monopolistic during a period when antitrust authorities were turning their eye on it.

Microsoft had resources that Apple needed. At the same time, by laying down the mantle of competition and choosing to collaborate, both companies became stronger. So we see how leveraging relational capital allows businesses to dramatically expand not just in terms of the bottom line, but multidimensionally: by penetrating new markets, acquiring news clients, and establishing durable networks of suppliers, buyers, and distributors.

You can utilize your contacts to mine third party opportunities (clients' clients, referrals, etc.). Relational capital means you're not just acting as a "business owner" per se, with a singular focus on what happens within the four walls of your own company, but as a relationship *matchmaker, dealmaker, finder, and catalyst.* It's a much more dynamic, flexible, all-encompassing conception of what entrepreneurship is, and it will deliver tremendous results.

We've identified nine benefits of tapping relationships, as follows:

1. Economies of scale. However thriving, or sizable, or prestigious your company may be, you're still just a drop in the vast economic ocean (there are tens of *millions* of businesses operating in the United States alone). Relational capital allows you to achieve advantages of scale, scope, or speed much greater than your own self-contained resources would ordinarily allow, by taking advantage of other people's infrastructure, their influence, their reach, and their resources.

2. Increase market penetration, locally, regionally, nationally, or in other niches.

3. You can enhance your competitiveness in local, national, and international markets because you've associated with a dominant force: somebody who's already built a market.

4. You can enhance product development by capitalizing on other people's research.

5. You can develop new business opportunities through products and services.

6. You can create new businesses at will by understanding that you're not limited to just your own company's product (recall the example of the sportswear company).

7. You can leverage (or even gain control of) tangible and intangible assets that organizations don't even know they possess.

8. You can reduce costs (and thus increase profits) by establishing strategic alliances and joint ventures.

9. You can afford to do things you otherwise wouldn't be able to, since in a partnership or joint venture, you pool risk and resources—for example, paying other organizations only in direct proportion to the revenue that comes in. So now you've reduced your risk while creating a new stream of income.

Every company has unused relational capital they can deploy to gain lucrative access to the all-important asset of OP___, or "other people's _____": OPM (money), OPT (time), OPW (work), OPE (experiences), OPI (ideas), OPD (distribution), and OPC (customers). One business's trash could be your "treasure."

No business should ever feel stymied by their lack of resources because someone else out there has the resources they covet. All they have to do is establish a collaborative relationship with their more resource-laden peers in a way that lets the smaller business share in the abundance.

But in a hyper-competitive market, you might ask, why would any business share its resources? "Collaboration" is the key word. The kinds of relationships that grow the bottom line are not zero-sum (my loss is your gain) or transactional (I sell, you buy), but collaborative, strategic, and ultimately exponential: yours times mine equals a value much greater than each of us could produce on our own.

Jay used to conduct extensive trainings in China for the country's top execs and entrepreneurs. During his first visit, a young man approached the mic. He seemed emotional, on the verge of tears even. Through a translator, he asked, "What do you do if your company is too small and the banks all refuse to lend you capital? I'm a local motorcycle manufacturer. If I could secure a loan, I could expand all over Asia, open new factories, recruit salespeople, set up a retail operation, all kinds of things. But I can't."

"What's the problem?" Jay said.

"I just told you. I don't have the money. No one will lend it to me!" the motorcycle man said.

"You don't *need* the money!" Jay said. "All you have to do is figure out that *your problem is the solution to someone else's bigger problem.*"

Talk to other business owners around Asia, Jay counseled. Not direct competitors but complementary companies in the same or a similar field. Create a mutually beneficial partnership with manufacturers, distributors, retailers, etc.

A year later Jay returned to China to give another presentation. Guess who shows up again? The same young entrepreneur. This time he walked up to the mic, smiling like the Cheshire cat and said, "Taking your advice, I traveled around the region talking with other business owners. In Malaysia, I reached out to Malaysia's largest lawnmower manufacturer, whose factory was operating at reduced capacity. It was underutilized. We struck a deal: I would supply the tools and dies, and he would provide the factory workers, salespeople, offices, and a network of thousands of dealers. In the last year we've made ten million dollars."

Your abundance is someone else's lack. And your lack is someone else's unproductive factory and team just waiting to be put to work in a collaboration that enables both parties to achieve tremendous growth instead of waiting around helplessly for some tight-fisted loan officer to extend the credit *you don't actually need.*

Partner or Perish

The myth of the solitary entrepreneur who needs nothing but his own bootstraps and a little bit of cash obscures the fact that the wealthiest entrepreneurs leverage the value of strategic alliances and partnerships. Doing everything on your own is a path to linear growth. Leveraging relational capital is how you achieve growth that is beyond exponential. If it works "profit wonders" for them and their businesses, there's no reason why it shouldn't create wonderful results for you, too.

Strategic alliances, joint ventures, licensing deals, and other types of partnerships lie where more short-sighted business leaders fail to look. But once you learn where to look, you'll see them everywhere.

Everyone is a possible joint venture, strategic alliance, or profit partner. You will be amazed at how many people, who in the brick-and-mortar world would ordinarily be considered our cutthroat competitors, are some of our best partners, because we know that working together, we can offer added value. Mathematically speaking, your company and my company are not "2X," they're "X^2." The profit is much greater than the sum of its parts. Exponential, in a literal numerical sense.

This process only takes two steps:

Step One: Ask yourself, "Who already has a strong relationship with the people I am looking to sell my (noncompetitive but related) product or service to?"

Step Two: Once you've got names on paper, contact those businesses and ask them masterfully to introduce and strongly recommend your product or service to their audience. Supply them with plenty of compelling language about what you sell along with some testimonials attesting to its high quality and demonstrating the specific value or benefit the buyers will enjoy.

There are hundreds of OBs—Other Businesses'—resources. You want access to other companies' sales teams, as well as their capital, brand, and distribution channels. Specifically, this includes help with manufacturing, sales, delivery, offices, commercial facilities, property, technology, procedures, and intellectual capital. You can license other companies' marketing, sales abilities, or management skills, as well as cash-flow management. Whatever your business needs to grow and prosper—equipment, employees, space, distribution, marketing, retail locations, manufacturing, or influence—can be found in other businesses, and you can surely create a partnering deal to get use of it.

How?

Think of it as a system of balance. No one in business has all the answers: there's always going to be another company out there with a problem that's polar opposite to yours. You bring strength to an area where they are weak, or maybe you have an efficient way to repurpose and reorganize an underperforming effort. In short, you can be the unexpected solution to someone else's problem, paying them a share of the revenue or savings the collaboration generates.

Here's another example:

> We all know that the cost of acquiring a client or a prospect can be enormous. Most businesspeople don't realize it, but they are in the client-and-prospect-generating business—that's the basic goal of all marketing.
>
> But what if you could eliminate a lot of the risk, expense, time, and inefficiency of "prospecting," and only spend your time and money on people who are ready to buy? Why spend all your energy, expense, and credibility-building activity to attract new clients from the outside market (who don't yet know or trust you) when there is a much easier and less expensive way already built in?
>
> You can get other people (companies, publications, and organizations) to get new clients for you, and they can do it faster, more efficiently, and for a fraction of the cost you'd spend doing it yourself. They may recommend or endorse your offering to their audience, who already respects and trusts them, which creates instant credibility for what you provide.

Endorse Other People's Products and Have Others Endorse Yours

You can increase the transaction frequency, increasing the number of times people buy, by endorsing other people's products to your list. It works like this: Company A agrees to let Company B deliver a sales message to people who are Company A's clients. Company A encourages their clients to purchase from Company B by providing an endorsement.

If you are Company A in this scenario, you would first do your due diligence to protect your clients. Don't abuse your customers' trust in exchange for a fast buck. Make sure you get more for your customer than they can anyplace else. You can do that because you are delivering the market on a platter to the company you endorse.

Jay recalls an instant endorsement deal with some colleagues in Australia, boosting income from $150,000 to a million in a year. Jay split about $400,000 in windfall profit and then showed them a way in which they could endorse 12 other people and not split the profit—just pay them a nominal amount for their product. The Australian colleagues made another million dollars profit for that. They made basically 4x as much money from what's called their "back-end endorsements" than they made from their front-line mainstream business.

One of Jay's more interesting ventures was a service that helped Japanese women immigrating to Canada. The genesis of the business was purely by endorsement from a person who had seen Jay doing some consulting. Within one week, he invited Jay to Japan.

Jay continued providing consulting services to the man, who happened to be the chairman of a 15,000-student private business school in Japan. That relationship led to introductions with two other friends who were also the chairmen of large business schools.

These individuals partnered with Jay and promoted Jay's academy on his behalf—effectively endorsing the program, thanks in large part to Jay's sterling reputation. It took very little active work on Jay's part—rather, he *levered* key relationships with people thousands of miles away.

Strategic Alliance Template: Endorsements

If you want to endorse other companies' products, you must communicate to your clientele why those products can benefit them. Here's a letter you can modify for any offering. You could say something like this: 'I've never done this before, and I'll probably never do it again, but there's somebody that I have met (or there's a company I have been introduced to) that has a product or service that is important, valuable, worthwhile, right, applicable, appropriate seemingly for you. I would be remiss if I didn't at least introduce you to them, negotiate for you a preferential price, and engineer a way you could try it out in your business or home without any risk or obligation."

That letter is easily adaptable to your particular situation.

The power of endorsement is so strong it may be the most overlooked tool in anyone's kit. Make a list of the five most logical products or services which you are in an excellent position to introduce to your customers, either through recommendation or endorsement or through strategic alliance or private label. Then search online which companies offer it. Every name on that list could be worth more on the back-end than the front.

Case Study: A Chiropractor Enters the Mulch Business

A chiropractor lived near a large national forest. Every year, the forest had to pay people to haul away the pine needles that fell from the trees. The chiropractor figured out that those pine needles, once turned into mulch, created a great fertilizer. It was an unacknowledged value, merely tree trash—but the chiropractor saw a grand opportunity.

First, he formed a joint venture with a trucking firm. He sought out a business that had delivery routes along the forest lines, specifically, with trucks coming back empty at the end of the day. A deal was made so that the truckers would take pine needles and deliver them to him for no fee, just a percentage of the revenue he would later get. Then he found an unoccupied used car lot where the trucks could drop off the pine needles. He made an agreement with the lot to let him access their space for free up front, later receiving a share of the revenue he would realize. Next, he went to the National Park Service, and underbid the company currently hauling and disposing of pine needles by 50%. In his first year selling pine-needle mulch, he made $300,000. How much money did he spend out of pocket? Not a cent.

Case Study: Cookie Empire

Mary, a brilliant advertising exec in Los Angeles, had made tons of money for her clients. One day she decided she wanted to go into business for herself. Her chosen product? Cookies. Specifically, chocolate chip macadamia nut cookies. Her original recipe was inspired in part by work she had done for King's Hawaiian Bread, which started as a small corner bakery on Oahu and, thanks to Mary's expertise, grew to a nationally recognized brand sold in supermarkets all over the country. On her many trips to Hawaii to service that client, she fell in love with macadamia nuts. When she came home and threw some nuts in with her cookie dough, everyone loved the taste. A new business idea was born.

But Mary had no suppliers, no distributors, no brand. What she did have was relational capital.

She took a big batch of these cookies back to the folks at King's Hawaiian, who were impressed by their taste and texture. She said, "I'd like to go into the cookie business. I'm an unknown cookie person. And getting people to sell my cookies in their grocery stores is going to be hard. So, I don't want to try to set up my own brand from scratch. I want to bring it out under YOUR brand name. I want to call these King's Hawaiian Macadamia Nut Chocolate Chip Cookies. And I want to put them right next to your bread racks and call them King's Hawaiian. You don't put up a dime. I'll put up all the money. All I want is a license allowing me to use your name and brand on my product."

She leveraged her marketing chops to show the King's people the value proposition of the offer: all they had to do was sit back and collect their royalty money from her.

They loved it.

Then, armed with that licensing agreement, she went back to California. But she now had a problem—she didn't have anyone to bake the cookies. So she went out to the suppliers of all the ingredients that she needed, showed them her licensing agreement with the King's Hawaiian company, and let them taste the cookie. So she persuaded all of her suppliers to agree that they'd sell her the ingredients and wait thirty days after she ships the cookies to the store to get paid their money. Now she had her ingredients, again without putting up a dime. She did the same thing with everything else she needed. Packaging, shipping, you name it—she deferred payment on everyone.

With all these deals in place, she was able to broker deals with a bakery to produce the product. She would put the orders through the bakery, with a concession in place that if her products hit 30% of the business volume in that bakery's sales, she wanted to *own* 10% of the bakery. When she hit 40%, she wanted to own 20%. When she hit 60%, she wanted to own 30% of the bakery.

Now why was this "no cash down," buy-in proposition attractive to those particular bakers? If you're a baker and you don't have a proprietary product, you're at the whim of the marketplace. It's a very unstable business—unless you've got a proprietary product.

So here was a proprietary product that she was willing to bring in and keep there. Then if it was successful—and ONLY if it was successful—she'd get a piece of ownership in the bakery. But, keep in mind, that even after she got her share of that bakery ownership, the remaining equity of the original bakery owner would produce much more profit than that owner would have earned had he not agreed to sell Mary's cookies. So, it was an attractive offer for the owner too.

She started marketing, shipping, and distributing their great cookies to all the same grocery chains who were selling King's Hawaiian Bread. The sales took off, defying even her rosy expectations. She reached her benchmark quotas with the bakery and thus ended up majority owner for absolutely nothing, plus was the owner of a thriving cookie business established with relational capital.

Case Study: Yoga Partnership

A yoga studio owner named Annie partnered with retailers in her neighborhood. She gave them valuable trial membership certificates to her studio, which they then gave away to clients who made purchases at their stores. Typically, these kinds of certificates are for one free lesson, but Annie gave away certificates for six months of lessons, worth $500.

The certificates had a very high perceived value, so the retailers were thrilled. They could say to clients, "I'll give you a $500 membership to this yoga studio if you spend $200 at my store." They made far more sales and solidified positive relationships with clients.

So what was in it for Annie? She knew that one out of four people who came in and redeemed their certificates would become a $2,000 member of her studio. The retailers were happy to add value for their clients; Annie was happy to get stunning back-end value from the joint venture; and, best of all, the clients were happy to get more for less.

Host-Beneficiary: Negotiation and Action Steps

You can arrange to gain additional benefits from the clients you've acquired, the prospects you couldn't sell, or the clients you sold to long ago. And you can find out who has already done your work for you. Some other business, or professional practice, has already spent time, effort, and advertising dollars to attract clients who can now be yours for little more than the asking. You're not rudely "poaching" clients. You're entering into a mutually beneficial partnership.

This process is known as setting up a "Host-Beneficiary Relationship." Company A (the Host) agrees to let Company B (the Beneficiary) deliver a sales message to people who are Company A's clients. Company A could even agree to encourage their clients to purchase a product or service from Company B and actually sing their praises.

Do you have a Visa, Mastercard, or American Express Card? What do you see every month when your bill arrives? Right in the middle there's an offer for another product or service. That's the Host-Beneficiary relationship at work.

If you are the beneficiary in this arrangement, it will bring you more clients and more cash right away.

It will also help you if you are the host in the process because your clients will respect you for helping them learn of a new value in the marketplace.

This is all you have to do:

Step One: Ask yourself, "Who already has a strong relationship with people to whom I might be able to sell a noncompetitive but related product or service?"

Step Two: Once you've got names on paper, contact those non-competing businesses and ask them to introduce your product or service to their audience. Supply them with plenty of information on what you sell, and some testimonials attesting to its high quality.

You should locate companies that have clients logically predisposed to your product or service. (e.g., real estate – carpet cleaner; stock broker – financial planner.) Negotiate with those companies to sell your product or service to their clients. Each company should give an endorsement to your product or service, and in return they would receive a certain percentage of the profits from all sales. Or offer other forms of compensation like donations to their favorite charity, help with their accounting expenses, etc.

Negotiating the Deal

Here is some advice on negotiating a Host-Beneficiary relationship and how to answer some of their possible questions.

Objection #1: "How do I know it's not going to take away my clients?"

Your answer: "First of all, we'll do a test to see if it works. We test it on a small percentage of your clients, not all of them. Then we'll compare the revenue from this test against the revenue you're making from the rest of the clients who were not approached in the test.

"We just want to augment your business, never supplant any part of it. We'll take as long as is necessary to get accurate results, and we'll be as conservative and as analytical as you want so we can prove to you that it's only going to make you money."

Objection #2: "I want control. I don't like you having control of my clients."

Your answer: "To assure you that you'll have control over the quality of our product, you can check us out as thoroughly as you want, and you can impose any kind of controls or standards that you want. We'll even create the kind of product or service that you feel most comfortable with. We can repackage it to be anything you want. If you want it to have a longer guarantee, a lower price, a higher price...it doesn't matter. We can do whatever you want."

Objection #3: "How do I know I'll get paid?"

Your answer: "Simple. You control the money and I'll collect from you. I'll trust you even if you don't trust me. Or, if you prefer, we'll have a separate account with a separate bank of your choice and we'll give the bank escrow instructions. Every time I deposit a dollar, and if 20% of sales is real profit, 10 cents out of every dollar is automatically transferred into your account. There's no risk that you won't get paid."

Remember: trust and transparency are key to successful negotiation and to cultivating strong relationships in the long run. Never fudge, exaggerate, embellish, or conceal (hidden fees, for example).

Another important point: when you cut the deal with the host, try your hardest to get a guarantee that when the test does a certain amount of business, your relationship with the host is automatically renewed on an exclusive basis for a set time period.

If you do, then the host can't bring in a competitor or do it himself. You want to be duly rewarded for showing him how to make all this money, so try to get an "automatic renewal and exclusive" agreement.

On the other hand, when you're the host, you don't want to get involved in a perpetual or exclusive relationship. You want the flexibility to work with other beneficiaries. So if you approach a beneficiary company and they want a perpetual exclusive, try not to give it to them.

When you're the beneficiary the worst thing you can do is to have a short-term deal where your brilliance brings something to somebody and then they dump you after they see how well it works. On the other hand, if you're the host company, you don't want to show a beneficiary company a good idea and not profit from your effort. Tie the beneficiary up. If you are the beneficiary, avoid the issue altogether.

Action Steps for Partnerships that Work

Start by making a list of products and services that complement, precede, or follow your product or service. Then make a list of businesses that sell those products or services.

Next, contact those individuals or businesses and propose setting up a Host-Beneficiary relationship. Don't expect anyone to say "yes" immediately. Think of this as a process. A letter should precede and prepare a potential Host-Beneficiary partner for your call or visit.

After your initial letter, follow it up with a call, then, if possible, a visit. Set up a logical, systematic progression of, for example, letter, call, visit, letter, call, visit, etc.

Compile numbers, facts, and logical reasoning and present the irresistible factors that make saying "yes" to your proposal the only ultimate decision your potential partner can make.

Start out with the sincere belief that it's only a matter of time before those you're contacting become your strategic partners and start contributing to your wealth and success. Don't wait until an agreement is signed to start contributing value to this relationship.

Barter

A common lament of upstart entrepreneurs is that their lack of resources, clientele, or capital impedes their growth, and in particular, makes it hard to partner with other businesses. This is false. You almost *always* have something of value to entice other companies into a partnership.

Trading your products or services for things your business needs or wants is called "Business Barter." Barter vastly increases your purchasing power—sometimes by as much as 5-10x over. Done right, barter also gives you the effect of having almost unlimited capital. It's like having a blank check. It allows you to acquire products and services now, but pay for them much later. And the longer you take to pay, the less it ends up costing you. You can make barter a major factor in your business growth strategy.

You can barter on a small scale: Charles Dickens didn't sell the first story he wrote for money. He bartered it for a bag of marbles. The French painter Toulouse Lautrec would trade his paintings for food and rent.

Or you can barter from small to large: the owner of a small radio station in Florida was having difficulty making payroll, so he traded advertising to a local hardware store for 1,400 electric can openers, which he easily "cash converted" (sold) over the air to generate enough income to save the station.

Sensing he was on to a good thing, he began trading for goods and services, then auctioning them over the radio to the listening audience. Within 60 days the small station was in the black. The "seller-on-the-air" concept was further tested on the local cable television channel. When this also proved successful, investors backed the concept into a satellite uplink and went national. The company's sales now exceed more than $1 billion a year, and it all started with 1,400 can openers. By the way, the company is now called "The Home Shopping Network."

Barter allows you to do things that you couldn't normally accomplish if you're short on cash or if you don't have unlimited buying power.

Case Study: Expand Your Advertising Budget Without Cash

An international air courier company in competition with Federal Express hired a barter firm to pay for its upcoming television ad schedule. The barter company put up the cash and ran the television spots. They took credits with the air courier service as payment, which it cash-converted over the next two and a half years. Only new accounts were allowed to use these credits. No existing ones could purchase or use the credits, so no existing "cash" revenues were ever displaced.

The barter company made a profit in the cash conversion. The courier had two and a half years to pay for the television—without any interest charge. And many of the cash conversion barter sales (some of which were Fortune 400 companies) continued to use the air courier on a full-cash-paying basis long after their barter credits were used up.

In other words, people who were originally not clients of the air courier service developed such a habit of doing business with them through barter usage that they stayed on and paid full cash after the barter credits were used up. We estimate that the cash business exceeds $3 million a year for the courier service. That means the initial one-time barter transaction produced a cash cow worth tens of millions in lifetime earnings.

Barter Action Steps

Start by making a list of all the products and services your business makes, sells, or markets on the left-hand side of the page. Make special note of excess or surplus goods, materials, equipment, inventory, capacity, space, technology, access, etc. your business no longer needs or doesn't fully use.

On the right-hand side, make a list of all key vendors you regularly buy goods or services from to see if any might be interested in directly trading with you for their products or services, or for a portion of the cost you pay for them. Also add the names of your current suppliers' competitors who might be even more eager to initially trade with you for product and service as a means to start a business relationship with your company.

Below that list, make a third list of companies with whom you might be able to triangulate for goods or services. See if there is any company to whom you'd like to start selling your products or services who would also trade whatever they make or sell in order to start a relationship. Then write down who you could either sell or trade those items to for things you or your business needs or wants.

Now, go wild with possibilities. Try putting a few small, easy trades together at first to get comfortable with it. Then with time, keep expanding your level of trading.

There are no less than 91 categories of profit explosion that we teach our clients. You've just been introduced to a handful of them. Obviously, in a book like this, we can't share our entire knowledge of profit-boosting strategies, but we have tried to be generous with you as we go through a number of different and exciting options. We have sought to stimulate, captivate, and animate your sense of all that's possible in terms of profit improvement, once you gain control of a business that can generate profits as never before.

We have also included a list of another 97 ways in which you can absolutely multiply profit performance without any major rise in risk or expense in the appendixes of this book.

If you want to learn all 97 techniques and become truly masterful at their implementation, we can enter into a partnership and profit-sharing relationship with you and with your business. Contact us at support@epicnetwork.com and we can discuss this further with you.

For more case studies, examples, worksheets, checklists, forms, scripts, and other resources, including quite a few that we simply could not fit in the book itself, we created a resources collection and all of these resources are available and waiting for you at BusinessWealthWithoutRisk.com/access. Visit the site now and enjoy a huge collection of resources at absolutely no money out of pocket for you!

Chapter Compass

We just unearthed the immense potential of "relational capital" and learned how to harness the resources of other businesses through strategic partnerships and collaborations—all at zero upfront cost.

We even navigated the tech landscape to discover how digital scalability and high customer lifetime value make technology companies fertile ground for these profitable alliances. Not to forget, we dove into Apple's history to understand how one strategic partnership with Microsoft served as a significant catalyst in its comeback story.

Now, let's venture into territory beyond just numbers and growth. Let's move into a realm where success is not just about leading but also giving, a realm we'll call "Preeminence."

The upcoming chapter will explore how achieving preeminence can offer sustainable, organic, and self-sustaining growth. We'll look at what makes preeminent businesses and their leaders stand out in their industry, often triggering hyper-exponential growth.

Preeminence isn't just about being an industry authority; it's about being an educator and provider of invaluable advice. You'll discover how looking outward, understanding and serving your clients, and contributing to society are integral to achieving this status.

The real charm of preeminence lies not in what you gain, but what you give.

BusinessWealthWithoutRisk.com/access

CHAPTER 11

GREATNESS AND GIVING

A STRATEGY OF PREEMINENCE

Preeminence, which by definition means, "surpassing all others," is literally priceless. Its value is impossible to quantify, but it is the kind of thing that elevates you to the upper echelon of business leaders who enjoy sustainable, low-effort, natural, organic, self-sustaining growth. Preeminence is an intangible quality that delivers tangible rewards.

Preeminent businesses (and their leaders) are recognized as having no equal in their industry, which is why preeminence often accompanies hyper-exponential growth. When you achieve preeminence, your reputation precedes you. You no longer have to chase clients, they will come to you (often in nearly overwhelming abundance). You become a market maven.

Ironically, being preeminent is not so much about *you* as it is about *them*. Look outward rather than inward. Fall in love with your client rather than your own business or product. As an entrepreneur, your *raison d'être* is to serve—to serve your buyers, to serve your industry niche, and more broadly, to serve society at large by putting into it more than you take out. Most people think, "What do I have to say to get people *to buy*?" They should say, "What do I have *to give*? What benefit do I have to render?"

Preeminence demands a *commitment to empathy.* How can you serve when you don't understand others' needs and wants on a deep and emotionally resonant level? After all, people are not merely rational actors motivated by economic self-interest. Sure, there may be a rational cost-benefit analysis behind every purchase one makes, but those decisions are also teeming with complex emotional factors that may have little to do with the tangible benefit that the purchase provides. In life, often the greatest rewards are the intangible ones. Preeminent entrepreneurs have strong emotional intelligence that enables them to read feelings and gauge others' emotional needs.

Preeminence is also characterized by being an authority in your field, which puts you in the enviable position of being an educator, of sorts. Educate clients about their options, what you offer, and how you can help. Provide clarity. Be decisive. Prospects don't want information. Information is overabundant and about as valuable as air. *Advice*, however—the kind of authoritative, ethical, enlightening, and actionable advice which preeminent leaders excel at giving—is in short supply. That is what your clients need, because it provides clarity and direction, which is what they lack.

Communicate authentically. Be trustworthy and hold yourself to the highest standards of moral conduct. Embody integrity in everything you do. People do business with folks whom they can count on, whom they know have the client's interests at heart and are not just pursuing the fast buck. The fast buck too often leads to slow decline. Chasing that short-term high is a poor means to long-term, sustainable growth.

A company that embodies many characteristics of preeminence is Headspace, a widely used meditation app. Interestingly, Headspace was kind of thrown into preeminence due to its high-quality offering and timely circumstances. When COVID-19 hit, everyone's anxiety levels rose. The need for more *headspace* became crucial, and the brand had already established itself through its free trials, calming meditations, and true dedication to its clients' well-being.

Organizational leaders began turning to Headspace to answer their needs with Headspace's workplace product *Headspace for Work*. As a result, Headspace's inbound funnel exploded. To handle the volume, the company had to pivot—they put a halt on outbound marketing and focused their energy on handling the incoming requests. Headspace was ready for preeminence and outside circumstances gave them an extra push. Now, 90% of Headspace for Work's qualified organic leads are inbound.

In summary, the strategy of preeminence turns the notion of entrepreneur as "center of the solar system" on its head, as the focus is shifted to the "receiver" and their best interest (and by "receiver" we mean not only prospects and clients but also team members, suppliers, and collaborators). It's a strategy that says, "I'm not trying to sell you, I want to *serve* you." Practice empathy, embody leadership, give helpful advice, and allow others to share in the power that comes from clarity. Offer solutions, not strategy, and offer the end result, not a drawn-out process to achieve it.

Operating from a position of preeminence is a rare and coveted gift in the business world, one few leaders have a chance to experience (it is, by definition, uncommon). When you manage to reach that summit, you discover that opportunities suddenly multiply as if by magic, and clients—and the wealth their business brings—materializes with little active effort on your part. It is another lever that produces exponential growth.

Multiplier vs. Diminishers

This concept was coined by one of our colleagues who is one of the top executive coaches in the world. It's like physics: nothing stays constant. Expand or contract. Grow or die.

Are you a multiplier or diminisher? Business owners either multiply (their situation, resources, opportunities, etc.) or they diminish. Multipliers make people's lives better, constantly create more value, elevate their team, and enhance their industry, product, category, etc. The more you multiply, the more asymmetric the result. The rewards dramatically outstrip effort. The parabola reaches toward the upper end of the chart. Things compound dramatically. And remember, multiplying the bottom line (profit) generates exponential growth more effectively than the top line (revenue).

Diminishers, unsurprisingly, do the opposite. Instead of producing a gargantuan output from a minimum of input, they're a drag on momentum, on progress, on passion. They siphon off resources and use them inefficiently in a way that is inimical to growth (growth in the broadest sense, not just the growth of your bottom line, though that, too, will suffer under a diminisher's myopic and self-absorbed stewardship).

Evaluate your own performance candidly. Do you supercharge the performance, the collaboration, the passion of your team, or are you a hindrance to their enthusiasm? Are you adding value to your clients' lives, to your industry, and really, to society as a whole? Is your net impact positive or negative? Are you innovating and improving in a way that pushes your product/service/company/industry one step closer to greatness, or is your vision narrowed by a singular preoccupation with profit for profit's sake?

Being a multiplier is as much a horizon-expanding mindset as it is a set of behaviors. Multipliers see growth, and the means to achieve growth, as being like a vast ecosystem of organisms seeking to thrive, each fulfilling its particular purpose, but also benefiting from the dynamic and symbiotic interaction between other members of that ecosystem. A healthy ecosystem thrives as one unit even though it is made up of many different species, some of which may be competing or doing their own thing.

Diminishers, in contrast, don't see the ecosystem; they see only a harsh and brutal world of scant resources and furious competition. They approach business with a zero-sum mindset; my loss is your gain, your gain is my loss. Yes, as an entrepreneur, you are competing with others, and that competition can be tough. We're not sugar-coating the reality of it. But viewing the problem of growth *only* through that lens will be self-defeating and, well, diminishing.

Multipliers look outside their organization for new ideas, fresh approaches, and innovative ways to motivate and develop their people and their relationships with their clients/prospects. They exemplify qualities of servant leadership and are open-minded and humble enough to adapt breakthrough ideas from within, and without, their organization.

CHAPTER 11 - GREATNESS AND GIVING

They encourage collaboration and give and earn the respect of those who work for them, and make their underlings feel like they are engaged in meaningful work. In short, they pursue—and epitomize—preeminence.

Stephen Covey is another leader who wrote extensively about greatness, giving, and servant leadership. He is best known for his perennially popular work *The Seven Habits of Highly Effective People*, but he also had a lot to say about how strong, admirable leaders cultivate trust, which, he says, is in short supply. Trust is good for business. Covey described a lack of trust as a "tax" on every business activity, since mistrust impedes strategy, communication, sales, marketing, and decision-making. Conversely, high trust organizations (and leaders) find that trust greases the gears—it becomes a "force multiplier."

Covey enumerated the following characteristics of a high-trust leader.[16] Practice them in your own business, and you will not only be acting with principle, purpose, and preeminence—the benefit will show in your profits too.

1. Talk Straight

2. Demonstrate Respect

3. Create Transparency

4. Right Wrongs

5. Show Loyalty

6. Deliver Results

7. Get Better

8. Confront Reality

---

16   Stephen M.R. Covey, "How the Best Leaders Build Trust," Leadership Now, n.d., leadershipnow.com/CoveyOnTrust.html

9. Clarify Expectation

10. Practice Accountability

11. Listen First

12. Keep Commitments

13. Extend Trust

What Do You Stand For?

One of the biggest mistakes people make in any business is they fall in love with the wrong thing. They fall in love with their product, service, or company. You should believe passionately in your product, service, or company, but you should fall in love with your clients. And we don't mean clients in the narrow sense, but in the broad sense of "stakeholders": not only the people and businesses who pay you for your goods or services but also your employees, bosses, team members, and vendors.

Falling in love with your clients means taking responsibility for their well-being and putting their best interests ahead of your own.

Most people think, "What do I have to say to get people to buy?" Instead you should say, "What do I have to give? What benefit do I have to render?" It has nothing to do with sales shenanigans or trickery or schemes. It has everything to do with what benefits you give your clients.

The more value you give others, the more value you generate. The more contributions you make to the richness of the lives of your clients, the more bonded you will be to them and they to you. And the more successful you will become.

See yourself as becoming an agent of change. A creator of value. A value contributor.

CHAPTER 11 - GREATNESS AND GIVING

Friendships have no terminus, and neither should the client-salesperson relationship. Life means constant dynamic change. People who are important, valued friends deserve to have the best reasoned, the best informed, the most objective and knowledgeable advice they possibly can get about important emotional decisions. Because if not, they could get into someone's unscrupulous clutches and make a critical decision that could negatively impact their lives and finances.

You need to recognize the impact you have on people's lives in the business you are conducting. What you render, the way you render it, has changed their lives. It has helped enrich them. It has helped their security.

Change the way you think about, deal with, and speak to your clients. Greet them on the phone and in person with the same joy, sincerity, and enthusiasm that you'd show any other valued friend.

Respect the importance of their time, their sense of security, and their comfort. Don't make them wait too long on "hold" or in your waiting room or at their home. Provide for their comfort.

Lend a hand when a client's in trouble—like the FedEx dispatcher who got a frantic call from a tearful bride-to-be whose gown had been misrouted the day before her wedding.

The alert dispatcher located the gown in a distant city and had it flown to the distraught client's city by private plane. The gown arrived in time for the young woman to wear it at her wedding.

The rescue effort was expensive, but it became the talk of the wedding reception—and no doubt caused many executives attending the ceremony to start using FedEx.

It means following up after the sale, not just to patronize but to contribute, acknowledge, and assure the client that you care about them.

It means thinking about the client as more than just a check-book. It means seeing him or her as a valued business partner, someone whose well-being and success is directly tied to your own.

Mastering the Strategy of Preeminence is really the understanding of human nature. When making decisions, whether large or small, you want to look smart and feel like you've done the best you can. But sometimes you're just not sure what the right decision is, so your first instinct is to take less action because you're afraid to take the wrong action, and you don't want to look dumb.

What you look for in those situations is a trusted friend. A confidant. Someone you know has your best interest at heart and will give you advice that will benefit you, not them.

Now, consider that everyone you sell to, individuals or corporations, reacts in exactly the same way. Because they are all, first and foremost, human beings. And, as such, they will always exhibit human behavior. Just like you.

Your job, therefore, is to understand and acknowledge the reality of human nature in your clients. Accept that people will work harder not to look foolish than they will work to gain an advantage. Become their trusted advisor, their friend. Treat them the same way you would want to be treated.

A successful business starts not with just a great idea or product. Rather, it starts with the desire to provide a solution to another's problem. In doing so you enrich your own life and the lives of those around you, your family, and employees or employers, by enriching the lives of your clients.

You need to understand that you have a higher purpose for being in business than simply making money. Your purpose must be understanding what you can do to help solve the problems of others and find ways to do it. Unless you understand that higher purpose, you can't begin to take advantage of your potential.

With that understanding, however, comes the realization that you can have an impact on people. That you can produce a positive response. A positive action. A positive result.

The beauty of the Strategy of Preeminence is that it applies to any business, whether you're selling life insurance or you own a hardware store. The steps you must take always remain the same. You must first identify what your client really needs, even if your client doesn't recognize what it is he/she needs. You might see that an entirely different solution will solve your client's problem, maybe even a less expensive solution. Now you have become more than a salesperson. You've become an advisor. You've begun the process of winning trust and, ultimately, additional business from your client.

We guarantee that when you practice this, the rewards will astonish you—and we don't mean just financial rewards. There is no question that you will generate more money than you ever imagined when you start putting your client's needs first. But it won't stop there: your business, your life's investment, the body of your work, will stand for something wonderful. You will have created value for yourself and your family. You will have provided livelihood and sustenance to your employees. And not only will you have enriched your own life materially beyond anything you ever thought possible, but you will have enriched your life because you will recognize the worth of your endeavor.

The Pursuit of Greatness

There's no one on this earth who strives to be mediocre. All of us want to be great in some capacity. Many of us desire to be great at everything. Yet vanishingly few people are great at *anything*.

The path from mediocrity to greatness is not linear. It is—you guessed it—geometric. When you realize how to operate in that rarefied stratum of greatness, the impact, the performance, the results, the connection, the relevance that emanates from it is asymmetric.

We've identified four steps to greatness.

The first is to define what it actually means, what it looks like. This is not the same for everyone. Paint a clear picture of what it would mean to be great, both internally and externally.

The second step is to create a roadmap to get there. The path may not be immediately clear to you. In that case, look to others, particularly those who have already achieved greatness. People you would like to emulate: your heroes and your mentors. Reach out and ask questions. People are willing to help. In fact, it is often a constituent trait of greatness, for great leaders are generous and recognize that greatness, while elusive, can be achieved by anyone with talent and drive, and they are eager to share their wisdom.

The path from mediocrity to greatness is almost always a long and winding one, with hazards along the way. It is not easy. People tend to want to achieve big goals in a single bound, but it rarely works like that. It's a series of starts and stops, of incremental steps which, when added up, catalyze into an exponential vault upwards.

The third step is to develop your self-confidence. That is the fuel that powers your vehicle on this long journey. As long as there is gas in the tank, you can keep charging forward.

The fourth step is to stay the course. Success is not an easy or straight road. You will be severely tested. The moments when you doubt yourself are precisely the moments when you need to draw on your wellspring of faith in yourself and reaffirm that you are capable, that you are worthy. You'll be tempted to throw in the towel and revert to the status quo. Don't give in. Here, too, mentorship can aid you a great deal because other great individuals have also been through these trials on the way to the top, and they can show you the way and restore your confidence in times of struggle.

For more case studies, examples, worksheets, checklists, forms, scripts, and other resources, including quite a few that we simply could not fit in the book itself, we created a resources collection and all of these resources are available and waiting for you at BusinessWealthWithoutRisk.com/access. Visit the site now and enjoy a huge collection of resources at absolutely no money out of pocket for you!

BusinessWealthWithoutRisk.com/access

Powerhouse Perspectives

We've embarked on an introspective journey into preeminence, an intangible quality that confers tangible rewards. We've talked about the fundamentals of sustainable growth, empathy, and authenticity in business leadership and how these are pivotal to achieving the status of preeminence.

Again, as preeminent leaders, it's not just about what we gain but what we give. It's how we serve our clients, our industry, and the society at large.

And that's where your journey to greatness begins. To truly understand and embark on that path, you must align yourself with principles that guide your actions:

1. The first is to define what it actually means, what it looks like.
2. The second step is to create a roadmap to get there.
3. The third step is to develop your self-confidence.
4. The fourth step is to stay the course.

Now, we're heading toward a place of introspection and decision-making to cultivate what we call "The Freedom to Choose."

In the upcoming chapter, we'll challenge the very purpose of this book by asking you two very important questions. We'll explore the concept of being the steward of our own destiny and the profound power of choice that each and every one of us has.

But remember, this journey isn't just about profit and growth.

This is about ethical business.

This is about serving others.

It's about making a difference.

CHAPTER 11 - GREATNESS AND GIVING

We've equipped you with the knowledge and tools, but embracing and utilizing them lies with you. As we progress, we hope to reinforce this commitment and help you understand the vast opportunities that lie ahead in our abundant world.

Let's explore "The Freedom to Choose."

CHAPTER 12

THE FREEDOM TO CHOOSE

So the questions we'd like to pose take us back to the purpose of the title and subtitle of this book. Do you want to use our methods to create business wealth without risk? And do you now see how and why it's highly probable that you can earn the income of a lifetime in just the next three years? If you can agree with both propositions, then we've accomplished our goal for this book.

Those of you who are our age may remember the actor Hugh O'Brien, who was best known for playing the titular character in the Western TV series *The Life and Legend of Wyatt Earp* that aired in the '50s and '60s. Later, O'Brien became a humanitarian who championed youth leadership and other causes. In an essay titled "The Freedom to Choose," O'Brien wrote:

CHAPTER 12 - THE FREEDOM TO CHOOSE

"I do *not* believe we are all born equal—*created* equal in the eyes of God, *yes*—but physical and emotional differences, parental guidance, varying environments, being in the right place at the right time, all play a role in enhancing or limiting an individual's development. But I do believe every man and woman, if given the opportunity and encouragement to recognize his or her own potential, regardless of background, has the freedom to choose in our world. Will an individual be a taker or a giver in life? Will that person be satisfied merely to exist, or seek a meaningful purpose? Will he or she dare to dream the impossible dream? I believe every person is created as the steward of his or her own destiny with great power for a specific purpose: to share with others, through service, a reverence for life in a spirit of love."

That last sentence is so profound and so on-the-money that it bears repeating: *the steward of one's own destiny...to share with others, through service, a reverence for life in a spirit of love.* Yes, the book that you are now on the cusp of completing is about business, it's about acquisition, it's about growth, it's about sales and marketing, it's about reaping enormous profit and achieving tremendous growth—the kind of growth that will make you and your family richer than you ever imagined. But we hope that you understand, above all, that it is not *only* about these things. If you are driven only by the desire for profit, without a broader, deeper sense of commitment to the world around you, to doing business ethically, and to serving others, then we have missed the mark.

But we're confident you *have* grasped the message, since you've made it this far, and you understand what animates and motivates us as investors and entrepreneurs too.

There is vast opportunity out there, in a world of abundance. Everyone who is willing to work hard for it, shift their thinking, take some risks, and apply the lessons we are teaching can claim their piece. In the first part, we explained how a vast reserve of businesses up for sale are ripe for the taking. EPIC investors—*people who ethically earn enormous profits in a time of crisis*—are uniquely positioned to lead the charge.

We've laid out a simple, actionable five-step plan for you to target and acquire businesses that are right for you, without committing your life savings or assuming outsized risk. **First**, work as an investor above your business. **Second**, never risk your personal credit or assets. **Third**, source and analyze desirable deals. **Fourth**, close those deals without any money out of your own pocket. **Fifth**, earn profits, get paid, and build wealth.

Whether you're a lifelong entrepreneur looking to enrich your portfolio or a novice who hasn't yet had any ownership experience these methods can work for you. Acquisition is only half the battle. While some entrepreneurs might stop there—"I've bought a profitable firm and I'm content with running it the way it has been run."—the truly great ones go beyond, and achieve exponential growth.

In the second part of the book, we showed you a myriad of strategies and tactics to add to the bottom line not merely incrementally, but exponentially and even *hyper-exponentially*: growth upon growth upon growth. Off-the-charts profit, no matter what industry you are operating in.

These "pillars of growth" are many and varied, but they revolve around some key themes. We call them our **Profit Maximizers**. Let's summarize those themes now, because they represent the mindset of the profit-maximizing and profit-multiplying business owner we want you to become:

1. Continually identifying and discovering hidden assets and overlooked opportunities in your business.

These are underperforming revenue activities, underutilized assets, undervalued relationships, both in and outside your business, that you harness. It's all about thinking differently. If you think differently, you will out-think, out-perform, out-earn, out-strategize, out-value create, out-position, out-risk/reward, and out-access the competition.

Broaden your perspective, avoid complacency, and continually expand your comfort zone.

2. Engineering success into every action you take or decision you make.

This sounds self-evident, but surprisingly, businesses stagnate because they fail to see the hidden potential that lies behind every action or decision. A less generous way of putting it is that entrepreneurs frequently act with no sense of logic, reason, or vision. We've seen it countless times.

3. Cultivating multiple sources of profit instead of depending on one single revenue-generating source.

This relates to the Power Parthenon. Athens' Parthenon is architecturally sound after 2500 years because it rests on the strength of multiple pillars that support its immense weight. Is your whole business edifice teetering on a single pillar? Is your company a magnificent wonder of the ancient world or a flimsy diving board that, if it snaps, will send you plunging precariously into the deep end of the pool?

4. Being different, unique, and advantageous in the eyes of your customers.

In other words, identifying a unique selling proposition while cultivating preeminence that will make you an industry standout and a recognized leader.

5. Creating real value for your customers and employees for maximum loyalty and results.

Preeminence means serving, not selling.

6. Gaining the maximum personal leverage from every action, investment, time, or energy commitment you ever make.

It's about maximizing your opportunities and making your resources work harder for you, whether that's through smarter systems, more efficient processes, or innovative uses of your time. Ideally, you want every minute you spend and every decision you make to produce a return on investment or return on the energy put into every action you take.

7. Networking /masterminding/brainstorming with like-minded, success-driven people who share real life experiences with you.

Your perspective may not be wrong, but it *is* limited. The more you can expand your mindset and look at things—at everything—in a more multifaceted, multidimensional way, the more you will understand other people's perspectives, and thus gain access to the covert opportunities that lie in wait. Learn everything you can about everything you can. There is great power in that.

8. Turning yourself into an idea generator and recognized innovator within your industry or market.

By doing so, you not only stay ahead of the curve but also position yourself as a recognized leader and influencer within your industry or market, which increases your leverage and opportunities.

9. Making "growth-thinking" a natural part of your everyday business philosophy.

Force yourself to grow in myriad ways beyond what you would normally do. Most people don't read more than a few books a year. Most people pay scant attention to what's going on outside their industry and make little effort to understand any business besides their own. Talk to other entrepreneurs. Ask questions. Strive to learn something new. Listen and evaluate—that's where breakthroughs come from, more often than from your own niche.

10. Reversing the risk for both you and your customers in everything you do.

So that the downside is almost zero, and the upside potential is nearly infinite.

11. *Using small, safe tests to eliminate dangerous risks and adopting funnel vision instead of tunnel vision in your thinking.*

Taking small, strategically calculated risks is the best way to mitigate losses. This approach enables you to scale winning efforts while discarding the losers. Additionally, employing the concept of 'funnel vision' opens up opportunities that others may overlook. While most companies are fixed on a narrow, singular focus, remaining flexible and adaptable to any landscape will give you a significant advantage over your competitors.

You now understand the theory and practice of what we call our business trifecta: acquire a solid but underperforming business; radically expand the profitability of the business; and then exit for a huge multiple...and then repeat this process again and again.

You are now fully able to fly on your own, but we are here to help you and work with you if you so desire. We hope that you will reach out to us and let us help you reach your goals...and then set even newer, higher goals for next year!

You have the freedom to choose the life and career you want. Be the steward of your own destiny. Nothing can stop you but your own mind.

Go where few others dare to go and reach beyond what you have thought is possible. We promise you'll be happy you did!

The Maze Exercise

Take a look at the image below. Open the clock on your phone and use the stopwatch feature to time yourself and see how long it takes you to trace the path from Start to Finish in the maze. You can do this with a pen or pencil or just with your eyes.

Take a minute now and time yourself. How long does it take you to get from Start to Finish in the maze?

Were you able to finish in 20 seconds or fewer? What path did you take?

Do you think that was the fastest way to get from Start to Finish, or might there be other paths you could have taken?

What assumptions did you make as you began the maze?

If you're like most people, you took the path shown in the image below:

But was that the best path? The fastest? If your assumption was to enter the lined maze at the Start point and then wind your way through it to the Finish point, then you are absolutely correct. However, we did not say that you had to get from start to finish that way.

Is there another path that would allow you to go from Start to Finish without crossing any lines or blockades in the maze?

As it turns out there is indeed another path that will get you from Start to Finish much, much quicker.

Take a look at the alternative solution below to see what happens when we question assumptions but abide by traditional rules. The rules for mazes that we all know is that you cannot cross a solid line to get to the finish. The assumption is that you must enter the maze and move forward through it. But what if you could avoid the twists and turns?

That's the path charted in the image below.

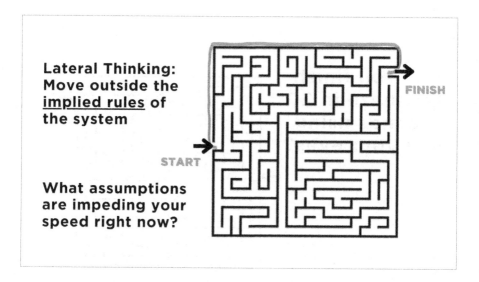

Lateral Thinking: Move outside the <u>implied rules</u> of the system

What assumptions are impeding your speed right now?

In the image above, we eschewed the assumption that we must enter the maze and find our way through all of its twists and turns. We still obey the presumed rules that we cannot cross any lines to find our way from start to finish, but while observing those rules, our changed assumption that we may get from start to finish any way possible just so long as we don't cross any lines does yield a much quicker path.

Three Ways to Grow a Business (Revisited)

Here is a lesson in the power of working on the geometry of the business. Growth begets growth; growth squared. There are a million ways to grow your business, and many of them can be categorized in one of three types:

1. *Increase the number of clients*

    a. Acquisitions
        i. Acquiring brands and zombie brands
        ii. Acquiring businesses that already have their own clients
        iii. Acquiring media
        iv. Acquiring qualified lists

    b. Advertising

    c. Affiliates and Affiliate Networks

    d. Content marketing

    e. Direct mail

    f. Earned media and public relations

    g. Email and list marketing

    h. Influencer campaigns

    i. Integrations, joint ventures, and strategic relationships

    j. Referral systems

    k. Search engine optimization/marketing

2. *Increase the average transaction value*

    a. Add physical products to services

    b. Add services to physical products

    c. Bundles

    d. Consulting add-ons

    e. Cross-selling

    f. Download insurance

g. Down-sells

h. Drops (limited quantity, limited access promos) +
    Special editions

i. Extended access offers (pay more for longer access)

j. Financing and payment plans (pay more over time/interest)

k. Multiples (ability to buy more than one item during checkout)

l. Price increases, and thus margins (raise prices)

m. Quantity discounts/Bulk Discounts

n. Recommendation engines (people who bought this, also
    bought that)

o. Recurring sales—annual and monthly recurring
    revenue, subscriptions

p. Sales development: training your team in advanced
    selling techniques

q. Sales enablement (tech enabled sales enhancement)

r. Tech-Support add-ons

s. Training package add-ons

t. Up-Branding: making your products/services more up-market

u. Upsells/upgrade offers

v. Warranties

3. *Increase the frequency of repurchase (squeeze more residual value out of each client)*

a. Add recurring services (scheduled maintenance, mow your lawn, etc.)

b. Add SaaS (software products with continuing MRR/ARR charges)

c. Calendared special events (closed door sales, limited pre-releases, etc.)

d. Consumables (e.g., toothpaste, detergent, toner, razor blades, etc.)

e. Credits based usage systems (pay for access and/or usage)

f. Deeper product/service line (developing a back-end product/ service line of multiple additional products/services that you can offer to clients)

g. Event-based marketing campaigns: current events and sports events-based campaigns (e.g., world series, world cup, movie release, tv show, season change, etc.)

h. Follow-up marketing campaigns: building relationships with clients by communicating with them personally

i. Frequent buyer program (discounts, punch cards, raffles, etc.)

j. Holiday calendar: holiday-based marketing campaigns

k. Loyalty programs

l. Membership programs (status/pre-release access/special shopping days)

m. Planned obsolescence cadence (new release, new/better model)

n. Subscriptions

Common Marketing Mistakes

Marketing mistakes are so deadly because just as drivers for growth compound and explode your profits, marketing mistakes inhibit growth. Each of the following marketing mistakes that you eliminate will have an exponential impact and help expand the bottom line geometrically, not just incrementally.

Mistake #1: Not testing all of your marketing ideas.
Remedy: Test them all!

This one is self-evident, but as we've said several times, as obvious as it seems, if business owners actually did it, it wouldn't bear repeating. You cannot gauge the effectiveness of a marketing technique if you don't test it in the field against the alternatives.

Mistake #2: Not articulating and differentiating your business.
Remedy: Develop a powerful unique selling proposition (USP) and use it in all your marketing.

You have competitors selling similar goods or services, so why should customers do business with you and not them? Carving out a clear, concrete USP is your means of distinguishing yourself from the herd and cultivating loyal, long-term fans of your brand.

You've probably heard the expression, "If you try to please everyone, you'll please no one," and that holds true for business as well. The most successful enterprises know exactly who they are—their brand identity and positioning. They don't seek to reach everyone; they target their ideal customer base. Cast too wide a net and the fish will slip through the holes. But narrow down the scope of your marketing and you'll reap abundant rewards.

Mistake #3: *Not having a back-end product or service.*
Remedy: *Create a profitable and systematic back-end.*

Customers may walk through your door (literally or figuratively) for the front-end goods, but the ideal customers stick around for the back-end (up-sells, down-sells, and cross-sells). Back-end marketing is effective because it targets customers you've already won over and who are thus familiar with your offerings, motivated, and even loyal to your brand. In our consultation with companies, we've developed numerous back-end catalogs to supplement their front-end, and often back-end sales end up being the primary drivers of exponential growth.

Also bear in mind that often, you break even on customer acquisition the first time around: it costs on average X dollars to win that client's business initially. You might even be losing money. But that cost is justified when that customer comes back again and again and again, for the same or a different product in your repertoire.

Mistake #4: *Not understanding your client's needs and desires.*
Remedy: *Always determine and address the real needs of your clients and prospects.*

This overlaps somewhat with Mistake #2. The flip side of businesses knowing through and through who *they* are and what purpose they serve is intimately understanding their target market. Don't push out products and services based on what you think is best and hope they'll attract someone. Market from the perspective of *your clients' needs.* What problems do they need solving, and how can you solve them?

Mistake #5: *Cutting the price and hoping for the best.*

Remedy: *Always recognize that you must educate your client as a part of the marketing and sales process.*

Marketing is not just pitching, and it is certainly not brow-beating or hard-selling prospects until you induce them to buy what you are selling. Rather, effective marketing consists of teaching your target market what you offer, why it's optimal, why you do it better than your competitors, and why their lives will be worse without it. Remember that education via marketing is much more than "providing information." It points people in the direction they need to go.

Mistake #6: *Making doing business with your company difficult, boring, or laborious.*

Remedy: *Make doing business with your business easy, appealing, and fun.*

This is self-explanatory. People tend to buy what makes them feel good and they tend to work with folks whom they like. Commerce is not just a transaction; it's an experience. When that experience is a positive one, customers keep coming back for more (and tell their friends and colleagues to do the same).

Incidentally, this is unquestionably part of the reason for Amazon.com's massive success. Not only is the website easy to buy from, but by offering a wide range of items with rapid shipping times and free returns, Amazon makes its customers' lives more convenient. It's no surprise that we all keep coming back for more.

Mistake #7: *Not telling your clients the "reason why."*

Remedy: *Always tell your client the "reason why."*

The "reason why" is likely multifaceted: the value you provide is more than meets the eye. For example, if you're selling diet pills, you understand, obviously, that your clients want to lose weight. But you must also market this with a deeper, more emotionally resonant motivation in mind: it's not just about the number of pounds on the scale. Your customers are motivated by a desire to *feel* fit, young, healthy, and attractive.

Those deeper "whys" are what really compel people to buy, to keep coming back, and to establish a long-term relationship with your business as a company that understands their fundamental needs and desires, not just the most obvious or superficial ones. People make purchasing decisions based on rational as well as emotional motives. It's essential you understand both.

Mistake #8: *Terminating marketing campaigns that are still working.*

Remedy: *Don't stop marketing campaigns that are still working just because you are tired of them.*

If it ain't broke, don't fix it.

Mistake #9: Not specifically targeting your marketing.

Remedy: When you prepare your marketing, focus on the intended prospect and no one else.

This was initially the mistake made by Pabst Blue Ribbon Beer (PBR), a beer that originally marketed itself as, "Good, old-time flavor, for those who feel beer is something special." Their vague, untargeted ads worked for a time, but by 2001, they had been on a 20-year decline and sold fewer than one million barrels.

Senior Brand Manager, Neil Stewart, noticed that the company had an interested customer they were neglecting to pursue: the hipster. While sales across the country declined steadily, sales in Portland, Oregon were ballooning. The anti-mainstream group appreciated PBR's vintage brand, cheap price, and unsexy marketing. So the company started a grassroots, word-of-mouth marketing campaign, deliberately designed not to appear flashy or mainstream, and used it to spread the brand name across the country to a similarly fringe target market. It worked. By 2012, they sold 92 million barrels of beer.

Mistake #10: Not capturing prospect addresses, email addresses, buyer data, and other pertinent information.

Remedy: Capture everything on a prospect or client that you can in an organized, retrievable system.

Failure to catalog prospect information is just squandering resources. Systematizing and deploying prospect data lets you nurture relationships, build your clientele, and keep prospects (and by extension, people they refer to you) within your orbit.

Mistake #11: *Not being strategic.*

Remedy*: Always having a strategy which tactical actions and methods are integrated into.*

We discussed this extensively in the section on "Sticking Point Solutions." Most entrepreneurs are effectively driving blind. They've got their hands on the wheel and their feet on the pedals but they're not looking beyond the 50-foot stretch of asphalt in front of them. They have no long-term vision, or they're trapped in a never-ending cycle of dealing with day-to-day minutiae, or preoccupied with *tactics* to the detriment of strategy. No wonder they aren't achieving growth.

This principle is as applicable to marketing as it is to any other aspect of the business. Without strategy, you're just "praying and spraying," throwing this thing and that thing at the wall and seeing what sticks. Strategy is the North Star that guides the ship.

Mistake #12: *Not having a marketing or sales system.*

Remedy*: Have a marketing and sales system in place and refine it continuously, using sequential marketing.*

It is essential to put a plan into place that will allow you to systematically close the deals that keep your business thriving. For example, sequential marketing. High-ticket prospects are often not closed on the first contact. Expect to conduct five to eight integrated, sequential follow-up efforts after the first conversation. This may take different forms; some combination, for example, of letter/call/letter/call or email/letter/call sequences. Test what works. Remember that *each contact* must provide something of value for the prospect: always transfer knowledge and ideas, provide vital information they didn't know, or give them a solution they can apply today. Respect your customers and their time and you will be rewarded.

Mistake #13: *Not taking advantage and integrating social media into your marketing and sales efforts.*

Remedy: *Leverage the power of social media and other digital channels.*

Yes, even in 2023, some business owners remain stuck in an analog mindset. The internet is, perhaps with the exception of television, the single most powerful marketing tool in human history. And if your business is still struggling to grow, it's unlikely you'll be airing TV ads. So the internet is your not-so-secret weapon.

Social media, in particular, is a massive engine of growth. The sheer breadth, reach, flexibility, customizability, and granularity of digital marketing provides a galaxy of options and abilities for business owners. If you aren't leveraging it, you will inevitably fall behind your competitors, who certainly are.

Mistake #14: *In sales situations, shooting from the hip.*

Remedy: *Constantly using and refining a sales script.*

We've seen that minute changes in a sales script can compound into exponential rewards. Examine what you're doing now. Evaluate (qualitatively and quantitatively) what works and what does not. Make changes. Measure their impact. Ramp up the best techniques accordingly.

Mistake #15: *Being stuck doing "what works."*
Remedy: *Always be willing to change.*

This is really a *sine qua non* of entrepreneurship: if you aren't evolving, you won't grow, and if you aren't growing, you're dying. Constantly be iterating, innovating, reconceptualizing, and trying new things. That said, do this *strategically;* if you approach it randomly, you'll find yourself committing Mistake #9: don't get rid of effective tactics (in marketing or otherwise) just for the sake of change, or because you're "bored" with them.

Mistake #16: *Not reinvesting your profits.*
Remedy: *Always parlay your success and momentum into greater achievement.*

A basic mantra of business: reinvest resources into growing the business, and success will quickly snowball.

Mistake #17: *Not knowing and leveraging the lifetime value of a client.*
Remedy: *Always understand the lifetime value of your clients.*

Acquiring a new client is costlier than leveraging the relationships you have with existing ones. Sky-high, sustainable growth tends to come from repeat clients who patronize your business over the long haul.

For more case studies, examples, worksheets, checklists, forms, scripts, and other resources, including quite a few that we simply could not fit in the book itself, we created a resources collection and all of these resources are available and waiting for you at BusinessWealthWithoutRisk.com/access. Visit the site now and enjoy a huge collection of resources at absolutely no money out of pocket for you!

BusinessWealthWithoutRisk.com/access

Rainmaker Revelations

Chapter 12 guided us through a profound exploration of the freedom to choose.

We engaged with pivotal questions, challenging the very essence of what this book aims to accomplish—creating business wealth without risk and potentially earning the income of a lifetime in just a few years. Drawing from the insightful words of actor and humanitarian Hugh O'Brien, we highlighted the significance of choice and our role as stewards of our own destiny.

As we reach the end of this chapter, we hope you've grasped the overarching message—the blending of profit-seeking with an ethical, service-oriented approach to business. The world offers vast opportunities, and you, as an entrepreneur and an investor, have an unprecedented opportunity to seize them while having an epic, positive impact on the world.

We hope you're ready for the exciting stage of your new *ACQUIREpreneurial* journey.

Assuming you've faithfully followed the lessons in this book, you're now ready to take your financial freedom to new heights by selling the businesses you've built and grown. The final part of this book will reveal our proven formula to help you exit your business in the most lucrative way possible.

PART THREE

Exiting at an Awesome Multiple

CHAPTER 13

TIME TO SELL WHAT YOU'VE BUILT

The 5 "Exits" of the Entrepreneur

Finally, we've arrived at the Exit stage! Now life gets really exciting and delightfully lucrative for you!

If you've followed the lessons of this book, you've already learned how to acquire businesses (often with little or none of your own capital), then grow them hyper-exponentially to explode profits far beyond what you thought was possible. Now you can reap an additional return by selling them for 5x, 10x, or even a higher multiple of their annual profits.

We're now going to show you how to exit. *So if you thought the prior sections of the book were exciting, buckle up, because this is where your financial freedom moves to a whole new level.*

Before we dive very deep into the exit process, let's take a moment to look at a concept Roland developed that will help you understand what it means to move through the entrepreneurial journey of "The 5 Exits of an Entrepreneur." To help you visualize this process, take a look at the graphic below as we explain.

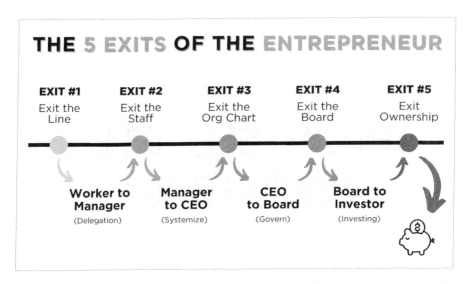

You begin your entrepreneurial journey in most cases almost by accident. We've referred to this both as being an incidental entrepreneur and being an accidental entrepreneur because most people never really consider the fact that they are going into business and becoming an entrepreneur when they start their business.

Usually, they are a talented technician, inventor, or employee tired of building someone else's business. They solve a problem for themselves that they subsequently discover is a problem for lots of other people who start asking them to share or sell their solution and before you know it, boom, another entrepreneur is born. As you can see, becoming an entrepreneur is frequently incidental to going into business and the people who find themselves faced with running businesses and doing business owner things very often get themselves into that position accidentally.

As most of these folks get into business, they find that they are doing the heavy lifting working directly in the business doing whatever they do, providing the product or service that they sell directly to the customer. At this point, they are working "in" the business as Michael Gerber would say, they are working on the Line.

That's where we find most entrepreneurs as they begin to contemplate their 1st exit of the 5 Exits of an Entrepreneur. The exit from the Line to Management, from doing to delegating. The first exit moves the entrepreneur from working "in" the business to working "on" it—they begin to hire other people to do the creating, manufacturing, serving, and maintaining functions and remove themselves to managing those people. Once they have a solid staff and find themselves doing primarily management functions vs. line functions, they have completed their first exit.

At that point, they begin to realize that with more business growth, more managers are needed and more line workers as well, and this is the point where they find they need to move from management to leadership of their business, they are exiting the Staff. This is the 2nd exit, moving from Management to Leadership, from Manager to CEO (Chief Executive Officer) of the business.

At this point delegation gives way to systematization, to the installation of operating systems, standard operating procedures, a business culture, processes for hiring, and more responsibility to establish a vision for the business and an over-arching mission the business seeks to accomplish. Sadly, most entrepreneurs never make the 2nd exit. They promote themselves with the CEO title, but they very seldom make it out of management and delegation into a true CEO leadership position. We say that most CEOs are managers with a title, not true CEOs.

Once the CEO is a true CEO, a true leader, crafting and executing their vision for the company, the next exit, the 3rd exit is to move off of the company's organization chart, to have no officer title in the business, no direct reports, no day-to-day responsibilities for the business. This is a move from Leadership to Governance, from CEO to Board Member. Now, we know that you're probably saying to yourself right now that you've seen lots of famous business celebrities that remain as CEO of their companies for years. Steve Jobs remained CEO of Apple until a few weeks before his death, Mark Zuckerberg stayed CEO of Facebook/Meta, and despite his age, Warren Buffett continues to act as CEO of Berkshire Hathaway. But many celebrity CEOs took their financiers' advice and moved on from day-to-day operations to serving as board members where the value of their company was no longer dependent on them working in it and they could prove that to investors, allowing them freedom to remain involved in the company at a high, visionary level, but escape the chains of being on the org chart. Great examples of this include Bill Gates, who moved out of the CEO role at Microsoft to let Steve Ballmer take the helm, followed by Staya Nadella. Sergey Brin and Larry Page accepted their venture capitalist, Sequoia's, recommendation to have Eric Schmidt serve instead of them as CEO of Google, and Jeff Bezos stepped down as CEO of Amazon to let Andy Jassy take over.

The challenge with remaining as CEO and staying on the business org chart is that very often anyone purchasing the business will require you to remain in the business for at least some period of time to reduce their risk while acquiring it and to ensure an orderly transition from your leadership to that of a professional manager who will take your place. The best way to ensure that you are not trapped into being the post-sale CEO is to make the move from Leadership to Governance, step up to the Board and step down from the CEO position, before you ever even think of listing your business for sale.

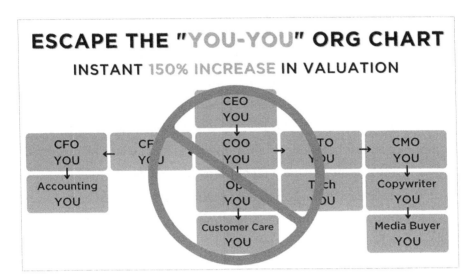

As a board member, you have power to elect the officers of the company, including the CEO and related C-Suite officers, to vote on important matters relating to the company's business, and to interact with the owners of the business. In big businesses, this might include several independent directors who serve on the board with you, as well as a myriad of shareholders including pension funds and professional investors like private equity companies. In smaller companies, you may be the sole board member and sole shareholder of the business, but no matter what the situation, if you want to truly exit the business, you're going to want to move off the org chart as soon as you can and install competent professional management.

The next exit, the 4th exit, is when you typically sell part of the business and decide to move off of the board. You see this with many famous founders when they decide to pursue something else. For yourself, you may want to stay on the board until you sell some or all of your business, or you may prefer to be free of board obligations and potential liabilities to other shareholders, and when you do decide to make the move, you will exit the board and move from Governance to Investor.

As an investor, you act just like you would as an investor in any company you might own through a purchase on a stock exchange. You are more removed from the company but still keenly interested in how it is doing and what its value is. You will monitor the company's performance and ultimately decide whether the income and value growth the company's equity (usually stock) provides you is worth continuing to hold, or whether, when compared to other alternative investments, it makes more sense to sell your interest and invest in something else you believe will be more lucrative for you.

When you make that last move, the 5th exit, the move from investor to exit, you Exit the Company by Exiting Ownership. That 5th exit is the subject of part three of this book, and that's what we are going to be exploring in depth in the coming pages.

The SPV Model

The next concept we need to explain to you before we move deeper into the exit process is the SPV model. This model is illustrated in the diagram below and comprises three overlapping parts: 1) Leveraged Sales, 2) Bankable Profits, and 3) Transferable Value.

We call this the Scalable Impact Framework, and we created an entire company called Scalable.co (GetScalable.co) to share our model with other business owners looking for a modern way to organize and run their businesses. To find out more about that and about this model, visit the book website at BusinessWealthWithoutRisk.com/ access where you will find tons of helpful free resources related to this book, along with updates that came in too late to get into this version.

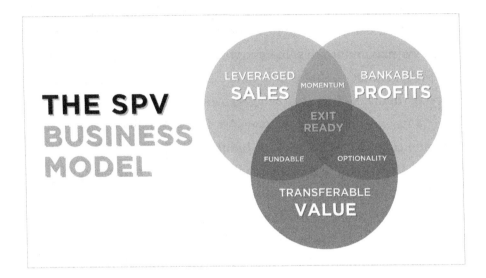

The SPV framework model includes three parts, and each of those parts includes three parts. If you would like to have a business with the maximum exitable value, you will want to put all nine of these parts in place.

Leveraged Sales

Leveraged Sales is a step above what you typically think of as sales. It involves getting more results from each sales-forward action you take than just selling one more product or service to one more customer. It focuses on how to generate multiple sales where each action creates a multiplier effect on total sales enterprise wide. Leveraged Sales comprises three subparts: Growth Engines, Authority Amplifiers, and Sales Accelerators.

While a complete explanation of each of these is beyond the scope of this book, suffice to say that growth engines are predictable selling systems that explain how customers happen in your business. To receive maximum exit value, you will want to have a diversified array of growth engines so that you do not suffer from platform risk (the risk that a particular selling channel goes away or dramatically changes).

You will also want to have Authority Amplifiers that clearly communicate and establish your brand's dominance as the leader in its class, from marketing messaging to content strategy that can drive brand awareness and communicate the business's brand promise, drive viral organic growth, and create an aura of preeminence around the company's business and brand.

Finally, with respect to Leveraged Sales, you will want to have Sales Accelerators that you can tap into to continually provide new strategies for generating more sales and customer growth. We have developed just over two hundred of these tools and strategies that we activate as needed to achieve Leveraged Sales in the businesses that we own, operate, or invest in. Here are a few of the two hundred to help give you ideas you can execute for your business:

20 BIG LEVERAGED SALES OPPORTUNITIES

___ Create Bundles + Multiples Packages

___ Extend Your Value Ladder

___ Optimize The Traffic Channel Grid

___ Adjacency, International + In-filling

___ Price Tests + As-Applied Pricing

___ E2P Cost Centers To Profit Centers

___ Use ZDOT To Acquire ICP Media

___ Franchise or License To Others

___ JV, Strategic, + Channel Partnerships

___ Create Product Integrations

___ Add or Expand Affiliate Program

___ License Other People's Products or Services

___ Create Bolt-On Businesses (BOB)

___ Vertically Integrate Supply + Distribution

___ Borrow A Salesforce or Rep Network

___ Create Recurring Revenue Products/Services

___ Add Services/Digital To Physical Products

___ Add Physical Products To Services/Digital

___ Micro M&A For Growth

___ Add Services To Digital Products

Sales Accelerators also contemplate that your business structure enables you to adapt to and absorb ever-increasing sales so that growth is possible without causing the wheels to fall off. Your business needs an adaptable model that permits it to scale in infrastructure and operations in concordance with sales growth. When you have a Scalable Framework like SPV, acquirers can reasonably expect that the business you built and that they are buying will be able to grow and achieve the financial returns that merit a high acquisition price.

Bankable Profits

Many businesses fail to survive due to poor financial planning and performance. A solid financial plan for your business contemplates systems for receiving, managing, and disbursing money as part of the day-to-day operations of the company, as well as the ability to work predictively to anticipate and arrange for cash needs throughout the vicissitudes of business operations, economic climate, labor needs, and unplanned disruptions.

When you have all these things in place, you should not only be able to cover your business operating expenses from operational income and profits, you should also be able to stack profits in the bank, take home more money for yourself, and provide savings for future growth, scale, and exigencies. The three key components to Bankable Profits include Profit Maximizers—of which we have 63, Cash Controls, and the House Cut.

Again, a much deeper explanation of each of these items is beyond the scope of this book, but can be found at Scalable.co. The short version of each of these three subparts to Bankable Profits is that Profit Maximizers are a set of 63 actions that you can take within your business to dramatically improve profits. These are separate and in addition to the 90 strategies and tools that Jay provided early in part two of this book. Here is a sample of some of those Profit Maximizers in each of the different categories where they live:

PROFIT OPTIMIZER TOOL

CHOOSE A CATEGORY

SELECT AN ACTION

FIND CURRENT COST

SET TARGET COST

SET TARGET DATE

Cash Controls are the budgeting and cash management devices used to handle the business's finance needs. These include tools like the Cashflow Waterfall (for managing cashflow) and Zero-Dollar Budget (for budgeting).

The House Cut is how you get paid in the business. We can't tell you how many times we are working with someone moving towards an exit or acquiring a business from an "accidental entrepreneur" when we get to determine the business profits and discover the owner has not been paying themselves a regular salary. Because we have to include a cost of management when determining what real profits are, that means we will have to reduce the existing profits shown on the income statement for the business by an amount equal to what the owners should have been paying themselves as salary, which will in turn reduce the value and sales price of the company correspondingly.

To show you the impact this can have, let's say that the three owners of a business with $1 million in EBITDA (profits) are selling at a multiple of 12x profits. The business shows EBITDA of $1 million, so $1 million x 12 = $12 million valuation. But, as we get into due diligence, we learn that none of the three owners have been taking any salary from the business, living instead on profit distributions as an alternative to salary. We do the research and learn that if the owners took a standard salary for the jobs they do one would be receiving $300k, and each of the other two would be receiving $150k. That's a combined total of $600k.

We will now need to adjust the business's EBITDA down by that amount, reducing it from a total per statements EBITDA of $1 million to a restated EBITDA of $1 million minus $600k = $400k. Now we apply the 12 multiple and get a revised valuation of $4.8 million vs $12 million. Worse yet, because the profit is now so much lower, the multiple decreases from 12 to 8, making the new net valuation of the business 8 x $400k = $3.2 million. This could have all been avoided and the owners may have chosen to wait to sell had they been aware of the need to take reasonable salaries for the work they were doing for the business.

As you operate your business and prepare to get Exit Ready, you will want to accurately reflect the true operating costs of the business by paying yourself an amount equal to what you would have to pay a similarly skilled and experienced worker to do your job. You can find these numbers on Salary.com and Payscale.com. You will also want to be sure that the business is paying you what you need to be motivated to remain there. Remember, the business is there to serve you, not the other way around. We recommend always taking at least 10% of profits as a distribution for yourself from your business. Think of it as the business's way of saying "thank you" to you for being there and doing what you do to support it. When you combine your reasonable salary with this 10% (or more if you can make it happen), that is what we mean by the "House Cut." It's the total amount that you take for yourself.

Transferable Value

That leaves us with one more very important part of the SPV model to explain, and that's Transferable Value. Transferable Value comprises our core set of 50 Valuation Amplifiers, the Goose+Eggs Structure, and the business Operating System.

VALUATION AMPLIFIER TOOL

Valuation Amplifier Tool

These are the 50 Valuation Amplifier Tools. Some Investor Goals are the same, but the Company Action is different, as well as the Tool + Impact. To return to the Index, click on the first tab titled "INDEX".

	INVESTOR GOALS	COMPANY ACTION	TOOLS + IMPACT
1	Acquire in desirable industry experiencing high valuations.	Focus growth efforts on industry segments showing greatest strength in terms of multiple valuation. Check multiples sheet to determine highest multiple segments existing business could fit within and refocus on attainable segments with higher multiples.	Tool: Use EBITDA Multiples Table to find high EBITDA industry segments. Impact: 1x to 20x increased EBITDA.
2	Reduce risk of business failure due to overdependence on owner/operator.	Professionalize management within the business. Remove or dramatically reduce owner operator dependence by cross-training, implementation of SOPs and business automation.	Tool: Scalable OS + You-You Chart Impact: 152% average increase in valuation from SDE valuations to EBITDA.
3	Realize valuation increases based upon growth of business size.	Increase sales and EBITDA business values. Acquire assets with programmatic M&A to increase EBITDA and sales. Consider roll-up within your industry to increase size or acquisition of Acquisition Wheel adjacent businesses.	Tool: Scalable OS, Acquisition Wheel, ZDOT, Size Affects Multiple Charts. Impact: 3.3x to 7.5x Valuation Increase.
4	Realize valuation increases based on industry growth.	Focus on industry segments experiencing greatest growth.	Tool: Size Affects Multiple Charts Impact: 2x to 5x Valuation Increase
5	Acquire the business assets delivering the targeted ROI in the targeted industry.	Structure your business using the Goose + Eggs structure to thin-slice the layers of desirable target acquisition profit centers. Appeal to exactly what acquirers want without giving away additional valuable assets.	Tool: Goose + Eggs structure template Impact: Create multiple exits
6	Acquire the business assets delivering the targeted ROI in the targeted industry.	Choose an entity type that provides the greatest flexibility for you as the seller from a tax and value cache retention aspect and appeal to acquirer's desire to acquire only the valuable assets they desire in a simple transaction.	Tool: Entity Choice Charts, Goose & Eggs Structure Template Impact: Save 10% - 100% of taxes on sale
7	Acquire businesses with simple cap tables.	Use the Goose + Eggs structure template to create simple cap table companies with value concentrated based on individual profit centers.	Tool: Goose & Eggs Structure Template Impact: Simple cap tables make attractive targets. Increase valuation the high end of the range.
8	Reduce risk of valuation damage due to businesses branded with the name of the founder or any individual's name.	Move branding away from any individual's name and to a corporate name. Consider re-branding early before large brand equity vests in the name of any individual.	Tool: Brand Value Transfer Worksheet Impact: Increase marketability of businesses. Increase valuation to the high end of the range.
9	Acquire proprietary intellectual property to increase and maintain competitive moat and reduce risk of duplication and perfect competition.	Increase ownership of in-house developed and acquired intellectual property.	Tool: Defensible IP Worksheet/ Acquisition Wheel Impact: Increase appeal and marketability. Increase valuation to the high end of the range.

Valuation Amplifiers are the many different things that you can do to increase the value of your business. A complete description of all of these is again beyond the scope of this book, but you can find out more at our book resource site BusinessWealthWithoutRisk.com/access.

The Goose+Eggs Structure will be explained shortly and is our optimal way to structure businesses for maximum exit valuation and flexibility.

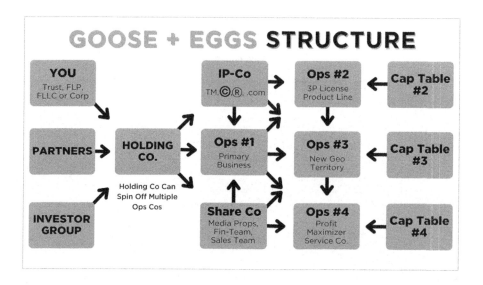

The Business Operating System can be any system for operating your business to permit it to thrive and scale. Gino Wickman created one of the most well-known Business Operating Systems called the Entrepreneurial Operating System. There are several others as well including our own Scalable OS, Verne Harnish's Gazelles system, and others.

BusinessWealthWithoutRisk.com/access

Entrepreneur's Epiphanies

In this chapter, we examined how the entrepreneurial journey often begins inadvertently and how most individuals don't recognize their entrepreneurial status when they start. Yet, if you've followed the lessons in this book, you're now poised to sell your businesses at high multiples of their annual profits, transforming this stage into an exciting and profitable experience.

WARNING: Most entrepreneurs are completely blind to the content in the next chapter. Skip over this next section, and you run the risk of missing one of the primary key ingredients that can significantly enhance your business's value—intellectual property. IP assets, such as copyrights, trademarks, patents, and trade secrets, can create a strong (and oftentimes, impassable) moat between your business and its competition.

Did you know that the more defensible IP your business possesses, the more valuable it becomes?

This next section will help you understand the various types of defensible IP and how to utilize them to maximize your business's worth at the exit stage. Financial freedom and entrepreneurial success are at your fingertips!

CHAPTER 14

CONSIDERATIONS BEFORE EXITING

Defensible IP (Intellectual Property)

One huge way to create a moat between yourself and your competition is to have intellectual property assets that your competitors cannot copy or use without your permission. This usually manifests itself in the form of copyrights, trademarks, patents, and trade secrets. Check out our chart on the various types of this "defensible" IP. The more of it your business has, the more valuable your business becomes.

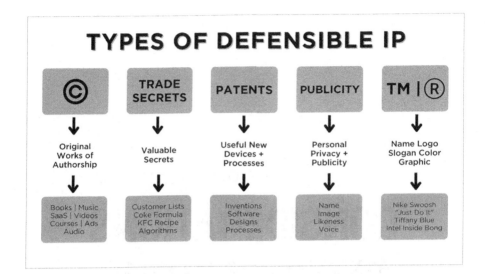

Entity Choice

Choosing the right entity to do business in is an important decision. Your typical buyer is usually looking for a familiar type of entity that most local business acquisitions take place with. Some common entities in the US, UK, and Australia are illustrated in the charts that follow. Take a look at the benefits and issues that each provides and determine what's best for your business.

ENTITY CHOICE: USA

OBJECTIVES → / VALUE CHOICE ↓	Limited Liability	Different Cap Table	Save Taxes	Prefer Law	Geo Diversity	Funding Friendly	Maintain Control	Prep For Sale
Profit Center	CORP LLC LP/LLP	CORP	CORP ?LLC?	CORP LLC LP	CORP	CORP	CORP VPS LLC (MM) LP (MP)	CORP LLC
Tangible Assets	CORP LLC LP	CORP	CORP LLC LP/LLP	CORP	CORP LP	CORP LLC LP	CORP (PFS) LLC (MM) LP (MP)	CORP LLC LP
Intangible Assets	CORP LLC	CORP	CORP LLC LP	CORP	CORP LLC	CORP LLC	CORP (PFS) LLC (MM) LP (MP)	CORP
Intellectual Property	CORP LLC	CORP	CORP	CORP	CORP LLC LP	CORP	CORP (PFS) LLC (MM) LP (MP)	CORP

ENTITY CHOICE: UK/EU

OBJECTIVES → / VALUE CHOICE ↓	Limited Liability	Different Cap Table	Save Taxes	Prefer Law	Geo Diversity	Funding Friendly	Maintain Control	Prep For Sale
Profit Center	PLC LTD-PCLBS LLP	PLC LTD-PCLBS LLP	PLC LTD-BS/BG LLP	PLC LTD-BS/BG LLP	PLC LTD-PCLBS LLP	PLC	PLC LTD-PCLBS LLP	PLC
Tangible Assets	PLC LTD (PCL-BS)	PLC LTD (PCL-BS)	PLC LTD (PCL-BS)	PLC LTD (PCL-BS)	PLC LTD (PCL-BS)	PLC	PLC LTD-BS/BG LLP	PLC
Intangible Assets	PLC LTD (PCL-BS)	PLC LTD (PCL-BS)	PLC LTD (PCL-BS)	PLC LTD (PCL-BS)	PLC LTD (PCL-BS)	PLC	PLC LTD-BS/BG LLP	PLC
Intellectual Property	PLC LTD (PCL-BS)	PLC LTD (PCL-BS)	PLC LTD (PCL-BS)	PLC LTD (PCL-BS)	PLC LTD (PCL-BS)	PLC	PLC LTD-BS/BG LLP	PLC

ENTITY CHOICE: AUSTRALIA

Business Structures & Rating Criteria:	PTY PTD Company	Trust	Partnership	Sole Trader
Simple Paperwork & Rules	X	X	—	✓
Expense of Setup & Maintenance	X	X	✓	✓
Personal Liability Protection	✓	—	X	XX
Tax Benefits	✓	✓	X	X
Overall Rating	✓	—	—	X

Do Not Be The Brand

Very often in service businesses, eLearning, and some SaaS businesses the business is very much based on and tied to a person. Many business owners are bursting with pride as they tell you how indispensable they are to their business. They don't realize that the indispensability that makes them feel so good, just might make their business unsellable at any price, even though it is wildly profitable. Always remember that the more valuable you are to your business, the less valuable your business is to someone else.

Having dealt with many personality-based businesses over the years, we have developed a strategy for de-personalizing a business and the checklist we use to accomplish that is included below to help you in the event that you face this type of situation.

BRAND VALUE TRANSFER **WORKSHEET**

Current Brand (Person Name)   Re-Brand (No Person Name)

_____   _____

Trademark Check Name/Class Available   ☐ Yes   ☐ No

Additional Spokespeople: _____

Brand Guidelines Checklist:
   ☐ Logo   ☐ Colors   ☐ Typography   ☐ Image   ☐ Voice

Brand Expansion Tools:
   ☐ Licensing   ☐ Partners   ☐ Affiliates   ☐ Franchise
   ☐ Ambassadors   ☐ Fan Club   ☐ Certification   ☐ Referral

Seek and Flaunt Your Media Wins

There are countless business awards and competitions and despite what you might think, they are extremely valuable in building your brand reputation and can transfer into increases in transferable value, particularly if your business receives national or international recognition from a well-known organization.

Shift or Pre-Capture COGS (Cost of Goods Sold)

The more you can insulate your business from financial risks, the more valuable it will be. One way to do this is to transfer the expense and therefore capital requirement and risk of cost of goods sold from your business to your customer. There are several strategies for accomplishing this as the next chart illustrates.

PRE-CAPTURE COST OF GOODS SOLD

T&C
Sell registration before event costs must be paid for.
Use proceeds to pay the costs of the event.

Sell computers before parts and labor must be paid for.
Use proceeds to buy parts and pay labor.

Sell + get payment for products before they exist.
Use proceeds to manufacture and launch.

Design, Curate + Measure CX (Customer Experience)

Studies have shown that happy customers create more valuable companies. Therefore, it is important to design and curate an exceptional customer experience within the businesses you intend to exit, and the best way to prove that you have done that successfully is by measuring customer satisfaction using NPS (Net Promoter Score).

Check out the impact of a good CX on valuation in the chart below.

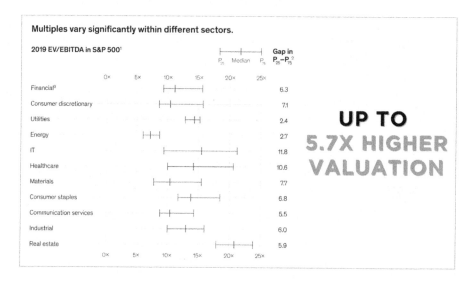

Once again, very detailed breakdowns of how to design, curate, and measure CX are beyond the scope of this book, but you can find more information about these things on the resource site for the book at BusinessWealthWithoutRisk.com/access. That said, below are two of the tools that we created and have found very helpful with respect to CX design and improvement.

BusinessWealthWithoutRisk.com/access

CUSTOMER TOUCHPOINT INVENTORY

PRE-PURCHASE	PURCHASE	POST-PURCHASE
Ads, Walk-By, Walk-In, Word of Mouth, Print Ad, Radio, TV, Trade Show, Referral, Website, Blog, Newsletter, Flyer, Search Engine, Email, Webinar, Landing Pages, Snap, Facebook, Instagram, YouTube, LinkedIn, UGC, Messenger, Chat, User Group, Forum, Review Site, Retargeting, Comparison Site, Competitor Sites, Online Store, Call Center, Physical Store, Amazon, Direct Mail, Samples, Trial	Add-To-Cart, View Cart, Customer Login, Guest Checkout, Pre-Pop Checkout, One-Click Purchase, Edit Cart Add/Remove, View Product From Cart, Zoom Detail, Persistent Cart, Shipping Methods, Delivery Times, In/Out of Stock, Payment Methods, Upsells, Down-Sells, In-Purchase Support, Thank You Page, Confirmations Chat, Messenger, Bots, In-Person Sales, Call Center	Email Order Confirmations, Messenger Order Confirmations, Bots, Ship Confirmations, Tracking, Delivery Time, Delivery, Unboxing, Box Open Welcome, 1st Product Contact, 1st Use, Use Instructions, Bundle-In Offers, On-Boarding, NPS, Consumption, Gifts Follow-Up, Support, UGC, User Communities, Testimonials, Follow-On Sales, Loyalty Programs, Retention, Referral, Re-order, Reviews

The Customer Touchpoint Inventory above is a comprehensive list of possible points at which your company is likely to interact or connect or contact your potential pre-purchase, during purchase, and post-purchase customers. You can take a current inventory of customer touchpoints and then design improvements for each point along the total path to purchase.

Another tool we developed to improve CX is the FAB 50 tool, where we conduct individual outreach to 50 top customers or customer category representatives to ask one-on-one questions about their Feelings, Actions, and Beliefs (FAB). Here's an example below:

FAB 50 FEEDBACK

FEEDBACK	FEELINGS	ACTIONS	BELIEFS
I buy most products online		"I like to buy this kind of product online."	
I think prices are better online			"I believe prices are better online."
I ask for friend recommendations		"I get recommendations from friends before I made a purchase."	
I'm nervous if it's not amazon	"I'm not comfortable buying from sites that I don't already know."		
I compare prices to not overpay			"I believe that you will overpay if you don't compare prices first."
I hate being upsold	"I feel like you should be able to buy without a bunch of upsells."		
I always look for coupon codes		"I search for discount codes before I make a purchase."	
I won't pay for shipping			"I believe all merchants should offer free shipping."
I search for reviews before I buy		"I search review sites before I make a purchase."	
I want a guarantee before I buy	"I feel reassured when they offer a money-back-guarantee."		
I need financing options			"I believe all merchants should offer financing options."
Save my cart or I'm gone			

Recurring Revenue (Monthly = MRR | Annual = ARR)

We talked a bit about recurring revenue way back in part one of this book with respect to the Acquisition Wheel for acquiring businesses, and here it is again. The truth is that businesses with recurring revenue are generally valued higher than those without it, so if you can create or acquire MRR/ARR for your business, that's only going to help its valuation.

Below are some tools to help you install recurring revenue in your business:

VARYING LEVELS OF MRR

CONSUMABLES: Food, gasoline, tape

SUNK-MONEY CONSUMABLES: Razor/blade, Verizon phone/minutes

MANUAL-RENEW SUBSCRIPTIONS: Magazines, Mastermind Membership

SUNK-MONEY MANUAL-RENEW SUBSCRIPTIONS: Bloomberg Terminal/Data

AUTO-RENEW SUBSCRIPTIONS: Cable, Home Phone, HBO, Garbage Collection, Power

CONTRACTED-TERM SUBSCRIPTIONS: Email Service Provider, Many SaaS

CONTRACTED-TERM AUTO-RENEW SUBSCRIPTIONS: SaaS

SUNK-MONEY, CONTRACTED-TERM, AUTO-RENEW SUBSCRIPTIONS: ESP

MRR STEP-BY-STEP

5X YOUR COMPANY'S VALUE IN 3 SIMPLE STEPS

#1 List Your Top 7 Income Streams:	#2 Static or MRR?		#3 How Could You Transform It? (circle one per line)
_____	Static	MRR	Buyer's Club SaaS Membership/Box Cert Assoc.
_____	Static	MRR	Buyer's Club SaaS Membership/Box Cert Assoc.
_____	Static	MRR	Buyer's Club SaaS Membership/Box Cert Assoc.
_____	Static	MRR	Buyer's Club SaaS Membership/Box Cert Assoc.
_____	Static	MRR	Buyer's Club SaaS Membership/Box Cert Assoc.
_____	Static	MRR	Buyer's Club SaaS Membership/Box Cert Assoc.
_____	Static	MRR	Buyer's Club SaaS Membership/Box Cert Assoc.

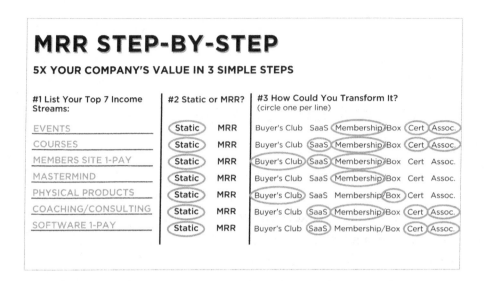

Simplify Your Product Offerings

Simplifying your products and services can often result in increased perceived and real value to your customers. Here are some ideas to help you with simplification:

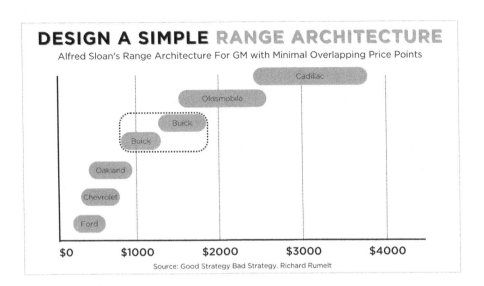

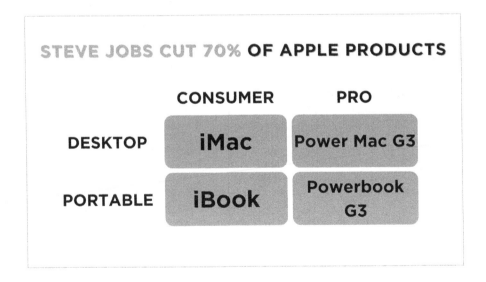

Scale + Cross-train Your Teams

The more your company depends on you, the less valuable it is to someone else. This also applies to a few key employees vs. well-trained, cross-trained employees who provide duplication of labor in the event something happens to any of the key employees in your business. But, this applies not only to key employees, but to all employees. All of your employees perform important functions, or you wouldn't employ them. Buyers worry that something may happen or one or more employees may leave the company post-sale and that would damage their investment and potentially reduce their ROI on purchasing the business. The best way to address this issue is by cross-training your employees. We use a tool to do this and have included a sample below to help you:

EMPLOYEE CROSS-TRAINING TOOL

JOB TITLE	EMPLOYEE	TASK TO TRAIN	WHO TO TRAIN	TRAINING DATES
ORDER ENTRY	Tiffany: Accounting Orders Processor	All tasks in job description except: [Except List]	Calvin: Sales Salesperson	Start Date: 9/12/21 ✓ Complete ✓ 9/14/21
PAYABLES	Juanita: Accounting AP Clerk	All tasks in job description except: [Except List]	Chu: Accounting AR Clerk	Start Date: 9/12/21 ✓ Complete ✓ 9/14/21
ORDER ENTRY	Chu: Accounting AR Clerk	All tasks in job description except: [Except List]	Juanita: Accounting AP Clerk	Start Date: 9/12/21 ✓ Target ☒ 9/17/21

Create a Long-Term Retention Plan to Incentivize Employees to Stay

There are lots of ways to incentivize employees to stay with your business no matter who owns it. The more retention plans you implement the less risk to the buyer, and therefore the higher the price you can expect to receive for your company when it comes time to sell. Here are some ideas to help you:

LONG-TERM RETENTION

COMPENSATION: Competitive or Above Market Salary + Benefits

INTERVIEWING: Motivation-Based Interviewing

ONBOARDING: Integrative Multi-Departmental Onboarding Program

SATISFACTION: Employee NPS + Satisfaction Monitoring

ENGAGEMENT: Provide Employees Voice In The Business

RECOGNITION: Implement Recognition + Reward Programs

DEVELOPMENT: Provide Management + Job Skills Training Opportunities

CULTURE: Create Strong Company Culture + A Compelling Mission

INCENTIVES: Merit-Based Bonuses + Incentive Equity Options

SOPs (Standard Operating Procedures)

Along the lines of retaining key employees and cross-training all employees, SOPs (Standard Operating Procedures) document all of the day-to-day functions of each of the employees and processes at a business. Having your business's SOPs well-documented helps reduce post-acquisition risk for the buyer and helps you command a higher price when you go to sell your business. You can document your SOPs by text, audio, or video, and they can be as complex as a series of process flowcharts to as simple as a written set of instructions. The only real thing that matters here is can someone not familiar with the job or process consume the SOPs and competently complete the task documented by the SOPs?

WAR ROOM CLIENT
INTAKE + ONBOARDING PROCESS

1. Online Application/Live Event Inquiry
2. Welcome Call
3. If they don't answer, email them and add the application as attachment.
4. Payment
5. Add to Facebook Group
6. Add to Member's Library
7. Add to Google Docs (Accounting Spreadsheet + Member's Spreadsheet)
   a. Member's Page
   b. Newsletter Page
   c. Attendance Page
   d. Name Badge Page
8. Add to Infusionsoft Accounts (MMS + Tag with WarRoom[Year] Tag
9. Mail WarRoom Welcome Box
10. Welcome Email -- Welcome to the Family
11. Directory Email

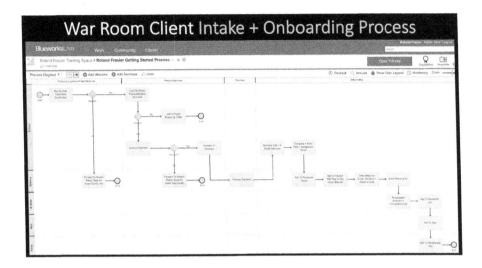

Plan in Advance

One key to successfully exiting is advance planning. This should start two to three years before your intended exit. First, make a list of potential buyers. The reason is self-evident. If you want to sell, you need a pool of buyers to sell to! Later in the chapter we'll talk more about the different types of buyers and the pros and cons of each.

Get all your legal and administrative ducks in a row with the help of an attorney. Audit or review your financials and get a professional valuation (more on that later). You'll also need to clean up any employment regulatory issues and HR compliance, register and catalog existing intellectual property, settle outstanding lawsuits, and resolve threatened claims.

During this two- to three-year window, you also want to make yourself redundant as the head of the company. That entails stopping being its public face or the key go-to person. Other things you must *cease* doing include suppressing profits to save taxes (this will inhibit your goal of maximizing valuation and sale price), paying personal expenses from the business (something you should generally avoid anyway), and paying down debt and investing in profit instead. Strive to prevent key employees, and key accounts/clients, from leaving. Eliminate unnecessary expenses.

Finally, for reasons we'll explain later, stop telling anyone and everyone you are selling. Later, you may want to go public with your exit intentions and advertise it far and wide. For now, it's better to be discreet.

Organization

You must be *organized*. Everything must be in order. No one wants to acquire a business with a lot of legal or financial loose ends—or liabilities.

Organize and audit your records, including those pertaining to intellectual property, contractor, supplier, customer, and employee relationships. Resolve pre-emptive, option, non-dilution, 1st right of refusal/ notice, approval and other rights/limitations in company documents. Review any director/owner meeting docs and equity and option ownership and issuance records. Get audited financials to reduce indemnification and holdback provisions in sales contract and post-closing claims.

These will all come up later and will have some bearing on the exit process. The time to handle these tasks is now, not when you're courting bidders or soliciting indications of interest.

Having a proficient management team is as important now as it was when running your business. Consider adding "bench strength:" hire experienced senior managers, add a retention program, fill depth, identify successors to exiting owners, and fill out your board of directors with the right people if you don't have them already.

You need to optimize value levers. Which lines of business will add to or take away from valuation? Fill product and service gaps. De-risk your revenue and customer base by identifying and correcting customer dependency, single/few product dependency, geo-limiting, and regulatory and related risks. Create recurring revenue and customer contracts that make the acquisition more attractive to buyers.

Institute and execute programmatic acquisition program to acquire competitors, IP, additional products and services, supply and distribution chain, teams, resources, and media.

Meanwhile, continue to grow your brand in your target markets.

Your Exit Dream Team

Every quarterback needs a squad of offensive linemen, backs, tight ends, and receivers. These are the people who make your championship-winning late game drive up the field possible. Hiring key advisors will ensure your company's financial, legal, and administrative health is intact and ready for an acquisition.

First, you need an exit advisor, someone who can counsel on any and everything related to the sale. You should also hire both an M&A attorney and a tax attorney. Finally, a wealth advisor, investment banker, and accountant will round out your team.

BUILD YOUR PERFECT EXIT ADVISORY TEAM

EXIT TEAM	PLANNING	OPERATIONS
Exit Advisor	Pre-Exit Entity Structuring	Continue operating as normal.
	Tax + Estate Planning	
M&A Attorney	Financial Due Diligence: Audits + Budgets	Hire and invest as usual but avoid extraordinary growth expenses.
Accountant	Optimize EBITDA	Continue existing expansion and growth plans.
	Employee Contracts + Key Team Retention Program	
Tax Attorney		Maintain confidentiality of Intent to sell until necessary. Reveal to
	Legal Diligence: Entity, IP, Documents, Governance	team on need-to-know basis.
Wealth Advisor		
	Commercial Diligence: NPS, Ops Review, SOPs, Org Chart	
Investment Banker	Cap-Ex + Op-Ex Initiatives Review	

Valuation and Sale Price

Is your business owner-operated or professionally managed? This influences your asking price.

A business is owner-operated if the owner cannot be away from the business for an extended period of time without that absence adversely impacting the business. Owner-operated businesses (OOB) sell for multiples of SDE (seller discretionary earnings) which is profit (sales minus expenses) including non-essential expenses and benefits the owner pays through the business (e.g., child-care, family trips, personal autos, meals, and other personal expenses).

A business is professionally managed if the owner can be away from the business for an extended period of time without that absence adversely impacting the business. In contrast to OOB, professionally managed businesses sell for multiples of EBITDA (which as you know by now is earnings before interest, taxes, depreciation, and amortiza-tion expenses.) Those expenses either do not affect cashflow or are not essential to operating the business so they are excluded.

When we say "multiples", what exactly do we mean? It's influ-enced by a variety of factors.

WHAT DRIVES THE MULTIPLE?

Market Conditions
Availability of Debt Capital
Industry Popularity
Supply + Demand
Investor Appetite
General Economy

Sales Process
Experience of Target's Team
Number of Potential Buyers
Management Availability
Data Room Quality + Completeness

Company Conditions
Financial Condition + Statements
Growth History + Opportunities
Customer Sentiment (NPS)
Management Team
Risk Factors

Valuation Models
Company Budget Pro-Forma History
Industry/Market Comparable Sales
Multiple Category Positioning
Buyer IRR Requirements

There is a handy chart that lists EBIDTA multiples by business type. Your business might exist in more than one category. This is not unusual and in fact can be strategically beneficial as you position your company for sale.

EBITDA MULTIPLES BY INDUSTRY

INDUSTRY NAME							
Advertising	8.86	Electronics (Consumer & Office)	18.96	Packaging & Container	10.34	Telecom Services	6.76
Aerospace/Defense	12.15	Electronics (General)	17.52	Paper/Forest Products	7.71	Tobacco	10.48
Air Transport	34.43	Engineering/Construction	10.85	Power	11.89	Transportation	12.96
Apparel	14.69	Entertainment	36.26	Precious Metals	10.30	Transportation (Railroads)	15.46
Auto & Truck	45.73	Environmental & Waste Services	14.98	Publishing & Newspapers	9.77	Trucking	10.06
Auto Parts	10.07	Farming/Agriculture	14.71	R.E.I.T.	22.72	Utility (General)	12.15
Bank (Money Center)	N/A	Financial Svcs. (Non-Bank & Insurance)	N/A	Real Estate (Development)	47.57	Utility (Water)	20.92
Banks (Regional)	N/A	Food Processing	12.88	Real Estate (General/Diversified)	25.25	Total Market	20.02
Beverage (Alcoholic)	17.61	Food Wholesalers	15.87	Real Estate (Operations & Services)	14.82	Total Market (W/O Financial)	16.52
Beverage (Soft)	20.74	Home Furnishings	9.73	Recreation	22.59		
Broadcasting	7.84	Green & Renewable Energy	22.94	Reinsurance	12.92		
Brokerage & Investment Banking	N/A	Healthcare Products	28.53	Restaurant/Dining	23.53		
Building Materials	13.27	Healthcare Support Services	10.36	Retail (Automotive)	11.56		
Business & Consumer Services	17.40	Healthcare Information & Technology	29.32	Retail (Building Supply)	12.59		
Cable TV	11.11	Homebuilding	9.54	Retail (Distributors)	13.88		
Chemical (Basic)	10.01	Hospitals/Healthcare Facilities	8.97	Retail (General)	12.29	Industry Determines Valuation	
Chemical (Diversified)	13.38	Hotel/Gaming	38.32	Retail (Grocery & Food)	5.75		
Chemical (Specialty)	15.56	Household Products	17.60	Retail (Online)	33.19	What Business Are You In?	
Coal & Related Energy	5.79	Information Services	31.70	Retail (Special Lines)	11.40		
Computer Services	10.70	Insurance (General)	9.99	Rubbert & Tires	9.84	What Valuation?	
Computers/Peripherals	24.76	Insurance (Life)	12.51	Semiconductor	18.04		
Construction Supplies	15.23	Insurance (Prop/Cas.)	9.69	Semiconductor Equipment	18.69		
Diversified	11.37	Investments & Asset Management	26.17	Shipbuilding & Marine	10.67		
Drugs (Biotechnology)	14.40	Machinery	16.70	Shoe	35.83		
Druges (Pharmaceutical)	14.32	Metals & Mining	13.90	Software (Entertainment)	25.09		
Education	14.43	Office Equipment & Services	8.82	Software (Internet)	19.21		
Electrical Equipment	15.96	Oil/Gas (Integrated)	10.77	Software (System & Application)	30.42		
Electronics (Consumer & Office)	18.96	Oil/Gas (Production & Exploration)	6.39	Steel	9.74		
		Oil/Gas Distribution	9.12	Telecom (Wireless)	10.14		
		Oilfield Services/Equipment	11.35	Telecom Equipment	13.92	Source: Stern.NYU.edu	

Obviously, your objective as a seller is to get the maximum selling price. There are various strategies to achieve this, one of which is using *multiple arbitrage*.

If your business is *not* owner-operated (professionally managed), then:

Step #1: It will sell for a multiple of EBITDA. Search the multiples charts that follow and circle all the industries that your business could currently be in.

Step #2: Circle other industries your business could move *into*.

Step #3: Compare the multiples of all the circled industries. Consider repositioning your business to qualify for the highest multiple industry it could be in. This is how to maximize your industry multiple to sell your business for the greatest possible price.

If your business *is* owner-operated, the process is a little different.

Step #1: Owner-operated businesses sell for SDE. Use the chart below (from Equidam.com) to locate the multiple and corresponding business value.

Step #2: Circle the multiples for the applicable industry and SDE for your current business. Note: larger size businesses sell for higher multiples.

Step #3: Determine whether you are happy to sell at the multiple your business currently qualifies for or whether you would rather grow it larger to sell for more.

AVERAGE SDE MULTIPLES BY SIZE

SDE	MULTIPLE	BUSINESS VALUE
$50,000	1.0 - 1.25	$50,000 - $62,000
$75,000	1.1 - 1.8	$82,500 - $135,000
$100,000	2.0 - 2.7	$200,000 - $270,000
$200,000	2.5 - 3.0	$500,000 - $600,000
$500,000	3.0 - 4.0	$1,500,000 - $2,000,000
$1,000,000	3.25 - 4.25	$3,250,000 - $4,250,000

SaaS Businesses

SaaS businesses are optimal for leveraging explosive profits, and if you've brought a SaaS enterprise to the exit stage, you're doing well.

Step #1: SaaS businesses typically sell for multiples of ARR (Annual Recurring Revenue).

Step #2: Using the chart below, circle the multiples for the applicable industry and SDE for your current business.

Step #3: Note: larger size businesses sell for higher multiples.

Step #4: Determine whether you are happy to sell at the multiple your business currently qualifies for or whether you would rather grow it to sell for more.

If your TTM (trailing twelve months) ARR is greater than $1 million, then your private (not publicly traded) company multiple will typically equal about 70% of current public SaaS company valuations in your industry, according to Equidam.com. Use Google, Crunchbase, or other research tools to find publicly traded companies most similar to your SaaS. Then look up their current market cap (total value of all shares of the company) and divide that by the current ARR for that company. You can find that in the company's public securities filings if it is not immediately available via Google.

If your business has TTM ARR of less than $1 million, then use an average private company multiple of between 3-10x TTM ARR.

Consider whether you can reposition the entire business towards the highest exit multiple. If not, can you spin-off the highest exit multiple business from others to maximize exit value?

For example, we owned a publishing business that intersected with several industries. In fact, our publishing business could have qualified for any of these categories.

INDUSTRY	MULTIPLE	INDUSTRY	MULTIPLE
Edu. Services	1.45	R.E.I.T.	11.43
Publishing	.91	Diversified	2.64
Business Services	1.83	Finance Services	31.81
Software/Internet	6.76	Retail Internet	2.99

As a publishing business, the multiple was only .91 at the time we wanted to sell. But it could also have qualified in these other categories that all had higher multiples at that time. We researched other potential multiple categories and determined whether to reposition the business in that direction.

We researched other potential multiple categories and determined whether to reposition **the business in that direction...**

INDUSTRY	MULTIPLE	INDUSTRY	MULTIPLE
Edu. Services	1.45	R.E.I.T.	11.43
Publishing	.91	Diversified	2.64
Business Services	1.83	Finance Services	31.81
Software/Internet	6.76	Retail Internet	2.99

If we could reposition as a Financial Services company, the multiple would be ~35x higher than a publishing company (31.81 / .91 = 35x)

We found that if we could reposition as a financial services company, the multiple would be around 35x higher than a publishing company (31.81 / .91 = 35x).

If we could reposition as a Real Estate Investment Trust (REIT), the multiple would be 12.6x higher than a publishing company (11.43 / .91 = 12.6x).

If we could reposition as a Software/Internet Business, the multiple would be 7.4x higher than a publishing company (6.76 / .91 = 7.4x).

So how you position yourself has a vast influence over the sale price.

Ultimately, it was best to reposition the business as a software company, so we acquired a software development team (by buying another software company) and turned our publishing business into a recurring revenue SaaS. Taking the time to convert our publishing assets into SaaS permitted us to reposition and increase valuation by 7.4x. You can do the same with your business. Just run the numbers.

How to Get a Higher Price for Your Business

Use *enterprise value (EV) acquisition arbitrage* to acquire low multiple entities and fold them into your higher multiple business to instantly and dramatically increase total valuation.

For example, if you position your business at an 8x multiple and you acquire three more businesses at a million dollars each, at a multiple of 3x, you add the difference of 5x (8x multiple for your business – 3x multiple paid to acquire the three businesses) to your business. 5 x $1 million = $5 million in exit value

The three sellers of the three acquired businesses receive their desired exit price and you add $5 million to your exit valuation!

Fortune Formulas

We will assume that we've sufficiently highlighted the importance of having defensible IP and how having unique assets like copyrights, trademarks, patents, and trade secrets that competitors cannot use without permission can significantly increase your business's value.

In Chapter 15, we'll bring everything together to help you navigate and select the most intelligent way to exit your business. Choosing the best option can be challenging as each transaction and process type has advantages and disadvantages.

Additionally, we will show you how to find hungry qualified buyers for your business. You will learn how to leverage the expertise and connections of your team, including exit advisors, investment bankers, business brokers, and M&A attorneys. These professionals are well-versed in handling processes, encouraging maximum offers, running auctions with multiple bidders, and overseeing negotiations.

Remember, the goal is not just to exit but to maximize your payout and mitigate risk.

BusinessWealthWithoutRisk.com/access

CHAPTER 15

THE SPECTRUM OF EXIT OPTIONS

FROM RECAP TO RESALE

There are multiple exit avenues you can pursue. The challenge lies in choosing which option is best. Each transaction and process type has its pros and cons, as the next table shows.

Understanding the balance between maximizing sale price and mitigating risk is a nuanced dance. Think of entering the market as you're playing a high stakes game; it offers immense opportunities but comes with significant challenges that need to be weighed.

WHAT TYPE OF TRANSACTION
IS RIGHT FOR YOU?

TRANSACTION	PROS	CONS
Do Nothing	Keep Control, No Dilution, No Distraction To Owners + Operators	No Immediate Payday, Maintain Ownership Risk, Ord. Income Tax On Distributions
Debt Recap	Keep Control, Small Dilution, Small Personal Payout	No Payday, Debt Risk, Covenants, Limited Flexibility + Distributions
Minority Recap	Keep Control, Medium Payout, Growth Capital, Smart Money, Big 2nd Payday @ Full Exit	Equity Dilution, Limits Future Options, Lower Valuation Than Majority Recap or Sale
Majority Recap	Big Payday, Growth Capital, Smart Partner, Small 2nd Payday @ Full Exit, Higher Valuation	Loss of Control, Debt Risk, Lower Valuation Than Full Sale, Loss of Minority Business Designation
Sale	Big Payday Now @ Highest Valuation. Possible Additional Paydays via Earn-Out, etc.	Loss of Control, Potential Earn-Out Dependence, Integration Issues, Potential Employment Required

WHAT TYPE OF TRANSACTION
IS RIGHT FOR YOU?

TRANSACTION	PROS	CONS
Buyer Approaches You	No Offer/Marketing process, Limited Distraction, Maximum Confidentiality Control	Likely Lowest Sales Price, Weak Negotiating Position, Can Drag On, Distraction to Operations
Target + Approach Buyers 1-On-1	You Control Process, Limited Distraction, Maximum Confidentiality Control	Lower Sales Price, Weak Negotiating Position, Can Drag On, Distraction to Operations
Target + Approach Buyer Group	Higher Sales Price, You Control Process, Create Competition Among Quality Buyers, Choose Your Buyer, Good Confidentiality Control	Fewer Potential Buyers Means Lower Sales Price. Some Risk of Confidentiality Loss
Take To Market In Auction Process	Likely Highest Sale Price, Max Competition Among Buyers, Potentially Fastest Time to Complete Process	Max Confidentiality Risk, Highest Disruption to Ops + Management, Expose Confidential Information to Competitors

What path you pursue also depends on your risk tolerance. There is an inverse relation between breadth of marketing your business for sale to receive the highest price and risk of exposure.

If you take it to the market in an auction, you'll likely garner the highest sale price since a wider pool of buyers will be competing. It's also generally a more expeditious method. However, exposure has risks of its own. It can be disruptive to operations, and it can expose confidential information to competitors.

The "target and approach buyer group" and "target and approach buyers one on one" has mediated risk. It's a middle of the road strategy.

When a buyer approaches you, there is, of course, the lowest risk of disruption or exposure of sensitive information. But the tradeoff is a longer process (it's a less efficient way of finding a suitable buyer) with a lower chance of maximizing your payout.

Finding Buyers for Your Business

So, where to actually find these mythical buyers? You were one of them once, searching for the next great opportunity, and probably competing with other buyers as well. So you know they are out there. Now the baton has been passed to you as you move to sell.

First, lean on your team. Exit advisors, investment bankers, business brokers, and M&A attorneys specialize in this—leverage not only their expertise but their connections. They already know potential buyers, and they're skilled in running a "process" to solicit the greatest number of offers. They can orchestrate an auction with multiple bidders vying for the chance to acquire your firm, and they can oversee the negotiations, including key terms and conditions that are probably unfamiliar to you.

Meanwhile, assemble a list of your *direct and indirect competitors* with a similar clientele and website keyword traffic, regardless of geographic location. Crunchbase.com, Pitchbook, or PrivateEquityInfo. com are excellent resources to find private equity funds that may be interested. In addition, research FamilyOfficeList.org and FamilyOffices. com to find family offices that invest in businesses like yours. Reach out and make an inquiry about selling.

Strategic vs. Financial Buyers

Understanding the two main types of buyers will let you narrow your search and strategize how to maximize sale price.

Strategic buyers look for acquisitions they can merge into existing operations. They seek growth, access to a talented management team, expansion of existing capabilities, forays into new markets, enlarging their customer base, synergies (equipment, headcount reduction, resources, purchasing power), industry consolidation that allows them to raise prices, and expansion of existing markets, products, and services.

Financial buyers are motivated by the prospect of an acquisition they themselves can eventually exit in six to ten years. They are attracted by high organic growth, a proven operational team, leaders in their industry or business category, firms that complement an existing portfolio, high-moat differentiated offerings, the ability to expand, exit the multiple, a simple cap table, and strong financials.

Naturally, each class of buyer offers respective pros and cons. Strategic buyers tend to offer a higher sale price. You gain a skilled partner who knows the industry. Potential merger synergies reduce costs by combining duplicated resources like assets and personnel. There exists the potential for improved management processes and resources when a larger company acquires a smaller one. The larger market share that results from the merger enlarges the lead pool.

The drawbacks of strategic buyers include a loss of control and direction of the company, the potential erosion of the company culture you've worked to build as the firm is absorbed by another, potential disputes with new management, the disclosure of confidential information to a competitor, potential loss of customers and sales due to integration challenges, contractual issues (newly required employment contracts or the need to sign non-compete agreements), and finally, minimal opportunities for a second payday upon a subsequent exit of the acquiring company.

The pros of selling to a financial buyer include gaining an experienced or prestigious board, professionalizing the company by adding experienced senior managers, gaining a skilled financial partner with access to growth capital, the potential of lucrative incentives for existing management based on achieving specified milestones, and the possibility of a second payday down the road when the financial buyer exits.

Cons of financial buyers include a loss of control over your company, clashes with the personnel of the acquiring company, required employment (likely) for existing owners and managers, non-compete agreements, the prospect of being sold off should your company underperform the acquirer's benchmarks, a lower valuation (typically) than a strategic buyer, and debt risk from acquisition financing.

Exit Process Timeline

The table below lays out an approximate timeline to follow as you get the ball rolling and formally move forward with selling the company. The length of the pre-exit planning and positioning phase is flexible, but once you progress to the marketing phase, during which you field first-round bids, the timeline is more rigid, and you can close the deal within five months.

EXIT PROCESS TIMELINE OVERVIEW		Flexible	Month 1	Month 2	Month 3	Month 4	Month 5
Pre-Exit Planning + Positioning	Determine Current Value						
	Research Multiple Arbitrage Opportunities						
	Re-position for Highest Multiple						
	Acquisition Arbitrage for Higher Multiple						
	Conduct Internal Due Diligence + Patch Holes						
	Research + Prep Buyer List + Initial Data Room						
	Prepare 1-Sheet, Confidential Info Memo (CIM)						
	Prepare Management Presentation (MP)						
Marketing: 1st Round Bids	Buyer Outreach With One-Sheet						
	Conduct Dry-Runs of MP with Management						
	Secure NDAs From Desirable Buyers						
	Distribute CIM to Desirable IOI Buyers						
	Buyer Indications of Interest (IOI) 1st Round Bids						
	Select Bidders For Management Presentation						
Select Buyer; 2nd Round Bids	Deliver Bid Packages + Grant Data Room Access						
	Pre-Bid Due Diligence / Contact Markup.						
	Deliver MP to Selected Bidders						
	Receive Final Bids (2nd Round Bids)						
	Negotiations + Select Winning Bidder						
	Confirmatory Due Diligence						
Close the Sale	Finalize Contract						
	Secure All Necessary 3rd Party Approvals						
	Sign/Close						

In the pre-exit stage, you'll prepare your one-sheet, a brief document describing the industry, region, and revenue/profit range. The one-sheet does *not* identify your company by name. At this stage, that is confidential (remember our earlier discussion about the relative risks of exposure vs. keeping things under wraps).

Acquirers whose interest is piqued by the one-sheet will reach out to you. At this point you have them sign an NDA (nondisclosure agreement) and a CIM (confidential information memo).

Acquirers offer their IOI (indication of interest) if they wish to proceed. Now, it's your job to be selective. Not all interested parties necessarily deserve a chance to move forward.

The IOI offers valuable information about the buyer's level of interest, their seriousness, and whether their capacity for acquisition is realistic. This stage also helps sellers adjust their expectations about the range of exit values. There are also some specifications about the IOI. It should be received within three weeks of sending the CIM. It is non-binding. Generally, it pertains to a range of potential acquisition valuations on a debt-free, cash-free basis. In the IOI, the buyer will outline their expected sources of funding.

The table below illustrates how you can analyze the potential benefits of various buyers. Not all buyers will hit all the marks. But some are likely to emerge as frontrunners based on the fact that they offer more advantages—or advantages that are of particular importance to you.

ANALYZE PROSPECTIVE BUYER BENEFITS

Potential Buyer	Operating Expense Reductions	Access to Additional Markets	Cross-Selling Possibilities	Tech-Stack Advantages + Compatibility	Access to Ops Sales, Dev + Other Teams	Overall Strategic Synergies	Capacity to Pay, Historic Acquisitions
BUYER 1	✓	✓		✓		3/5	3/5
BUYER 2			✓		✓	2/5	4/5
BUYER 3	✓	✓	✓			3/5	2/5
BUYER 4	✓			✓		2/5	4/5
BUYER 5		✓			✓	2/5	3/5

So, review the IOIs and determine which responders will be invited for a management presentation (MP).

After the MP, the company selects the acquirer and submits a LOI (letter of interest), which we talked about in part one of the book.

In the final stages of the process, negotiations over the finer points of the deal take place, and you select the winning bidder. A confirmatory due diligence process ensues, and then the contract can be finalized, along with securing all necessary third-party approvals.

After that, the seller and buyer sign on the dotted line, and the deal is closed. Congratulations! You've now successfully exited the business. Savor the satisfaction of this great achievement and think about what you can do next. The possibilities are boundless. You can repeat the acquisition/growth/exit process again and again, building your wealth beyond your wildest dreams.

Final Thoughts

You now know how to buy, grow exponentially, and exit a business. The secrets are all in these pages, and they now belong to you to apply and enjoy. We made a huge, sweeping promise when we started, that you could enjoy astonishing levels of wealth by applying these ideas, even if you don't have a college degree, tons of capital, connections, or the "right" appearance to succeed in business—however that's defined at any given moment.

Will these ideas work? Of course they will. We can guarantee that, because they have worked so well for so many, starting with the two of us and spreading out to thousands of individuals to whom we have taught these concepts. The real question is whether they will work for you. And the answer depends on whether you will work with them—whether you will put them to use.

If you're saying, "It's too good to be true, it's hype, and it's not going to work for me," there's not much we can do for you, other than hope and pray that you shift your mindset to something more positive! We'll leave you with a brief story to illustrate this point. A native Alaskan tells a story about two boys who wanted to play a trick on a wise man. They got a bird and one of the boys held it in his hands behind his back as they stood before the wise man and asked, "Old man, is the bird alive or dead?"

They had decided if that old man said that the bird was alive, they would snap its neck and kill it. If the old man said it was dead, they would show him that the bird was still alive. They would make him wrong either way.

But the old man was truly wise. Instead, he replied, "The answer, boys, is in your hands."

And the same is true with the contents of this book. Will it work for you? The answer is in your hands.

We feel certain that if you give these ideas a try, the answer will be a resounding, wealth-creating, truly life-changing YES!

For more case studies, examples, worksheets, checklists, forms, scripts, and other resources, including quite a few that we simply could not fit in the book itself, we created a resources collection and all of these resources are available and waiting for you at BusinessWealthWithoutRiskBook.com. Visit the site now and enjoy a huge collection of resources at absolutely no money out of pocket for you!

Also, keep in mind that in addition to a desire to share with you and give back in gratitude for all of the good things that we have both experienced in our lives, we also wrote this book in the hopes that some of you would read it, take action on it, and make it to this page where we want to let you know that we are also very interested in working with you, to help you with your deal, be a part of it, and enjoy success together. Reach out to either of us on social if you feel that you have a deal we should take a look at. Who knows, you may just be our next business partner!

Here's What Next

Now that you have the insights you need to choose the best path to exit your business, it's time to wrap this up.

We trust that you've found value, direction, and transformative potential within the pages of this book. But the real adventure, the journey of implementation and seeing tangible change, is only just beginning.

In closing out this book, we'd like to share the best ways we can support you on your journey. One of the worst mistakes a business owner can make is to think that they should embark on this journey alone, without any help. NOTHING COULD BE FURTHER FROM THE TRUTH.

Inside the final pages of this book, you'll discover potential collaborations and strategies that can help to take your success to the next level.

Remember, you are not alone. We are here, excited to be a part of your journey, cheering you on every step of the way. As you turn the final pages, keep in mind that implementing what you've learned is just the beginning.

Reach out, get more help, and always know that we're here to support you. We eagerly anticipate your achievements and the possibility of surpassing even your wildest dreams. So here's to your success, your growth, and an exciting journey ahead!

BusinessWealthWithoutRisk.com/access

CHAPTER 16

WHERE TO GO FROM HERE?

Alright, my friend, you've journeyed with us this far. And we hope, no, we truly believe that you've found a wealth of insight, direction, and real potential for transformation. We've poured our hearts and souls into this work because we're passionate about YOUR success and about taking YOU to the next level. You see, we don't just write to inspire or educate; we write to create change, to shape lives, to ignite that spark of greatness that we know exists within every reader.

Yet, the real journey is just beginning. The wisdom you've gleaned from these pages is potent. It's true, but it's just the tip of the iceberg. The gold mine we've discovered together—this arsenal of strategies, insights, and opportunities—it's a mere fraction of what can be achieved together. We want to dive deeper with you, work closely with you, become a part of your journey to the top. Because, let's be clear, success is not a solo sport; it's a team effort.

Now, in the appendix, you'll find some ways in which we could collaborate, learn, and grow together. These are not exhaustive lists by any means. They represent an invitation to break the chains of ordinary, to transcend limits, and to journey with us beyond the confines of this book. We want to see you thrive. We want to be there with you at every step. Because nothing would make us happier than to see you not just achieve, but surpass your wildest dreams.

As you turn the final pages of this book, remember, implementing what you've learned is just the beginning. Reach out. Get more help. Don't be a stranger. You're not alone in this. You've got this—and we've got you. So here's to your success, to your growth, and to an exciting journey ahead! Goodbye for now, but we hope, not for long.

Private Consult with Roland Frasier

EpicNetwork.com/private-consult

With over 40 years of experience, Roland Frasier and his team have worked with companies in virtually every industry to achieve financial growth, acquisitions of other businesses and assets for growth, leads, sales, profits and wealth building, and multiply the transferable value of any company in a fraction of the time that it typically takes using proven and tested approaches.

Whether you are looking to expand operations, grow sales, reduce customer acquisition costs, eliminate inefficiencies, or need a profitable exit strategy, your answers are a single consult away.

Private Consult with Jay Abraham

Abraham.com/coaching-consulting

Jay provides high level advice, strategic high performance long (and short) term "hands-on" consulting, and serves as a masterful 360-degree thinking partner to CEOs, Entrepreneurs, and P&L-responsible managers throughout the world.

He works in uniquely different ways with each company (and private client) he serves, depending totally on the mission critical opportunities and issues at hand.

His fee structure is value based, meaning it's predicated on the size of the problem he's asked to solve and/or opportunities he is challenged to help mine.

He also conducts elite, small group weekend, multi-modality, makeover experiences for company heads preferring shorter-term access to his expertise.

To understand how Jay might best serve your company's outsized growth and profitability goals, contact him c/o

Jay@abraham.com

Book Jay Abraham to Speak

Abraham.com/jay-speaks

A different slant on "keynote" addresses, Jay approaches group presentations differently from most keynote speakers. He does not merely do the standard one-hour canned presentation, instead he typically does a hybrid of principles and examples, followed by 2+ hours of problem solving, Q&A, and opportunity mining clinics with participants.

His forte is the ability to think "way outside of the box" while thinking "way inside of the box" when addressing multiple potential scenarios that has enabled him to find creative, preemptive solutions (with high performance results) to very complex problems on demand, live at events.

When time permits, he interacts with participants in special VIP mini-masterminds and meets with sponsors all for the same fee equivalent to what experts charge for a simple one-hour presentation.

If you would like to book Jay to speak at your next event, simply reach out to his office at The Abraham Group at 1 (310) 465-1840

Abraham.com/jay-speaks

Book Roland Frasier to Speak

RolandFrasier.com/speaking

For nearly three decades, Roland Frasier has been educating, entertaining, motivating and inspiring entrepreneurs to acquire, scale, and exit their businesses. His unique style inspires, empowers, and entertains audiences while giving them the tools and strategies they need to acquire, scale, and exit brands and businesses.

For powerful keynotes packed with real-world, actionable content that moves your audience to innovate, profit from technological change, disrupt industry incumbents, and transform their businesses with proven rapid growth strategies, book Roland for your next event.

To book Roland Frasier for your next event, simply fill out the form online at RolandFrasier.com/speaking or you can email his team at support@epicnetwork.com.

Other Opportunities with Roland Frasier:

EPIC NETWORK LIVE Events

RolandFrasier.com/events

Imagine learning how to do deals using M&A strategies and Consulting for Equity in 2 days with Roland Frasier and his entire team.

The next step is to contact his team at support@epicnetwork. com and find out how you can get a ticket to his next live event.

MASTERMINDS

EpicNetwork.com/epic-board

RiseNationMastermind.com

Several times per year, Roland invites clients that he is working with, people that he wants to work with, and thought leaders to come to gather for mastermind meetings. He has traveled to London, Paris, and all over the US and world hosting these mastermind meetings. He has different mastermind meetings that he participates in. He has an exclusive network of elite entrepreneurs and investors who rise to take their business and life to the next level.

If you would like to find out more on how to get involved with one of his masterminds, please email support@epicnetwork.com.

BusinessWealthWithoutRisk.com/access

APPENDIX

TOOLS AND STRATEGIES TO ENHANCE YOUR SUCCESS

This appendix offers you our collective expertise distilled into a few lists that will help you maximize your growth and business success. We'll explore points to leverage marketing, ways to maximize relational capital, and categories that can grow your business.

From these, we encourage you to adapt them to enhance your own strategies. They offer you tangible steps to follow as you embark on your unique journey. And be sure to tell us about all about it!

First, let's dive into our 62 points to leverage marketing. They prompt you with questions as you embark on your business future to ensure that you are fully prepared for all of the various challenges you might encounter. So from us to you, here are some considerations to make sure you are ready to embrace each new phase of your business's life cycle.

62 Points to Leverage Marketing

1. When hiring people, ask yourself, "What can they teach me that I don't already know?"

2. What allocation of your budget is set aside for trying wild, innovative things?

3. Do you acquire one competitor, or acquire a complimentary business, every year on an earn-out basis?

4. In what ways are you defining, distinguishing, and delineating your product/service/company/people?

5. Do you study all of your competitors' sales material, sales approaches, marketing approaches, websites, communications, etc.?

6. How can you make the media you use more high-yielding?

7. Can you move your media cost from fixed to variable?

8. Can you use barter instead of cash to get your media and thus reduce your cost of acquisition?

9. Are you looking at all the performance metrics of everything and everyone?

10. Where could you put incentives or bonuses to increase your yield?

11. What have you done to make your database provide more performance yield?

12. Have you looked at better lists? Endorsements? Sub-strata within your lists?

13. In what ways are you continually optimizing and maximizing the three ways to grow a business?

14. How have you built your Power Parthenon? Have you built multiple impact and access points? How many do you have working for you?

15. How many of the 21 Power Principles are you utilizing?

16. How many of the 34 X-Factors are you utilizing?

17. Are you continually looking at the Nine Sticking Points and engineering breakthroughs for each?

18. How are you using your time? Your ability? Your opportunity cost?

19. How might you go to your competitors and try and buy their non-sold prospects (or even buyers)?

20. How much earned media are you trying to get?

21. Do you look at categories of buyers and analyze where they came from to see what unique correlations and implications exist?

22. What are all the facets you're testing with your sales force? What else could be tested?

23. Have you tested multiple different variables? Different ways to open a relationship? Different ways to advance the relationship?

24. Have you tested a multitude of sequential communications that involve call, letter, email, text and more?

25. Have you tested different messaging that is value-based or provocative, sustainable, and progressive? Can you build upon this?

26. When communicating with someone, do you test different premises, propositions, and preemptive ways of addressing issues?

27. Have you tested what you can do to accelerate the purchase?

28. Have you tested what you can do to upsell the purchase?

29. Have you tested what to do after the purchase?

30. Have you tested making arrangements with other people who have additional and/or complementary products and services?

31. How many different sources have you tested for your online (and offline) marketing?

32. How many different headlines, copy points, positioning elements, etc. have you tested?

33. Are you exploring and testing new access vehicles to your market?

34. Who might be someone that would endorse you to their list or that would be an influential advisor who would recommend you?

35. How many referral strategies do you currently have in place?

36. How many relational capital strategies have you applied? What's your method and system for continually engineering Power Partnerships and Joint Ventures?

37. Do you have anybody on your list that is influential?

38. Are you leveraging testimonials and success stories?

39. Who is a non-competitive mind in your field that would be valuable to sit down with/call/talk to?

40. Did you form your own mastermind group in your community with non-industry successes you collaborate with and discuss problems and opportunities?

41. Who is in your industry, left the company they were with, and has superior knowledge and skill you could bring into your company either as a hire or consultant?

42. How could you leverage thought leadership locally, nationally, or in your industry?

43. Whose bigger problem can be solved by figuring out how to solve your problem?

44. How could you arrange with conference providers to get the rights to video or audio and use segments to give away as value-adds to your market?

45. Are there people in other markets that have produced selling, marketing, operational, cash flow, production, fulfillment processes that are better than you, that you can find and license from them? Do you have things you can license to other people?

46. How do you leverage everyone else's knowledge base?

47. How do you leverage everyone else ethically? How do you leverage your team?

48. What can you do that blows people's minds?

49. Where are all the places and activities in which you are embedding the strategy of Preeminence?

50. What value do you create above and beyond your competitors?

51. Once you get a buyer, how do you enrich the relationship with that buyer after they have purchased?

52. What do you do that is extraordinary for your buyers? Do you contribute other things? Do you speak differently to them? Are there areas where you're taking them for granted? Or do you

relish them and treat them as special? Do you really and truly, in a preeminent way, fall in love with them?

53. Are you really working on distinguishing yourself and your business? How?

54. Can you make your communication style and voice distinctive (or more distinctive)?

55. How many different ways are you using to bring in prospects and first-time buyers?

56. How many ways are you trying to ethically improve the sale?

57. If you don't have products or services to add, how many ways are you trying to find them? How many products or services have you acquired? Are you adding one more product every year?

58. How many ways are you trying to continue the sale?

59. Are you adding one more market every year?

60. How are you leveraging the front-end and back-end of your business?

61. What can you do to make it easier to start the relationship?

62. What would happen if you added one more dimension of purchase revenue that was more expensive and advanced at the end of the purchase cycle?

How was that? Do you feel better prepared now? It's ok if some of these questions left you stumped. Do some research, reach out to your colleagues, and forge ahead! We're here for you too, so feel free to reach out with any questions or requests for additional information.

Now, let's turn to ways to maximize your relational capital. These are tips we've discovered along the way to help you seek out the hidden potential of every facet of your business, your network, and the capital you already have.

40 Ways to Maximize Relational Capital

1. Strategic alliances and joint ventures only add to your own selling efforts (power of geometry).
2. It increases your sales significantly, and thus your profitability.
3. It lowers the barrier of entry into new territory.
4. It boosts your market presence.
5. It provides added value to customers.
6. It contributes substantially to perceived customer or client benefits.
7. It facilitates your entry into emerging markets.
8. It expands your horizons, goals, aspirations, and vision.
9. You can expand beyond your geographic boundaries and even can gain a foothold in international/niche markets.
10. You can control other people's markets.
11. You can gain a competitive advantage.
12. You can rapidly overpower the competition.
13. You can joint market with people and share the cost.
14. You can do joint selling or distribution.

15. You can collaborate to design new products or combinations with other people, using their resources, technology, staff, or talent.

16. You've got total flexibility in the way you operate.

17. It's less risky.

18. It requires less/no cash; you give away no equity, either.

19. You can acquire a technology license.

20. You can get someone else to fund research and development and share R&D they've already completed.

21. You can access knowledge, expertise, and talent beyond company borders.

22. It strengthens *your* expertise in an industry as a result of the relationship association.

23. It extends your product/service offerings.

24. It widens your scope of innovation.

25. You can secure your position as front runner in your market in any new/niche markets you address.

26. You can provide marketing or sales or have someone else provide marketing or sales.

27. You can easily establish purchasing and supply relationships.

28. You can set up instant distribution networks all over the country, industry, nation, continent, or world.

29. You can capitalize on all kinds of hidden assets and overlooked opportunities (underperforming activities, underutilized relationships/credibility).

30. You can make much higher ROI and ROE on alliances than from your core/main business.

31. You can remain focused on your own core business while expanding, exploiting, and harnessing this vast, expanded stream of possibilities.

32. It lets you maximize and stretch your own management, talent, economic, technical, and operational resources.

33. You can outsource every non-core competency, make it more profitable, and only pay for it in direct proportion to its results to your bottom line.

34. You can reduce your overhead through shared costs, lower pricing, and outsourcing.

35. It reinforces a growth/expansion mindset.

36. You're capitalizing on all the goodwill other entities have created over years.

37. You can flip business opportunities.

38. You could do equities in all kinds of strategic partnerships.

39. You can totally reinvent business opportunities.

40. You can access production that you can't afford because there's always going to be somebody somewhere who's got excess production. You can license other people's marketing, or other people's sales ability, or other people's management skills, or other people's cash flow management. You can get access to delivery, facilities, technology, procedures, and intellectual capital that before were out of reach.

Are you inspired yet? We hope so! Our final list of information offers you specifical categories to grow your business. These categories each represent tools you can use to build your network, develop your growth potential, and maximize your impact.

Jay Abraham's 97 Categories That Can Grow Your Business

1. **Brunch Stories, Mindshift (Also Known as Bedtime Stories for Business Owners):** Jay's Stories that illustrate how to creatively implement opportunities to grow a business.

2. **Tunnel vs. Funnel Vision:** Moving from a narrow perspective and limited focus to a strategic practice that is always adding more perspective and insight into every decision you make.

3. **Leverage Your Human Hedge Fund "Investment":** Treat your business like a hedge fund. How can you beat the market? If you aren't, what is your plan to do it or exit?

4. **Going Beyond Exponential with Your Business:** It is mathematically possible to grow your business beyond exponential, so if it is possible, then why not live in the exponential zone?

5. **Preeminence (Becoming the Go-to Advisor):** A gravitational force that attracts business because of ethical behaviors, trust, leadership and so much more that elevates your stature far beyond the maddening crowd.

6. **The Reason Why - Your Wonder Marketing Drug:** Sharing your reason why connects your target market to the reasons and connected emotions for what you do and puts them into your story where they are more likely to buy.

7. **Only 3 Ways to Grow Your Business**: It is easy to believe that there are millions of ways to grow a business, the reality is there are only three ways. These three ways will give you clarity on where to focus your efforts to create profits.

8. **Advanced 3 Ways To Grow Your Business**: Once you master the the ways to grow your business, there are an additional three ways you can add new methods to profit.

9. **Parthenon Strategy**: Most businesses settle for one or two ways to generate revenue. This is not stable, thus the Parthenon strategy illustrates the value of adding new revenue streams under your business roof.

10. **Force Multiplier Effect**: In every military objective, what matters is winning the objective, thus by adding multiple strategies to overcome objections, eliminate threats, enhancing logistics, and over deliver a destructive payload to decimate an enemy the certainty of winning increases.

11. **9 Drivers of Exponential Profit**: Nine areas in business where a small improvement can leverage huge profits.

12. **Social Media**: Connecting to experts that give you insights to access social channels to improve your reach, grow your prospect lists, and convert to new clients that will engage with you for life.

13. **Power Pivots**: Multiple inflection points you can use to turn your business around from being stuck to maximizing profitability.

14. **De-Risking Risk Factors - Eliminate, Limit, or Minimize Your Downside**: Knowing how to take on, minimize, limit, or eliminate risk for your clients so they can more easily choose to do business with you.

15. **What Kind of Investor Are You?**: Knowing yourself—are you a safe preserver, a growth accumulator, a follower, or exponentially independent?

16. **The Golden Numbers**: to get the gold, here are the numbers you need to know: What does it cost to acquire a buyer and what is (or could be) their yield and lifetime value?

17. **Start with the End in Mind**: Knowing what you want to sell your business for and developing the strategies to get your value in place so you can get even more than your asking price.

18. **Crushing the Glass Ceiling**: Make other people's imagined limits your foundation for exponential growth.

19. **Windows of Short-Term Opportunities**: What is going on in the market right now, and how you can take advantage of these conditions?

20. **Performance Gaps**: How to create wins on the front end in business and inspire your clients to cross the gaps left by your competitors.

21. **Yield Gaps**: How to create completions and add value even after the first sale is made.

22. **Maximize... Then Multiply**: The key heuristic (Rule of thumb) on how to start and continue in implementing these exponential profit strategies, and the danger of going too big, too soon.

23. **Profit Prism**: A one tactic business will create profits that get eaten up by market, a profit prism takes in a spectrum of profit producing potential to create shining profits, or it can take the clear light of strategy and apply it to multiple aspects of doing business to grow them all.

BUSINESS WEALTH WITHOUT RISK

24. **Access Denied:** You've lost your buyers' attention, interest, trust, and fallen off of their radar, how can you move back into their awareness?

25. **The Sticking Points Solution:** It is easy to get stuck in business, sometimes it is difficult to notice how stuck you are especially when you are successfully stuck. This category highlights where business owners typically get stuck and how to get back your momentum towards success.

26. **20 Marketing Mistakes and Multipliers:** Marketing is fraught with pitfalls. These 20 points warn of common marketing dangers and how to leverage growth in those areas.

27. **Multiplier vs. Diminisher:** You either multiply value or detract from value. This strategy asks you to give your behaviors an honest look to see where you might be out of alignment with an exponential preeminent growth strategy.

28. **Critical Consequential Thinking and Socratic Interviewing:** How can you ask better questions?

29. **Relational Capital:** The power of relationships to get access to everything you need to grow your business without investing money to get it. Your helping others solve their problems creates the capital for you to solve yours.

30. **Unlimited Checkbook:** The math of relational capital. When you use relational capital, you gain access to an unlimited checkbook.

31. **12 Pillars of Strategic Business Growth:** Practical actions you can apply to grow your business right now, and structuring your thinking and business strategies to align with exponential growth.

32. **61 Points of Leverage Marketing:** 61 questions to unlock profit potential leverage points in your mind and business.

33. **Consultative and Advisory Selling:** A preeminent approach to selling that verifies your clients will get the full value of their decisions and empowers them to begin a lifetime relationship with you.

34. **Relevancy Rules and Rectifiers:** It's easy to break the relevancy rules and fade from prospects' and clients' good graces. This strategy gives an insight into the rules and how to win back people you may have lost.

35. **Activating Absolute Advantage:** This is an integration of strategies so that you can win in the strategic compounding value game.

36. **Radical Rebound:** We might not be able to go back in time, but we can reset. When things are in decline these are strategies and mindsets that can give you a bounce.

37. **Testing:** Insights from Deming, Multivariate testing, and Jury Picking illustrate the critical need for testing, why it works, and how to work it.

38. **PEQ - Optimizing Your Performance Enhancement Quotient:** Every element of every process has the capacity to be optimized.

39. **5 Ways to Create Business Wealth:** Find your key wealth creation levers in business.

40. **Sunk Cost Marketing:** Avoid the sunk cost trap and profit from your non-performing investments.

41. **Modeling for Millions, Borrowing from Billions:** Success is built on the shoulders of giants. This strategy demonstrates how to model the success of millionaires and use the systems, insights, and resources of billionaires.

42. **Beyond Bartering:** The art and fun of deal making. Jay gives examples of how business owners create massive advantage through value exchanges.

43. **Tom O'Neil Theory - The Equity Playbook:** Methodology to build the equity in your business so it can eventually sell for a much higher evaluation.

44. **Proprietor vs. Entrepreneur:** You have a choice to do business at a competitive disadvantage or create a system that builds value to continuously exceed market needs and expectations.

45. **Understanding Meaning to the Other Side:** How to understand what your clients and prospects value is the key to guiding them to buy and profit from your offers.

46. **10x Moonshot Alternative:** There is a hidden danger in moonshots without doing the alternative first.

47. **Spending vs. Investing:** How you and your team think about spending and investing shapes your results, give examples on how shifting thinking shifted results.

48. **Low Hanging Fruit:** We know that this is the ripe and ready fruit that is easy to harvest. It is obvious when you know what to look for, after understanding these strategies in detail, your orchard of opportunity is filled with low hanging fruit.

49. **The Law of Infinite Returns:** Expectations can unlock opportunity or limit growth, see the proof in record breaking examples.

50. **Ideator:** The Power in the Mind of Jay Abraham Unlocked - How to Shift Perspectives, See Unseen Connections, Identify Undervalued Implications, and Grasp Unrecognized Correlations.

51. **Decision Scientist:** Decisions guide everything that happens in your business, understanding the science of better decision making will empower your leverage in every decision you make.

52. **Private Equity vs. VC:** Many owners gamble on unlimited downsides when there are ways to strategically leverage a diversified upside.

53. **Avatar of Exponential Business:** What does an exponential business look like?

54. **Performance Opportunity Assumptive and Yield Gaps:** Finding what your clients do before, during, and after (or instead of) doing business with you.

55. **Ultimate Leverage and OPR:** No Fixed Investment, No Downside, Only Infinite Upside.

56. **Social Intelligence:** There are a multitude of ways to improve our Emotional Quotient that can also improve your client engagement, retention, compelling copy, and so much more.

57. **Trust:** The factors that can grow your business 300%.

58. **Greatness - Four Rules and Eight Categories:** The Mindset and Methods to align with your deepest wish for your life and business.

59. **Six Sigma:** The insights from one of the best Six Sigma experts in the world.

60. **How You Are Seen:** The world's perception of you = the results you can get and grow

61. **How You Are Heard:** Your messaging and how it is delivered matters, and there are many ways to improve it.

62. **The Reason Why - A Marketing Wonder Drug:** Sharing your reason why will inspire clients and prospects to connect with you.

63. **2 Way Licensing:** Stories that illustrate how You can win, they can win and both your clients win too!

64. **Strategic Soft Skills:** A multitude of ways to improve people skills, teams, communication, and strategies that lead to impressive improvements in business profits and the enjoyment of doing business... and life.

65. **Flipping Your Business World View:** Rapid Result Mastery

66. **What Do You Stand For?:** Questions that will guide you into areas you believe in.

67. **CIA Continuous Intelligence Accumulated:** Most people are in love with knowing and being right, it is better to fall in love with learning and fixing what was wrong.

68. **Amazon.com AKA Mind of the Market - School of Business / Research:** How to improve your understanding of your prospects and clients minds, and ways to improve your copy to connect with them.

69. **9 Forms of Thinking:** There are multiple ways of thinking - which are your strengths - The essential addition to all of them is being strategic.

70. **Uncovering What you don't know:** Expand your knowledge Paradigm - to find the correlations, implications, anomalies, quantifications, connections and relationships.

71. **Pattern Recognition:** There are many ways to develop understanding, to see the ways we can program Augmented Intelligence (AI) we can gain insight into how to better program our own minds and

72. **Partner or Perish:** We all know the power of people, but it is even more powerful in business, without connecting businesses are more likely to die.

73. **Power Partnering - Joint Venture - Strategic Alliance – Endorsements:** How working with others can often double profits or half the costs of doing it 100% on your own. It can speed

74. **Creative Collaboration:** Where you can connect to other people's genius, connections, strategies and insights.

75. **Friction Factors:** You are keeping people from buying - These are your friction factors that create buying resistance.

76. **Profit Pinata:** It takes multiple touches to break through market resistance and unleash the profit connection.

77. **Perspectives:** Hindsight, Insight, Foresight: The power of understanding the past, future, and the connections to this moment can give you perspective to improve your decisions.

78. **3 P - Passion Purpose & Possibility:** How to create the Energy to grow your business.

79. **Loyalty Royalty:** Investing Preeminence Into Clients and Prospects will engender a loyal following, and a long lasting royalty from their investing back into you.

80. **Aikido School of Marketing:** How to use the energy of the competition (enemy) against themselves.

81. **Moat Strategies:** How to protect your profit making strategies from the competition

82. **Attention Deficit Syndrome:** Of All the Critical constraints... Lack of Attention is often the biggest.

83. **The RCP System - Relevance, Competency, and Passion:** The Answer to the question what creates success in one of Jay's Client's Life.

84. **Masterminding:** Designing and gathering Masterminds that Improve your business and connect you with your market.

85. **Knowledge Trapping /Asymmetry:** Gaining an unfair advantage in learning and applying information.

86. **Compete with Yourself:** When you are the best in the world you become your competition, and how to keep winning...

87. **Story Telling:** The way to create understanding in others is through telling stories.

88. **Types of Growth:** Making A Growth Choice... If you don't keep building momentum you will decline.

89. **Barter - Becoming a Barter Barron - Barter Profit Centers:** There are hundreds of nuances to creating profits in the world of trading products, services, strategies, connections and information.

90. **7 Concepts they Don't Teach @ Business School:** Specific Areas to Focus on that can unlock profits that build from an easily understood insight X 7.

91. **Victor or Victim:** What will you choose? To Win? Or let life win over you?

92. **Types of Thinkers:** Can you break out of the status quo, linear thinking? And See into a new dimension of exponential profits?

93. **Mind-Stein - How to Think Like Albert Einstein:** Modeling Einstein's strengths is possible for a non-genius but will get you results that will get people to think you must be a genius.

94. **The Action Bias:** Movement is far better than meditation - how to create the action habit.

95. **What Happened:** The power of reflection and review - what will you take away and apply to grow your business?

96. **ROI of Big ideas:** You only need one of these ideas to build an incredible business, and adding two more will create exponential growth.

97. **Exponential Entrepreneurship:** In a world where exponential growth is possible, why would you want to be any other kind of entrepreneur?

BusinessWealthWithoutRisk.com/access

ABOUT THE AUTHORS

Typically, when you venture into the initial pages of a business-oriented book, what greets you is an array of glossy photographs accompanied by standard, often monotonous biographies. This is where we diverge from the norm.

The authors are seasoned veterans in the realm of business success. They are entrepreneurs who have triumphed over and over again, in the face of adversity and changing markets, and have amassed significant wealth and success along the journey.

In your hands, you hold a compelling roadmap to prosperity, sketched by these exceptional architects of wealth creation. Jay & Roland have fostered, nurtured, and cultivated businesses across an expansive spectrum, again and again. They have not only survived the unforgiving corporate battlegrounds, but have consistently emerged victorious. They haven't merely played the game; they've revolutionized the rulebook.

Read further to learn a little about the authors of this book.

Meet Jay Abraham

Abraham.com/about

As a founder and CEO of The Abraham Group, Inc., Jay has spent his entire career solving complex problems and fixing underperforming businesses. He has significantly increased the bottom lines of over 10,000 clients in more than 1,000 industries and over 7,200 sub industries, worldwide. Jay has dealt with virtually every type of business scenario and issue. He has studied, and solved, almost every type of business question, challenge, and opportunity.

Jay has an uncanny ability to increase business income, wealth, and success by looking at the situation from totally different paradigms. He uncovers hidden assets, overlooked opportunities, underperforming activities, and undervalued possibilities unseen by his clients. This skill set has captured the attention and respect of CEOs, bestselling authors, entrepreneurs, and marketing experts worldwide. Jay's clients range from business royalty to small business owners. But they still have one thing in common: virtually all of them have profited greatly from Jay's expertise. Many of his ideas and strategies have led to millions of dollars of profit increase for his diverse clients.

Jay has identified the patterns that limit and restrict business growth. He is a unique industry leader who shows clients that most industries only know (and only use) one particular marketing approach. He teaches that there may be dozens of more effective and more profitable strategies (with far lower risk) and options, available to them. Jay shows his clients how to take different success concepts from different industries and adopt them to their specific business. This gives Jay's clients a powerful advantage over their competition.

446

Meet Roland Frasier

RolandFrasier.com

Roland is a "recovering attorney" and co-founder/principal of five different *Inc. Magazine* fastest growing companies in the e-commerce, e-learning, real estate and Saas spaces.

He is a serial entrepreneur who has founded, scaled, or sold over two dozen different businesses ranging from consumer products to live events to manufacturing companies with sales ranging from $3 million to just under $4 billion.

Roland has been featured in *Entrepreneur, Forbes, Money, Business Insider, Fast Company,* and on major television networks.

He has interviewed Sir Richard Branson, Martha Stewart, William Shatner, Jesse Itzler, Spanx founder, Sara Blakely, and many other industry leaders on his award-winning Business Lunch podcast.

He has produced infomercials with Guthy-Renker, completed publishing deals with Simon & Schuster and Random House, negotiated shows with major hotels on the Las Vegas strip, funded over one hundred private and public offerings, run an international hedge fund, and advised major brands (from PepsiCo to Uber to McDonald's) on a variety of business issues.

He currently lives in Rancho Santa Fe, California, and invests in and advises business owners on how to leverage, grow, scale and exit their companies.

TOOLS AND RESOURCES

Free Download

BusinessWealthWithoutRisk.com/access

Made in the USA
Middletown, DE
01 October 2023